Varieties of Religious Conversion
in the Middle Ages

Edited by
James Muldoon

University Press of Florida
Gainesville/Tallahassee/Tampa/Boca Raton
Pensacola/Orlando/Miami/Jacksonville

02 01 00 99 98 97 6 5 4 3 2 1

Library of Congress Cataloging-in-Publication Data

Varieties of religious conversion in the Middle Ages / edited by James Muldoon.
p. cm.
Includes bibliographical references and index.
ISBN 0–8130–1509-X (alk. paper)
1. Conversion—History of doctrines—Middle Ages, 600–1500.
2. Conversion—Case studies. 3. Church history—Middle Ages,
600–1500. I. Muldoon, James, 1935–.
BT780.V37   1997
248.2'4'0902—dc21   96–39216

The University Press of Florida is the scholarly publishing agency for the State University System of Florida, comprised of Florida A&M University, Florida Atlantic University, Florida International University, Florida State University, University of Central Florida, University of Florida, University of North Florida, University of South Florida, and University of West Florida.

University Press of Florida
15 Northwest 15th Street
Gainesville, FL 32611

CONTENTS

PREFACE

This book had its beginning in several conversations with medievalists decrying the lack of a general book on religious conversion in the Middle Ages. There are, of course, numerous narrative sources describing the conversion of specific individuals, such as Augustine of Hippo, and of entire societies, such as Bede's *History of the English Church and People*. What is lacking is a general understanding of what conversion is—and is not. To use the same term for both Augustine's lengthy, emotionally intense search for God and the corporate or communal acceptance of a new god by an Anglo-Saxon people at the behest of their king and leading men is to stretch the meaning of the word *conversion* to the extreme. As is often the case in academic life, these conversations about conversion eventually led to a panel at a scholarly conference, in this case at the 27th International Congress on Medieval Studies at Western Michigan University in May, 1992. Interest in the topic among the members of the audience at that session led to two more panels in the succeeding years.

One result of this early interest was a tentative proposal for a book that would discuss the full range of conversion experiences in order to provide a baseline or starting point for further study of the conversion experience. That goal turned out to be beyond the scope of a single volume. For example, it would have been useful to examine the concept of conversion by comparing the Christian notion of conversion with that found in non-Christian religions. It would also have been interesting to compare the conversion of the Old World with that of the New World. These topics and several others will have to await another volume. Religious conversion is a broad and varied category that will require a great deal more study before it is fully understood. Analysis of the conversion of individuals and societies in medieval Europe will require the efforts of scholars in a variety of disciplines—anthropology and psychology—for example, before we can fully understand it. The present volume is a contribution by a group of medievalists to that larger task.

As is usually the case in wide-ranging projects such as this one, the editor owes a debt of thanks to a number of individuals who have contributed to it. To thank them all would make this preface too long. So to all those who suggested topics, potential authors, and titles for the book during the first phase of this project, thank you. I trust that you like the result.

On the campus of the Camden College of Arts and Sciences of Rutgers University, several people were especially helpful in getting the various contributions into readable form for the computer. Edward McHugh, Robert Young, and David Gwalthney of the campus Computer Center were always cheerfully helpful when I appeared in their offices to resolve a problem with computer disks or to convert obscure word-processing programs. Finally, I owe a great debt to our departmental secretary, Loretta Carlisle, who handled many of the tedious and time-consuming activities that accompany a project such as this.

A special note of thanks is owed to Alexandra Cuffle, a graduate student at New York University, for her help in translating Cordula Nolte's article.

Above all, I owe a great debt of thanks to the scholars who have contributed to this volume. They have all been wonderfully cooperative in the process, making editorial revisions, meeting deadlines, and making suggestions to improve the book. Thank you all very much.

Finally, I must thank Walda Metcalf, former editor-in-chief of the University Press of Florida, who suggested doing this book on the basis of the original panel at Western Michigan University; without her encouragement, this project would not have seen the light of day. I thank also Judy Goffman who saw the manuscript through the process with good-humored efficiency.

Introduction: The Conversion of Europe

Conversion, the rejection of one religious tradition in favor of another, is a fundamental concept in the history of Christianity. The word itself comes from a Latin word that means to change or transform one thing into another. In the modern mind, religious conversion is usually associated with a dramatic, life-changing experience such as St. Paul's stunning experience on the road to Damascus. On a larger scale, conversion is associated with Constantine's victory at Milvian Bridge and the subsequent emergence of Christianity as the official religion of the Roman Empire or with the conversion of the Franks under Clovis. Textbooks for courses in Western Civilization and in Medieval History often refer to the conversion of Europe or the conversion of the barbarians, the transformation of the invaders of the Roman world from paganism to Christianity, as the fundamental event in the creation of medieval Europe.

By using the term *conversion* to describe a wide range of related religious experiences, however, we oversimplify its meaning. St. Paul's intense personal experience is equated with the gratitude that Constantine felt toward the deity who insured his crucial victory. The result is a far too simple model of that experience, one that places too much emphasis on a single traumatic experience that causes a rapid, radical change in an individual's or a society's way of life. In reality, these experiences form a range or spectrum of experiences that we label conversion rather than a single moment.

Between the experience of St. Paul on the one hand and that of Constantine or Clovis on the other, there exists a variety of transforming experiences. For example, the Christian who moves from one level of Christian life to another is a convert, as when a layman enters a monastery or when a monk or nun seeks a higher level of spiritual development. The monastic life as St. Benedict outlined it in his *Rule* is in fact a series of stages of spiritual development, "a school for the Lord's service," leading to the transformation of the individual.[1] In other words, the monastic life is a series of lesser transformations or conversions that, taken collectively, change the individual monk over a lifetime.

At each point along the conversion spectrum there is a process involved, not just an event. St. Paul's conversion only began with his experience on the road to Damascus. The meaning of that experience had to be explained to him (Acts 9:1–22) before he understood its meaning, and he continued to develop spiritually over the rest of his life. Likewise, Constantine's or Clovis's experience, the models of collective, corporate, or communal conversion in the Middle Ages, did not immediately lead to a complete and total renunciation of a previous way of life, much less to the immediate transformation of the entire Roman or Frankish worlds.[2] As in the case of St. Paul, the meaning of the experience had to be explained before they could proceed to recognizing the Christian God. Here again, however, there was a process involved as the Christianization of the Roman world proceeded slowly over three generations, beginning with the Edict of Milan in 313, in which Constantine reissued previous imperial edicts of Galerius and Maxentius, legalizing the Christian religion in the Roman world. He did not become a Christian at that point, receiving baptism only on his deathbed in 337.[3] Furthermore, it was under Constantine's Christian successors during the remainder of the fourth century that Christianity gradually become the official religion of the empire, a process that reached its climax in 382 when the Emperor Gratian ordered the statue of Victory removed from the Senate House in Rome.

Among the various barbarian invaders of the Roman world about whose conversion to Christianity we have some knowledge, the turn to Christianity is often described as following a path similar to that followed by Constantine and his successors. A king, such as Clovis, becomes a Christian at the prodding of his wife and after winning a victory that he attributed to the Christian God's intervention. A bishop, Remigius, provides instruction in Christian doctrine and then baptizes the king and his soldiers.[4] With local variations, this story can be found in the histories of a number of barbarian peoples who became Christian in the early Middle Ages. In fact, this kind of corporate or communal conversion is the way in which most European peoples were introduced to Christianity.

Given the importance of conversion in both Christianity itself and in the formation of European society, it is interesting to note that the literature devoted to analyzing and understanding it is rather small. The first and until recently the only book-length discussion of the nature of conversion remains A. D. Nock's *Conversion: The Old and the New in Religion from Alexander the Great to Augustine of Hippo.*[5] As its title indicates, this volume ended at the point at which the Middle Ages began and did not deal with the conversion of entire peoples that characterized the experience of the barbarian peoples who entered the collapsing Roman world. Its focus was entirely upon effects of a change in religious orientation upon the life, both interior and external, of individuals.

Likewise, in William James's older, classic work, *The Varieties of Religious Experience: A Study in Human Nature,* two chapters are devoted to conversion, again focusing on individual experiences, not group ones, and stressing conversion in the modern world, not the medieval.[6] There has also been an attempt to place the notion of individual conversion in a broader, comparative context, Alfred Clair Underwood's *Conversion: Christian and Non-Christian; A Comparative and Psychological Study.*[7] Rather than seeing conversion as a uniquely Christian experience, Underwood saw it as present in Judaism, Hinduism, Buddhism, and Islam as well as in various other religions, ancient and modern. Here again, however, the emphasis was upon the conversion of individuals, not groups, and the author paid little attention to the European Middle Ages.

With the appearance of Karl F. Morrison's *Understanding Conversion,* there is now a major work analyzing the concept of conversion in the Middle Ages. But even this work does not analyze all the forms of religious conversion that occurred in medieval Europe. Instead, Morrison has focused "in great part on writings by members of the Benedictine, Cistercian, and Augustinian orders." He also recognizes that his reader might "question whether ideas nurtured by an ascetic, male, literate, and aristocratic class were shared by other orders in society." His response is that "in the period under review, persons committed to the monastic life were, as we might say, specialists in the ideology and techniques of conversion."[8]

Although Morrison centered his analysis on the way in which twelfth-century monastic intellectuals understood conversion, he also recognized that this particular understanding of conversion was the product of a longer historical development. In fact, it was a "metaphor," which when "unpacked" is found to contain "a variety of models of conversion, some quite incompatible . . . all cobbled together."[9]

The observation that the twelfth-century conception of conversion can be unpacked is the central contention of the present book. In the Middle Ages, the term *conversion* described not only the complex experience that sophisticated monastic intellectuals knew; it also included a wide range of experiences that such intellectuals might have had some difficulty in describing as conversion in the true sense. Several terms have been used to describe the acceptance of Christianity at a level less than true inner conversion. Nock, for example, contrasted conversion, that is "the reorientation of the soul of an individual" with what he termed "adhesion," the "acceptance of new worships as useful supplements and not as substitutes" for previous forms of worship. Furthermore, adhesion "did not involve the taking of a new way of life in place of the old."[10]

As we shall see, many of the converts in medieval Europe were at a stage between adhesion and true conversion because their Christian rulers imposed social and cultural changes required by the Christian way of life. The conversion of Europe was at least as much a process of introducing large groups of barbarian pagans to a Christian way of life as it was a matter of personal spiritual experience. The process might better be called the acculturation or perhaps the Christianization of the barbarians rather than their conversion.

At the same time, as several of the articles here demonstrate, those who narrated the conversion stories often had other agendas when they wrote. As a result, it is necessary to compare what the classic writers on conversion wrote with other sources in order to appreciate fully what actually happened.

The plan of the present book stands in sharp contrast to Morrison's *Understanding Conversion*. Rather than focusing on a narrow time and place and on very sophisticated understandings of conversion, in this volume a wide range of conversion experiences is surveyed, beginning with Augustine of Hippo's examination of his own conversion, his *Confessions,* in the fifth century. The long span covered here reflects the fact that the experience of conversion was not restricted to the early Middle Ages but was, rather, a process that extended throughout the entire medieval era.

Because in the final analysis conversion is a personal experience, the first section of this volume examines conversion as an intense personal experience in the lives of two individuals who lived a millennium apart. The goal of the missionary who baptized an entire people was to enable each individual eventually to become fully transformed in Christ. Augustine of Hippo, who provided the classic spiritual autobiography, his *Confessions,* explains how and why a successful public figure turned to Christ. Augustine saw his life as a series of conversions, but as Frederick Russell reminds us, his conversion was not from nonbelief to belief but from the fringes of Christianity to its very center, from one level of Christian life to another. Almost a thousand years later, Margaret Ebner (1291–1351), a Dominican nun whose order's rule of life was influenced by Augustine's ideas about spiritual development, wrote of her gradual transformation from lay Catholic to nun to mystic. It was within the framework of the Dominican rule and way of life that Ebner underwent another conversion, a lengthy process of spiritual transformation. Leonard Hindsley emphasizes that one of the purposes of the formal religious life was to facilitate spiritual conversion, a purpose that went back to the *Rule* of St. Benedict. Whenever a new wave of spiritual enthusiasm arose in medieval Europe, new foundations emerged to institutionalize that spirit. In the thirteenth century, the experience of Francis of Assisi led to the creation of the Franciscans and other orders of friars, including the Dominicans. Ebner's story is a reminder that the call to a higher level of individual Christian spirituality was a constant factor in medieval Christian life and one for which the Church provided an institutional structure.

As we have seen, however, the individual conversion experience was only one part of the medieval spectrum of conversion. With the establishment of Christian kingdoms and with the creation of an ideology of Christian kingship, conversion of a kingdom's enemies—as part of either a policy of defense or one of expansion—became a responsibility of the Christian ruler. With that arose an issue that had troubled St. Augustine, the legitimacy of force in the work of conversion. During the early Middle Ages a number of nonbelievers, facing at least an implicit threat of war to the death if they did not accept Christian baptism, agreed to accept Christianity. As Lawrence Duggan points out, Charlemagne required the Saxons whom he had conquered to accept baptism or die. This was clearly not simply an effort to bring Christianity to a benighted people; it was also part of a long-term effort to pacify a threatened border. To convert the Saxons was, presumably, to bring peace to the frontier. Over the next several centuries, a number of Christian rulers engaged in activities designed to turn their enemies into Christians as well as to pacify foes and to extend their own domains. Conversion of nonbelievers became a matter of foreign policy. The missionary and the warrior traveled and worked together in the process of extending both Christ's kingdom and that of the king.

As John Howe points out, the concept of conversion or Christianization can also apply to changes in the physical world within which Christians live. Just as there is a Christian sacred history, there is also a Christian sacred geography. The Christianization of Europe meant that even the countryside was spiritually transformed, as the Christian God and His saints displaced the deities and spirits that had inhabited the previously pagan sacred space. Pagan sacred spaces could be transformed into Christian places of worship in the same way as some pagan religious practices could find their way into the Christian liturgy.[11]

Once we become aware of the lengthy and complicated process that eventually led to the Christianization of barbarian societies, various issues that were submerged in the main narratives rise to the surface. One of the most important of these is the role of women in this process. In many cases, a ruler's introduction to Christianity came through his mother or wife. The role played by Clovis's wife in eventually achieving the baptism of her husband and his people is well known. Less clear is the way in which these women had become Christian and the precise nature of the role they played in the process that led to baptism of their husbands. The traditional sources mention but do not discuss at length the role of women in the conversion of various peoples. Cordula Nolte argues that in reality women often played an important role simply by remaining faithful to Catholic Christianity in the face of strong pressures to abandon it. Furthermore, women often acted as "convert makers," teaching and instructing their spouses in Christian doctrine.

For Ruth Mazo Karras, the failure of the basic sources to deal at length with the role of women in conversion comes as no surprise. She points out that in the case of the sources dealing with conversion of the Scandinavian peoples to Christianity, the narratives describing these events were written centuries after the events actually occurred. In the intervening centuries, Scandinavian societies underwent significant changes, changes that undercut the role of women in those societies. The result was that the power of women was associated with pagan religion, with a rejected past. In addition, conversion came to be identified with a transfer of allegiance from one god to another, a process similar to the feudal relationship between lord and vassal, a relationship that involved only men and in which women played no part.

Nolte and Karras seek to understand why the writers who described the conversion of the Merovingian and the Scandinavian regions downplayed or omitted the role of women in that process. Jennifer Goodman, however, examining the romantic literature of the late medieval and early modern periods, points out that in the literary tradition, women continued to play a significant role in stories involving conversion. In her opinion, these late-flowering romances, a literary form more often associated with the thirteenth century than with the sixteenth, portrayed women in two distinct roles. The first was the traditional role of the Christian wife who converts her husband. The second was the tale of the Saracen princess who becomes a Christian as a result of marrying a dashing Christian hero. In both cases, the consequence is the conversion of an entire people achieved through the female character.

Although the stories of corporate conversion suggest that all the inhabitants of Europe became Christians, there in fact remained small groups of people who did not convert to the Christian faith of their rulers. Jews and Muslims living in Christian societies often remained unconvinced by efforts to convert them. Even when Jews did convert, there remained some suspicion about the sincerity of both their spiritual and their cultural transformation. At one level, there was the obvious fear that the conversion was only superficial, designed to win social and economic benefits, not spiritual ones. As Jonathan Elukin argues, to Christian neighbors, converted Jews remained just that—converted Jews. Religious conversion did not transform them so completely that they became fully assimilated into the surrounding Christian society. They remained outsiders, not completely participating in the Christian community, as did their descendants over the next several generations, a circumstance destined to have tragic consequences for the Jews of early modern Europe.

In the kingdoms that crusaders established in the Holy Land, it was Muslim converts who raised difficulties for Christians. Muslim slaves sought baptism in order to claim freedom, a practice that threatened the economic position of their Christian masters. As Benjamin Z. Kedar emphasizes, this also caused tension between the Church and the crusaders, adding to the stresses found in these kingdoms. Furthermore, conversion went both ways, as Christians for one reason or another became Muslims. Here again, conversion appears as something less than an intense and personal spiritual experience. In an ironic twist, Kedar presents a variation on the traditional story of the Christian who falls in love with a Saracen princess and seeks both her hand in marriage and her conversion. In this version, a Muslim man loves a Christian woman and eventually converts and weds her.

The theme of corporate or communal conversion that underlay many medieval conversion narratives emphasized what we might term the politics of conversion, a politics that existed on three levels. The first level was the obvious one, the situation of a ruler such as Constantine or Clovis, who saw in his victory over his enemies a proof of the Christian God's power, and whose conversion assured him not only of that God's support but also of the support of those subjects who were already Christian. At the second level, the politics of conversion meant insisting upon baptism as the price of peace with a Christian society, something that Alfred of Wessex demanded when making peace with the Danes. The final level of the politics of conversion concerns the written narrative of the conversion experience. In this case, the narrative might transform the facts of the experience into a form more acceptable to the audience for which it was written. This kind of reconstruction of the historical events occurred when the writers described the change from pagan to Christian as something sudden, rather as the long, drawn-out process that we know it to have been. In terms of missionary propaganda, a story of sudden, dramatic conversions was no doubt more attractive than the reality of a process that took decades, even generations, before true Christian conversion of the sort that Augustine experienced could occur.

The fact that conversion had a political aspect also meant that a pagan ruler who understood that fact might be able to manipulate his Christian neighbors in his own political interest. Rasa Mazeika points out that the rulers of Lithuania did just that when dealing with the Teutonic Knights.

What she describes as the Lithuanian rulers' "flirtations with Christianity" were part of a careful plan to strengthen their position in the face of German Christian expansion. The Lithuanian situation is especially interesting because it is one of the few cases in which we can see the politics of conversion from the non-Christian side. It is clear that the Lithuanians did not understand conversion as demanding an major inner transformation or even any changes in the Lithuanian way of life. Furthermore, it is striking that the conversion, or at least the Christianization, of Lithuania only finally occurred in the late fourteenth century when the pagan Duke of Lithuania, Jagiello, married the Catholic heiress to the Polish throne and united the two states.

The farther Christian missionaries moved out from Europe in the search for converts, the more difficult the work became. As the situation in Lithuania clearly demonstrated to anyone who cared to learn a lesson from it, the stories of Constantine and Clovis, the traditional stories of miraculous events that led to the rapid conversion of entire peoples, did not provide models for what was actually happening in the East. The crusades and the desire to find allies against the Muslims gave rise to myths about the existence of Christian rulers such a Prester John in Asia, who would happily ally with European Christians against the ever-expanding Muslims. When the kingdom of Prester John evaporated as more Europeans penetrated the Mongol-dominated regions of central Asia, there emerged stories of Christians, especially women, in the household of the Great Khan, giving rise to expectations that these women might play the role that Clotilda had played in Clovis's conversion. Stories of supposed conversions to Christianity in the East circulated throughout Europe. Even some Muslim rulers were identified as belonging to families who had once been Christian and who were interested in returning to the faith. In all of these cases, conversion was seen as an essential element in any alliance against the Muslims.

The presence of what Adam Knobler has termed "pseudo-conversion" in popular stories about potential allies and converts in Asia stands in sharp contrast to what James D. Ryan sees as the beginnings of modern evangelization in the attempts to create in Asia Christian communities that were not based on the baptism of an entire society.[12] Instead, some missionaries began to emphasize the baptism of converts only after a lengthy period of instruction. In other cases, although baptism was conferred quite early in the process of conversion, the missionary assumed that the process of education and spiritual development would continue. Seen in this light, baptism became only one stage in a conversion process rather than the sign of its completion. This emerging emphasis on the conversion of individuals who were not part of the local power structure marked the beginning of the end for the medieval practice of seeking the conversion of entire societies, although belief in such an approach continued to exist in Catholic missionary circles until modern times.

The final stage, or last gasp, of the medieval approach to conversion came in the wake of the European encounter with a variety of new worlds following Columbus's first voyage. Many of the early missionaries who went to the Americas or to Asia had visions of replicating what they understood to have been the European experience of conversion, that is, the mass baptism of entire peoples. In Asia, where strong governments existed, this seemed a plausible outcome, a dream that kept Jesuits working at the Chinese imperial court long after reality suggested that it was not going to happen.[13] In the Americas, wholesale conversion might, theoretically, have occurred if the Aztec and Inca empires had not collapsed in the face of Spanish troops and the rebellion of previously subject peoples. Perhaps the closest the Spanish came to seeking the conversion of the people of Mexico in the traditional manner was the establishment of a school in Mexico City to train the sons of chiefs to become priests, a move that collapsed in a few years.

In the final analysis, the experience of the late Middle Ages and the early modern era demonstrated that whatever the truth of the stories about the conversion of Constantine, Clovis, and other rulers in the early Middle Ages, that experience would not be repeated in the sixteenth and seventeenth centuries. Furthermore, the Protestant Reformation caused serious reconsideration of what conversion was, how it was achieved, and what role baptism played in it.[14] Protestants, as well as some Catholics, criticized the Catholic practice of baptizing entire peoples without extensive doctrinal instruction. Protestants condemned this practice in the Americas, implying that when such practices had been employed in the conversion of Europe, they had led not to conversion to true Christianity but to an evil, corrupt version of the true faith.[15] In effect, the Reformers argued that the sixteenth century marked the beginning of the conversion of Europe to Christianity.

Notes

1. *The Rule of St. Benedict,* ed. Timothy Fry, O.S.B. (Collegeville, Minn.: Liturgical Press, 1981), 165.

2. The terms *corporate, communal,* and *collective* as applied to the conversion of entire societies are from Christopher Dawson, *The Movement of World Revolution* (New York: Sheed & Ward, 1959), 79.

3. The basic documents dealing with Constantine's religious experience are in *A New Eusebius: Documents Illustrating the History of the Church to* A.D. *337,* ed. J. Stevenson (rev. ed., London: SPCK, 1987), 282–86.

4. Gregory of Tours, *History of the Franks,* trans. Ernest Brehaut (reprint, New York: W. W. Norton, 1969), 38–40.

5. A. D. Nock, *Conversion: The Old and the New in Religion from Alexander the Great to Augustine of Hippo* (Oxford: Oxford University Press, 1933; reprint, 1961).

6. William James, *The Varieties of Religious Experience: A Study in Human Nature* (New York: Longmans, Green, and Co., 1902; reprint, Harmondsworth, Eng.: Penguin Books, 1982).

7. Alfred Clair Underwood, *Conversion: Christian and Non-Christian; A Comparative and Psychological Study* (London: George Allen and Unwin, 1925).

8. Karl F. Morrison, *Understanding Conversion* (Charlottesville: University Press of Virginia, 1992), xix.

9. Ibid., xv.

10. Nock, *Conversion,* 7.

11. Howe's views are in contrast with those of Lynn White, Jr., "The Historical Roots of Our Ecological Crisis," *Science* (March 10, 1967): 1203–7, reprinted in *Dynamo and Virgin Reconsidered: Essays in the Dynamism of Western Culture* (Cambridge, Mass.: MIT Press, 1968), 75–94.

12. Adam Knobler, "Pseudo-Conversions and Patchwork Pedigrees: The Christianization of Muslim Princes and the Diplomacy of Holy War," *Journal of World History* 7 (1996): 181–97.

13. C. R. Boxer, *The Church Militant and Iberian Expansion 1440–1770* (Baltimore: Johns Hopkins University Press, 1978), 95.

14. Marilyn J. Harran, *Luther on Conversion: The Early Years* (Ithaca, N.Y.: Cornell University Press, 1983), 19–53. Harran surveys medieval ideas of conversion and their relation to Luther's conceptions, stressing the individual conversion experience.

15. Kenneth Scott Latourette, *A History of the Expansion of Christianity,* vol. 3, *Three Centuries of Advance,* A.D. *1500–*A.D. *1800* (New York: Harper, 1939), 51.

Conversion as Personal Experience

I

Augustine
Conversion by the Book

Frederick H. Russell

Conversion looms large in the life and thought of Augustine; indeed, he sees the whole of his life as a process of conversion, and the motif of conversion can be found in the very interstices of his thought. His own "conversion," so elaborately and rhetorically narrated in the thirteen books of his *Confessions,* written about 400, served as role model and inspiration for centuries of Christian experience. And yet, taken in its entirety, his own conversion experience was unique to him and could not be wholly replicated. He wrote no systematic treatise on the theory or phenomenon of conversion, and so his program of conversion must be teased out, a task made difficult by the multiple agenda of so many of his works. So it is perhaps not surprising that there is no systematic and comprehensive modern treatise on what conversion in all its senses meant for Augustine.[1] After a first approximation of the meanings of "conversion" and of its meanings to him, I will examine his autobiographical account of his own conversion (*Confessions* 1–9) and then how he generalized from his own experience so as to make it emblematic for all Christian conversions (*Confessions* 10–13).

The term *conversion* is rich in meaning, even deceptively so. In the popular imagination it seems to mean a sudden and complete change of belief. The term itself is a metaphor borrowed from the arts and crafts, meaning a transformation of some material into a different object.[2] Hence whenever it is applied to the kind of experience we are investigating, it is used metaphorically rather than literally. Etymologically it means to turn, a turning from something to something else.[3] Thus "conversion" is only half of a process, the other half being "aversion," or, as Robert Markus puts it, "disenchantment."[4] In conversion there is always something left behind.

Disenchantments may be as important as conversions, for the past is never wholly discarded, and so the continuities of a person's life facilitate a certain coherence in the process of change.[5] Scholars have discerned many conversions over the course of Augustine's career. He was successively converted to philosophy upon reading Cicero's *Hortensius* (now lost) at the age of nineteen, then to Manicheanism, to skepticism, and to the neo-Platonism of Plotinus. These can be seen as the changes of heart and mind of a sensitive and intellectually gifted young adult, but they do not directly explain Augustine's conversion to Christianity, or the conversions of others that he relates in the *Confessions*. Conversion in his works can also refer to the conversion of ordinary people from paganism (or better: polytheism or idolatry) or from heresy, and to the conversion of educated people narrated in the *Confessions*.[6] In addition, the concept describes the growth in the Christian life of those who were already Christian, as in Augustine's self-analysis in *Confessions* 10. A further caution before we emerge from this terminological thicket: Augustine had been raised as a Christian. He was never far from the outward life of the Church, thanks to his mother Monica, and he never—even during his violent swings of sentiment and conviction—expressly renounced the Christian faith.[7] So in effect his conversion in the garden at Milan (*Confessions* 8) can actually be seen as a *re*conversion, or as a series of connected events within his narrative.[8]

As we shall see, conversion in Augustine functioned on two formal levels, the supernatural and the human. The supernatural concerned the individual's affective or empathetic relationship to the Godhead, while the human concerned the words used to describe that relationship and the effects of that relationship on one's life in the Church. The human aspect functioned within human nature and institutions and was validated by the supernatural dimension of the conversion experience.[9] Conversion as experienced by an individual cannot be strictly equated with any account of that experience. Even with a person as articulate about his feelings as Augustine, an account such as the *Confessions* cannot convey the experience itself but only the person's reflective rendering in words or other signs of the feelings and meanings of that experience. So in dealing with the rhetorically sophisticated *Confessions*, we must allow for the play of fictive elements. While the *Confessions* is probably not a work of "fiction," it is not to be taken as factual truth on a narrative level. It is rather as a surrogate for Augustine's conversion experience that it commands our attention.[10] The approach here will look first at what might be called the phenomenology of sin and conversion as Augustine related it in the first nine books, seen as structured reflections on his early life. In the last four books he shifted from microanalysis of his own life to the macro tableau of salvation history, from the personal and singular to the universal and plural.

The details of Augustine's life before his conversion, the details he chooses to tell us, are reasonably familiar. Augustine sees himself as an intellectually gifted yet morally dissolute young man, much addicted to the worldly lusts of I John 2:16: lust of the flesh; lust of the eyes; and pride. After much experimentation he came to a personal crisis about where his life should go. In the depths of despair, he was summoned by a child's voice to read in the Pauline epistles, whereupon he resolved to undergo baptism. This conversion took place in 386, with baptism following the next spring. More than a decade later he produced his own reconstruction of these events in the *Confessions*. But, for him, the bare details of the events were but the tip of the iceberg.

In effect Augustine wove three themes into his narrative: sin and its resulting misery; God's initiation of the conversion process; and the perilous and incomplete nature of his conversion. Two entry points allow us to penetrate the density of the autobiography. First, as Augustine observes at the conversion scene, "you converted me to yourself" ("convertisti me ad te," 8.12.30). Divine activity is at work in every moment of every conversion. Second, of the depths of his earlier despair he remarked, "I had become a question to myself" (4.4.9). At the time of writing, long after his conversion experience, his present condition remained much the same (10.33.50). His conversion was incomplete, not an event fixed in time. As a result of his sins he remained problematical, alienated from himself. Only God could make him whole. God had interrupted his despair in the garden at Milan, when Augustine, bewailing his inability to be good, heard the voice of a child, chanting "pick up and read, pick up and read." Seeing this as a divine oracle, Augustine picked up a copy of Paul's Epistle to the Romans, and read: "Not in riots and drunken parties, not in eroticism and indecencies, not in strife and rivalry, but put on the Lord Jesus Christ and make no provision for the flesh in its lusts" (13.13–14). Instantly he felt relief from his agonies, and now all shadows of doubt were dispelled (8.12.29). This was indeed conversion by the book, or better yet, conversion by means of the book! Converted to God by God, Augustine felt no longer torn by desires for a wife and worldly success (8.12.30).

This is Augustine's conversion from the depths of intractable sin. Earlier he had seen his sins multiply (6.15.25). He was keenly aware of the role habit (*consuetudo*) played in human actions, and to him habit usually meant bad habits.[11] Frequently one's acts were at odds with one's motives, such that righteous acts were done for the wrong reasons (1.12.19; 3.9.17). Even after attempts to rise to spiritual contemplation, Augustine was again dragged down by the weight of his *consuetudo carnalis,* and his pride and lust returned. His weakness reasserted itself and he returned to his accustomed habits (7.17.23), remaining firmly bound by woman (8.1.2). More generally, he saw the burden of this world (*sarcina saeculi*) weighing him down. His distorted will fostered his passion. By servitude to passion, habit was formed, and habit became necessity. This process formed a chain (*catena*) that kept him in harsh bondage so that his new resolve was not strong enough—yet (8.5.10). "The law of sin is the violence of habit" (8.5.12); Augustine was so bound by the chain of sexual desire (and the trap of secular affairs) (8.6.13), that he uttered his famous anguished lament: "Grant me chastity and continence, but not yet" (8.9.17).

Yet God was always there for Augustine. Even in the spiritual and not-so-spiritual wanderings of early adulthood he was never far from Christian influences. He affirmed that he had never lost his belief in God and Providence and assumed that he would eventually return to the Christian faith (6.5.7; 7.7.11).[12] His fear of death and divine judgment restrained him from further erotic indulgence (6.16.26). Even in the depths of his despair, God's secret providence was working within him (5.6.11). The worse his pain, the greater would be his joy in returning to God from his alienation (8.3.8). Through these very pains of earthly life, God's laws disciplined humans for their improvement, from the beatings of schoolmasters to the ordeals of martyrs (1.14.23). Pains were lessons (2.2.4), or the rod of divine discipline (6.6.9). Inward goads (*stimula*) and salutary sorrows stirred inward perceptions leading to Augustine's spiritual health (7.8.12), enabling him to tame his lusts (9.4.7). God used human authorities to care for the health of souls, even if, like the surgeon's knife, they delivered a harsh reproach.

In short, God was converting Augustine back to himself (8.12.30). He snapped the chain so that Augustine could reject his own will in favor of God's will; Augustine no longer needed to scratch the itch of lust (9.1.1). Duly baptized, he rediscovered the good habit of living with his mother (9.12.30). To the chain that had formerly bound him he now opposed the chain of faith by which Monica had bound herself to the sacrament of redemption (9.13.36). The sacraments served as merciful remedies for spiritual illnesses (9.4.8). Book 9 closes as Augustine resolved to dedicate his life to the service of the Church, the mother of all Christians, where he hoped Monica would be remembered at the altar by all who read the *Confessions*.

Augustine saw the life of someone undergoing conversion as unstable and insecure. The lonely quest was made a little easier with support from others in similar predicaments. In Book 6 he began his ascent toward conversion in the company of close friends. His narration of his own conversion in Book 8 is preceded by accounts of the conversions of the pagan rhetorician Marius Victorinus, Antony the Desert Father, and some un-named government officials in Trier. And, shortly after Augustine read Romans 13 in the garden, his friend Alypius read, in the next chapter, "Receive the person who is weak in faith," and taking it to heart, likewise resolved to be baptized (8.12.30). He thus bracketed his own conversion between the similar experiences of others before and after him.[13] More generally, Augustine showed sensitivity to the moral dilemma of those are making progress (*proficientes*) in the faith. When they committed sins, strictly speaking they should be punished, but they should rather be encouraged to persevere. So, when their acts offended neither God nor the consensus of the community, they should not be punished (3.9.17).

Several times Augustine sought intellectual enlightenment through personal visions of higher truth. In Book 7 he sought union with the Plotinian One, as part of his meditation on the "books of the Platonists." While during the experience all doubts left him and he came intellectually to understand the nature of evil and the goodness of God's creation, the vision was a fleeting one, and his old habits returned (7.10.16–17.23). The so-called "vision of Ostia" in Book 9 found Augustine and his dying mother deep in prayerful contemplation. Step by step they removed their attention from creaturely things to glimpse eternal wisdom. Augustine realized that if all things were silent, God would speak himself, and all of us could hear him directly. But again the vision did not last: from this "out of body experience" Augustine returned to the world of time and human speech, of conventional signs and lesser visions. The moment of understanding had passed quickly (9.10.23–25). Even a convert such as Augustine still had a long way to go.

Scholars have long debated over the organization and structure of the *Confessions*. How were the last four books related to the first nine? Were they simply "tacked on" or did they belong to some other work? Happily these debates need not concern us here, for regarding conversion Augustine employed thematic linkages that manifest the integrity of the entire work. Two of these lead us into Book 10, easily the longest of all the books. There Augustine recounts his further attempts at spiritual vision, remarking that at times he feels a strange sweetness when contemplating God, but the feeling never achieves perfection, whereupon he lapses miserably back into his old habits (10.40.65). And, while lamenting his continuing sinfulness, he observes, "In your [God's] eyes I have become a problem to myself, and that is my sickness" (10.33.50). Alienated from God, he cannot understand even himself.

These two passages give us a profound clue to Augustine's condition as he sees it, writing about 400, and to the organization of his autobiography, for the postgarden Augustine, the convert now become rising bishop, still cannot achieve a lasting vision of God (cf. 7.10.16; 9.10.25), and remains his old, problematical, pregarden self. In Book 10 Augustine is writing about himself in the present tense, and he finds that more than a decade after his conversion and baptism, he is still convalescing.[14] "Confessing what I am now" (10.3.4–4.6), he begins a long meditation on his self-understanding and his many faults, a meditation framed by his discussion of memory. Memory, which makes it possible to speak in present time, enables the narrative reconstruction of the self (10.2.2–3.3).[15] In a poignant passage he laments: "Late have I loved you, beauty so old and so new. . . . You were within me and I was in the external world and sought you there. . . . You were with me, and I was not with you" (10.27.38). Not adequately filled with God, Augustine is a burden to himself (10.28.39). With this he begins a confession of his continuing temptations that, taken out of context, would seem a self-lacerating scrupulosity. Given the strength to resist concupiscence even before becoming a priest, he is nevertheless still bothered by memories of sexual delight (10.30.41–42). He is too fond of the pleasures of food and wine, even though they are proper in moderation (10.31.43,47). He sins without even realizing it (10.33.49). Admitting that he is too hard on himself, he still finds himself radically problematical (10.33.50).

These seemingly trivial sins are not enough, for Augustine is fearful of his desire for human praise. As a bishop he takes pleasure in being either feared or loved by others, in place of God. He cannot wholly reject admiration and fears hostile criticism. He feels he should show a more restrained love for the admiration of others (10.36.59–37.61). As a bishop he is very unsure of himself, since he knows God better than he knows himself (10.37.61–62). What is the solution to his dilemma as he has constructed it? If memory shows the force of habit, God's power is constantly healing his wounds (10.39.64–40.65). Christ must have something in common with both God and humanity. He is both mortal and righteous. As God he is the Word; as human he is mediator. Being our servant, he makes us sons, not servants. As Book 10 ends, Augustine finds healing in the Eucharist of the incarnate Christ (10.42.67–43.70). The abyss between creator and creature has finally been crossed.

The last three books of the *Confessions* are all part of the same piece. Augustine invites his readers to share in his lifelong process of convalescence. He demonstrates his striving for knowledge of God by giving an extended interpretation of Genesis 1, where the single chapter stands for all the books of Scripture. In effect, the last three books present the three persons of the Trinity.[16] Thus Book 11 treats God the Father, the first person of the Trinity, Being, and contrasts his eternity with our temporality and contingency. We are captives of time and change. Book 12 contrasts the eternal Word (Christ, knowledge) with the words of Scripture and the words we use to interpret Scripture. If our words are many, conflicting, and obscure, they are still a means of understanding God. Augustine, and humankind, struggle to interpret the Word, so as to unite God and his books of Scripture. Since words are signs of the invisible things of God (Romans 1.20), they can give us information about creation, divine eternity, and divine omnipotence, but these words tell us little about the work of the spirit in the world of humanity. Through luxuriant and intricate allegorical interpretation, Book 13 holds out the prospect of the dynamic union of the soul with God under the action of the Holy Spirit in the world and in the Church, whereby the breach of sin can be mended.

In Book 11, Augustine struggles to understand Scripture, the meaning of which God has made obscure, to bring Augustine closer to perfection (11.2.3–4). In the Gospels, the Word speaking through the flesh is heard externally but believed internally. Augustine feels both love and terror at the Word as revealed (11.8.10–9.11). This brings Augustine to his famous discussion of time: in the present time of our memory we have an image of our past, and this is where we can discover God. The mind measures time, expecting the future, attending to the present, remembering the past (11.27.36–28.37). Since time is fleeting, Augustine seeks stability and solidity in the eternal God (11.30.40). Knowledge of God allows one to escape from the disintegrating effects of time (11.29.39; cf. 9.4.10). Time is the medium in which the convert passes through the painful and anxious stages of approaching closer to God.

In Book 12 Augustine runs into problems of interpreting Genesis 1, because the poverty of human intelligence yields an ignorance based on knowledge (12.1.1; 12.5.5). The movement of the will away from God toward what has less being constitutes fault and sin (12.11.11). The Scriptures reveal their awesome depth, and so when different interpretations conflict, the twofold command of love of God and neighbor must guide the interpreter (12.18.27; 12.25.35). Augustine generally admits that as signs, the words of Scripture are bound to be ambivalent. Further, biblical signs convey spiritual mysteries and so are particularly open to varied interpretations. Some interpreters so love their own opinion not for its truth but because they are proud of it as their private possession, but scriptural truths should be the possession of all, for the benefit of all. Still, Augustine allows for a diversity of correct spiritual interpretations (12.25.34).[17]

In Book 13 he pursues the meaning and operation of conversion on the more general and less personal level of salvation history. Augustine proceeds on two complementary and intricately related tracks, the abstract and theological, and the practical and ecclesial. The book opens with his consideration of the theological meaning of conversion (13.2.2–5.6).[18] Creation is only a beginning, a program rather than a completed process, for creatures remain alienated from God unless called by the Word to receive form (13.2.2). Creatures are undetermined, unformed, and imperfect; they merely live (*utcumque*: 13.3.4). Spiritual creatures ratify the call by their own movement, seen as a turning to the Word. They are thus able not only to live but to live wisely (13.2.3). This process, called *formatio,* like the original creation, is the gratuitous gift of God. In this formation—which Augustine, in his shifting terminology, also calls conversion—the creature imitates, according to its measure, the Word, the Son of God (13.2.3–4.5).[19] The relationship between creator and spiritual creature is personal; the Word addresses the soul, which responds by turning to the Word. The result is a metaphysical dialogue wherein created liberty responds to creative liberty. *Formatio* is thus the work both of creatures and of God, a turning to the origin of creatures through appeal and illumination. Thus *conversio* replicates *creatio* or is a new kind of creation. *Formatio* is not imposed once and for all but is rather repeated at each moment in the existence of the spirit and sustains the whole life of the creature in its historical development (13.10.11; 13.12.13–14.15). The relationship between creature and God must be acknowledged and reevaluated in what amounts to a constant process of reformation.

The contingent historicity of the individual human creature caught in time is the essential grounding for the creature's ultimate relationship with God. There is also a social complement to the individual's historical development, for human creatures are gathered together in a community of destiny, of progress in time, a community whose human meaning depends on the attitudes of each person toward God and the community. (This is the story told at length in the last twelve books of the *City of God*). Within each person there is a conflict of loves, and persons freely determine their allegiance between the two cities, the earthly and the heavenly, according to their loves, especially their relations with God (13.7.8).[20] Conversion is the historical process in which the various human loves seek integration with the love of God. History records the conflicts of human wills, on the horizontal plane of interpersonal relations, until those conflicts achieve composition on the vertical plane of their destination in God.

Passing from the historical to the moral dimension of conversion, Augustine sees that baptism in the Trinity initiates a sort of second creation.[21] Moral conversion through penitence transforms persons from darkness into light in the Lord. The linkage *conversio-formatio,* now joined to *illuminatio,* takes on an ecclesial dimension. Here below, the Christian lives, in the Church, dialectically stretched between the earlier and the later, in the present of mortal existence, suspended between the abyss of sin and the abyss of the divine being. In this destabilized position hope supports faith, and the promise of the heavenly city supports efforts at perseverance (13.13.14–14.15). Salvation is now realized only in hope, but penitence continues the constant effort to flee the profanity of the world and to maintain the person at an adult level (13.13.14). Those who are saved aspire incessantly to the full salvation of the heavenly life. The mediation of faith and hope is God working historically and morally in the Christian.

This analysis may seem too metaphysical, too abstract, but it is the fruit of Augustine's long *Confessions,* where he explained his own conversion experience and its continuing aftermath and then sought to show how he was Everyman, how his own experience could stand for the human condition throughout history. In many ways Book 13 is the climax of the *Confessions,* for it joins Augustine's past experience, his self-analysis, and his biblical hermeneutics into a program for conversion that explores the prospects for the expansion of the faith in Christian times. His personal activity is now transposed into the key of salvation history, to make Christianity fit to travel across time and space through the continuing work of the third person of the Trinity. The abstract triad of formation-reformation-conversion now receives concrete application. Essentially Book 13 treats the creation of the universe and then turns to the divine reformation or conversion of sinful humanity. If Christ is the Word (thanks to the opening of John's Gospel), he is directly involved in the original creation. To the Son, by whom the Father made things, is added the Holy Spirit. Through allegory Augustine is able to find the Trinity announced in the first verses of Genesis, since he equates the "spirit of God" with the Holy Spirit. The whole Trinity is thus the creator (13.5.6–6.7; 13.9.10). Again through allegory, Augustine finds the Church prefigured in Genesis 1 (13.12.13).

Addressing fellow Christians in the Church, that community of wills now undergoing conversion, Augustine contrasts the love diffused in our hearts by the Holy Spirit with the cupidity that pulls us down (13.7.8). The conflicting vectors or "weights" on our souls make us restless and anxious, since we are not in our intended positions. Here Augustine utters his famous epithet *pondus meum, amor meus:* "my weight is my love" (13.9.10). The soul is carried wherever its loves take it, and the soul can even fall into a bottomless pit. But disturbed souls remember God and are converted to him (13.12.13). Yet we are made light only by faith in things unseen, not with a clear view, and so our salvation remains a matter of hope, not sight.

The soul often slips back into the depths and bears remnants of its former darkness. Given the uncertainties of human knowledge, only God can distinguish the souls of light from the souls of darkness (13.14.15).

The continuing divine activity of the Word comes to our rescue in the books of Scripture, which provide a solid firmament of authority over those who submit to it, through the ministry of the biblical authors (13.15.16–17; 13.34.49). This firmament restrains our departure from God (13.21.31) and enables us to discern truth through contemplation, but for the present only through signs (13.18.23). The sacred signs of the Word are appropriate to our anxious condition (13.20.27). In short, signs are a kind of verbal sacrament. Corporal signs and intellectual concepts evidence a multiplicity that allows one idea to be expressed in several ways and to bear several meanings (13.24.37) These signs are often mysterious to carnal persons, but these "infants" living in darkness are not without hope of the divine, since Scripture speaks to them in time-conditioned (*temporaliter*) language (13.15.18–19.25; 13.29.44).

The first formal step in conversion is, of course, baptism, that "second creation." As God in Genesis created the waters that became bitter with sin, so now the sweet water of baptism is available to all. Now the earth, Augustine proclaims, is believing and baptized and rejoices in the Eucharist. Human unbelief made the Gospel necessary, but now the baptized are supported by the work of ministers who dispense the sacraments of baptism, the Eucharist, and preaching, which serve as a visible ladder to spiritual things (13.20.26; 13.21.29–30). As such, ministers should be imitators of Christ (13.21.31). The miracle of conversion becomes possible because God formed humankind in his own image and likeness (Gen. 1.26), such that within the human self there is the triad of being, knowing, and willing that reflects, imperfectly and at a great distance, the Trinity (13.11.12). This image and likeness is what makes conversion possible.

Persons being renewed can now understand the Trinity above them (13.22.32; 13.24.45) and can rightfully exercise authority over irrational animals by their reason and intelligence (13.32.47). Renewed according to God's image and likeness, the mind will be subject to God and will have no need of a human model to imitate. For now, however, it is necessary for ministers to bring the faithful to perfection in this life (13.34.49).

Augustine naturally sees the Church as a necessary instrument of salvation, as the bride of Christ assisted by the apostle Paul, who acts as a friend of the bridegroom as well as a member of the bride (13.13.14). The renewed must perform works of mercy, such as loving our neighbor in relief of physical necessities and in rendering aid and protection to rescue someone from the injustice of the powerful (13.17.21). These lower good works lead to the delights of contemplation (13.18.22). God's heavenly blessings to earth include the words of wisdom that makes of human minds an elect race (13.19.25). Ministers should now be role models for the faithful (13.21.30). In the Church, spiritual judgment is exercised not only by those who spiritually preside, but also by those subjected to them, including women. No one is entitled to judge the Scriptures, or whether individuals are spiritual or carnal, or to judge whole peoples. Spiritual persons judge rather what is right and censure what is wrong in the sacraments and verbal signs governed by Scripture and in the deeds of the faithful. Their power to correct abuses (*potestas corrigendi*) is expressed through counseling and absolution (13.23.33–34).

God works in time to bring order out of our disorder. He justifies the impious and separates them from the truly wicked, and establishes the authority of his book over all those who are subject to him (13.34.49). The result is human fecundity: human beings and their works increase and multiply even in the intellectual realm. The earth is filled with human energy and its mastery by reason (13.24.37). Allegorically, the fruits of the earth are the works of mercy, owed to ministers as models of ascetic restraint. These works derive their worth not from the merit of the recipients but from the good intentions of the donors (13.25.38–27.42). Augustine ends the *Confessions* on a note of high optimism, obviously an attitude toward the future of the human race. Both earthly prosperity and eternal salvation are possible through the Church as the locus of the salvific work of the Holy Spirit. Now, Augustine implies, he can get on with his life, and Christians with theirs.

The *Confessions* is obviously an extraordinary work. Its structure gives us a clue to Augustine's purpose. Augustine is sketching out the basic outlines of a program of conversion that would be used in succeeding centuries. Therein lies the unity of the work: the retrospective conversion of Augustine's self paves the way for the prospective conversion of others.[22] What is crucial for him in this effort is that the reading or hearing of a text, for him primarily the Bible, is capable of transforming one's life. As a text, the *Confessions* was similarly intended to transform the lives of others. His idiosyncratic biblical exegesis (Books 12–13) resulted from the imperative to ground his conversion program in Scripture, which provided a kind of safety net to ensure that other conversion attempts would never be wholly fruitless.

The rhetoric of conversion in the *Confessions* demanded a total commitment, one never completed here below, that embarked the convert on a perilous journey. The hope of salvation was balanced by constant reminders of one's moral shortcomings. The experience of those who were making spiritual progress (*proficientes*) was always liable to setbacks.[23] In writing the *Confessions*, Augustine perhaps exaggerated his euphoria of 386–87 to highlight the contrast with his own unfinished agenda of about 400. The convert achieved a vision of moral and spiritual enlightenment, only to have that vision quickly recede in a kind of intellectually and psychologically destabilizing striptease. God's revealing and concealing could lead to almost unbearable tension.

Indeed, the fear of recidivism, of backsliding from a moment of enlightenment, was so terrifyingly real for Augustine that he rhetorically exaggerated his ups and his downs. True conversion could only be effected through incessant pain. William James observed: "[Conversion denotes] the process, gradual or sudden, by which a self hitherto divided, and consciously wrong, inferior and unhappy, becomes unified and consciously right, superior and happy, in consequence of its firmer hold upon religious realities."[24] In Augustine's case at least, James exaggerated the happy consequences of conversion, at least until the confident and optimistic ending of the *Confessions*. And Augustine would later impose stricter limits on the human freedom to answer God's call. Still, Augustine reflexively sought knowledge of God to acquire knowledge of himself. He felt that in the economy of salvation, God would do what was absolutely necessary, and no more, while leaving much initiative to individuals and to empirical groups to answer his call, to participate in their own salvation. Augustine was convinced that the Church and its ministers were an absolutely necessary component of the process, but here the Church was not the bureaucratic church of hierarchy and subordination, not a clerocracy, but a mutually loving ministry. ("Priests" are not mentioned explicitly.) The individual, cleric and lay alike, must in the spirit of charity show humble obedience to the Church and to the rule of faith that should govern it. In its role as vehicle of the Holy Spirit, the Church was more nurturing than disciplinary. Its work took place not in the past but in the present, for the sake of the future. With the *Confessions*, theology now became salvation history, and Scripture as a safety net provides the core knowledge of the faith that prevents the dynamic and historical (time-conditioned) conversion efforts on the periphery from misleading the faithful. Conversion lies at the center of Augustine's theology of creation, redemption, and human history. All of a Christian life, rightly lived, is conversion.[25]

Beyond the *Confessions*, Augustine showed an abiding concern for the conversion of others. Just as God had converted Augustine inwardly through words and other external signs indicating his will, so the divine intentions were similarly manifested to others. This possibility Augustine grounded on Romans 1.20. Referring to the ungodly, the apostle said: "For the invisible things of him from the creation of the world are clearly seen, being understood by the things that are made, even his eternal power and Godhead; so that they are without excuse." To Augustine this meant that sense data can reliably reveal something of the divine nature, so that those who do not understand the message, even non-Christians, are culpable. Yet, because of sin, we cannot perceive divine truths directly but only through signs. As verbal signs the words of Scripture are especially privileged, since they are the product of Christ, the Word. If Scripture is a trustworthy guide to divine truths, its messages are often obscure and mysterious, so readers and hearers are forced to stretch their spiritual insight.[26] Shortly before writing the *Confessions,* Augustine had probed biblical hermeneutics in the *De Doctrina Christiana* ("On Christian Teaching"). Humans communicate via conventional signs, including language. Since these signs are variously interpreted by different people, a plurality of interpretations is possible. The common good sense of the whole Church acting in the spirit of charity constitutes the rule of faith that distinguishes useful from invalid interpretations.

About the time he was writing the *Confessions,* Augustine also produced the treatise *De Catechizandis Rudibus* ("On Instructing the Unlearned"), which applied the fruits of his study and experience to the conversion of non-Christians.[27] The treatise details the rhetorical strategy and tactics of the catechetical process, with much down-to-earth advice on how the catechist's words about Scripture could be persuasive. Augustine treats both the medium and the message of conversion. The treatise is not as nuanced as the *Confessions,* but the theology is put simply and cogently so that catechists who were not as gifted verbally as Augustine could still get across the Christian message. They should seek to establish a bond of love through their words. The narration of salvation history should produce charity, good conscience, and genuine faith, while at the same time instilling a salutary terror of God's severity. Augustine would have the learners empathize through the medium of the catechist's words with the complex double message of love and fear that he himself had experienced. Once the catechetical moment has been successfully reached, the learner can then seek the invisible things of God through membership in the Church.

In this treatise Augustine made two contentions that resonate with *Confessions* 13 and that he would later invoke against the Donatists. First, he insisted that bad Christians and others whose conversion remained incomplete would continue in the Church until their winnowing at the last judgment. Second, the Church in the meantime must exercise its pastoral role in the continuing work of conversion. In effect Augustine's pastoral strategy employed both the carrot and the stick: when rhetorical persuasion was ineffective, the Church could turn to coercion. Indeed, coercion was an integral component of conversion. As God had brought about Paul's and Augustine's conversion through external pressures, in short through signs, so the Church could pressure its wayward members to the unity of the faith. This was applied in Augustine's confrontation with the Donatists, a north African splinter group which claimed that the efficacy of the sacraments depended on the morality of the officiating priest.[28] The details aside, the essential bone of contention was God's role in the sacraments. Augustine's position was that Christ was the agent at work in the sacraments, whose effects then depended on the receptivity of the individual. To assert, as the Donatists did, that only a morally pure priest could administer an effective sacrament limited God's freedom of action in the conversion process.

The Donatist schism ruptured, in Augustine's view, the charity conferred on the Church by Christ and the Holy Spirit. At first he hoped to return them to unity through force of argument, but they remained obdurate. Meanwhile, imperial coercion was goading many Donatists to return to the Catholic fold, and they appeared grateful for the external discipline that had brought about their change of heart. In response, as Augustine explained in Letter 93, he broadened the tactics of his pastoral strategy to include coercion that broke the shackles of inveterate habit (5.17–18). In the repressive atmosphere of the late Roman Empire, pastoral severity could take the forms of harshness, fear, threats, fines, exile, and other secular misfortunes that went far beyond mere physical force. Such severity was the work of love (1.1; 1.3; 5.19). The parable of the Great Supper (Luke 14:15–24) served Augustine as a proof text for religious coercion. As the master of the household ordered his servants to compel those in the highways and byways to come to his feast, so the Church could compel the wayward Donatists to come into (*coge intrare*) the orthodox Church (2.5). Just as God used constraint and fear to discipline his people, so pastoral discipline could exert external pressure to bring about internal moral improvement (5.17). Compulsion was not incompatible with free choice, since Christ said "coge intrare" so that external necessity could give rise to inward free choice.[29] This is of profound psychological significance: thought control or behavior modification is possible through the continued application of external pressure.

In effect God legitimated religious coercion carried out by his agents. His external impingements on the individual will could be expressed as his own secret admonitions such as dreams, or as temporal laws.[30] When Christian imperial officials acted, the Church was acting in them.[31] In seeking the eternal welfare of its enemies even at the expense of their temporal well-being, the Church imitated God in carrying out justified persecutions.[32] The Church, not the imperial government, had the duty to exercise religious coercion, and so individual Christians who were imperial officials functioned as agents of the Church.[33] This attitude conformed to Augustine's general conviction that God's inward work of conversion could be effected not only by the Word but by external signs produced by human agents.

While he never advocated the death penalty for heresy, Augustine's justification of conversion by coercion left a dangerous legacy to the medieval Church, for it was prone to misuse and distortion in the hands of others.[34] Still, it reinforced the conversion program of *Confessions* 13, where he saw conversion as a joint effort of the Christian people against God's enemies as well as being a personal encounter with God. His legacy became part of the destabilizing, scrutinizing energy of medieval Christendom.[35]

As life can imitate art, so conversion by the book entailed conversion by means of Augustine's own books. If St. Patrick entered Ireland with the Bible in one hand and Augustine's *De Doctrina Christiana* in the other,[36] he and others should have had the *Confessions* in their knapsacks.[37] Few medieval missionaries could hope to understand, much less emulate, Augustine's literary sophistication, but their methods and examples, their trials and tribulations, were similar.[38] It could also be said that the monasticism of the Benedictine Rule assimilated Augustine's notion of conversion as a gradual process, one accompanied by asceticism, self-doubting criticism, and the terror of apostasy.[39] Penance could entail persecution; preaching the Gospel could merge with the manly blood sport of the Crusades where the brotherly love of Chaucer's knight-errant could hardly be distinguished from hatred.[40] Augustine's conversion experience as mirrored in his texts fostered an endless variety of individual variations and improvisations. Without it, medieval conversion by the book would have taken an entirely different course.

NOTES

Author's note: Research for this chapter took on additional dimensions during my participation in a 1993 National Endowment for the Humanities Summer Seminar, led by James J. O'Donnell, on Augustine and his influence.

1. Though old, Arthur Darby Nock's *Conversion: The Old and the New in Religion from Alexander the Great to Augustine of Hippo* (Oxford: Oxford University Press, 1933; reprint, 1961) is still useful. The literature on Augustine's own conversion is immense. I cite here only some helpful recent works. Foremost, of course, is the biography by Peter Brown, *Augustine of Hippo* (Berkeley: University of California Press, 1967), esp. part 2; a careful study of the semantic nuances of *conversion* is Goulven Madec, "Conuersio," *Augustinus-Lexikon* 1 (fasc. 7–8)

(1994): 1282–94; Paula Fredriksen, "Paul and Augustine: Conversion Narratives, Orthodox Traditions, and the Retrospective Self," *Journal of Theological Studies* n.s. 37 (1986): 3–34; E. Ann Matter, "Conversion(s) in the Confessiones," in *Collectanea Augustiniana*, ed. Joseph Schnaubelt and Frederick Van Fleteren (New York and Bern: P. Lang, 1990), 21–28; R. A. Markus, *Conversion and Disenchantment in Augustine's Spiritual Career* (Villanova, Pa.: Villanova University Press, 1989); Karl F. Morrison, *Conversion and Text: The Cases of Augustine of Hippo, Herman-Judah and Constantine Tsatsos* (Charlottesville: University Press of Virginia, 1992), and *Understanding Conversion* (Charlottesville: University Press of Virginia, 1992); James J. O'Donnell, *Augustine* (Boston: Twayne, 1985), esp. chaps. 5–6; Anton C. Pegis, "The Second Conversion of St. Augustine," in *Gesellschaft. Kultur. Literatur*, ed. Karl Bosl (Stuttgart: Hiersemann, 1975), 79–93; Geoffrey Galt Harpham, "Conversion and the Language of Autobiography," in *Studies in Autobiography*, ed. James Olney (Oxford: Oxford University Press, 1988), 42–50. Diane Jonte-Pace gives the state of the psychohistorical question in "Augustine on the Couch: Psychohistorical (Mis)readings of the Confessions," *Religion* 23 (1993): 71–83.

For the *Confessions*, I use the translation and notes of Henry Chadwick (Oxford: Oxford University Press, 1991) and also the Skutella edition of the Latin text as found in the Bibliothèque Augustinienne edition, vols. 13–14 (with introduction and notes by A. Solignac; hereafter cited as B.A.) (Paris, 1962). Recently James J. O'Donnell has published the text and an extensive computer-generated commentary that is a gold mine of information on particular points: *Augustine, Confessions: Text and Commentary*, 3 vols. (Oxford: Oxford University Press, 1992).

2. Morrison, *Understanding*, 185.

3. Matter, "Conversion(s)," 22; Nock, *Conversion*, 8.

4. Markus, *Conversion and Disenchantment*, esp. 2.

5. Markus, *Conversion and Disenchantment*, 2–3; Morrison, *Text*, viii; Morrison, *Understanding*, 143.

6. Cf. R. A. Markus, *The End of Ancient Christianity* (Cambridge: Cambridge University Press, 1990), 28–33.

7. *Conf.*, 3.4.8; Nock, *Conversion*, 263–64.

8. Cf. Madec, "Conuersio," 1290.

9. Morrison, *Text*, xii; Morrison, *Understanding*, 185.

10. Cf. Morrison, *Text*, vii, xi; Morrison, *Understanding*, 124; Fredriksen, "Paul and Augustine." The *Confessions* can be seen as a conversion of the experience of the self into narrative discourse: Harpham, "Conversion and Language," 42, 46.

11. Cf. B.A. 14, Note complémentaire 3: "*Libido* et *consuetudo* d'après Augustin," 537–42; J. G. Prendeville, "The Development of the Idea of Habit in the Thought of Saint Augustine," *Traditio* 28 (1972): 29–99.

12. Cf. Nock, *Conversion*, 263–64.

13. Cf. Harpham, "Conversion and Language," 43.

14. Cf. Brown, *Augustine*, 177; Markus, *End*, 54.

15. Cf. Wallace Fowlie, "On Writing Autobiography," in Olney, *Studies in Autobiography* (see n. 1), 166; and Germaine Brée, "Autogynography," ibid., 173.

16. Cf. O'Donnell, *Augustine,* 117–22; O'Donnell, *Confessions,* 1.51, 3.343.

17. Cf. *De Trinitate,* 15.11.20.

18. The discussion here draws upon B.A. 14, Note complémentaire 27: "Conversion et formation," 613–17; O'Donnell, *Confessions,* 3.347–8, 362; Gerhart Ladner, *The Idea of Reform: Its Impact on Christian Thought and Action in the Age of the Fathers,* rev. ed. (New York: Harper and Row, 1967), 168–69, 194–99, 237–38; Madec, "Conuersio," 1288–89; Harpham, "Conversion and Language," 48–50.

19. Cf. *De genesi ad litteram,* 1.4.9–5.10.

20. Cf. *De gen. ad litt.,* 11.15.20; *City of God* 14.28.

21. Cf. B.A. 14, Note complémentaire 29: "L'interprétation spirituelle de l'Écriture," 626–27.

22. Cf. Harpham, "Conversion and Language," 44–45.

23. Cf. *Conf.,* 3.9.17; *De Catechizandis Rudibus,* 25.49; *City of God,* 15.4.

24. William James, *The Varieties of Religious Experience* (New York: Modern Library, 1929), 186; cf. 168–72.

25. Pegis, "Second Conversion," 90; Morrison, *Understanding,* xii, 25.

26. *Conf.,* 3.5.9; 8.17.23; 11.9.11; 13.14.17.

27. For this treatise see F. Van der Meer, *Augustine the Bishop* (New York: Sheed and Ward, 1961), 453–67.

28. Fuller discussions of Augustine's anti-Donatist polemic can be found in R. A. Markus, *Saeculum: History and Society in the Theology of St. Augustine* (Cambridge: Cambridge University Press, 1970, 1988), 105–53; H. Deane, *The Political and Social Ideas of St. Augustine* (New York: Columbia University Press, 1963), 172–43; Brown, *Augustine,* 212–58; G. G. Willis, *Saint Augustine and the Donatist Controversy* (London: Society for Promoting Christian Knowledge, 1950); G. Bonner, *St. Augustine of Hippo: Life and Controversies* (London: SCM Press, 1963), 237–75.

29. *Sermo 112,* 8: "foris inveniatur necessitas, nascitur intus voluntas."

30. *Epist. 105,* 4.13.

31. *Epist. 134,* 4.

32. *Epist. 185,* 6.23; 2.11.

33. Cf. Markus, *Saeculum,* 149–53.

34. Cf. Deane, *Ideas of St. Augustine,* esp. 216–20; Markus, *Saeculum,* 133–53; Peter Brown, "St. Augustine's Attitude to Religious Coercion," in his *Religion and Society in the Age of Saint Augustine* (New York: Harper and Row, 1971), 260–78, and "Religious Coercion in the Later Roman Empire: The Case of North Africa," ibid., 301–31; E. Lamirande, *Church, State and Toleration: An Intriguing Change of Mind in Augustine* (Villanova, Pa.: Augustinian Institute, Villanova University Press, 1975).

35. For the restless demand for reform that conversion entails, cf. Morrison, *Text,* 148.

36. E. Kevane, "Augustine's *De Doctrina Christiana* in World-Historical Perspective," *Collectanea Augustiniana—Mélanges Van Bavel,* 2 vols. (Louvain: University Press, 1990), 2:1031.

37. The *Confessions* were as well known in the Middle Ages as the *De Doctrina Christiana:* Matter, "Conversion(s)," 25; on Augustine's influence generally, see James J. O'Donnell, "The Authority of Augustine," *Augustinian Studies* 22 (1991):7–35.

38. These include intercession of the clergy to defend marginalized persons; conversion by catechesis and coercion; asceticism; the use of signs; the struggle against idolatry; and the development of a Christocentric liturgy for the Church as a praying community; see Edward Peters, ed., *Monks, Bishops and Pagans: Christian Culture in Gaul and Italy, 500–700* (Philadelphia: University of Pennsylvania Press, 1975), and J. N. Hillgarth, ed., *Christianity and Paganism, 350–750: The Conversion of Western Europe,* rev. ed. (Philadelphia: University of Pennsylvania Press, 1986).

39. Morrison, *Understanding,* xviii, 14, 70.

40. Cf. Morrison, *Text,* 8; Morrison *Understanding,* xvii, 47, 65, 114, 139, 163.

2

Monastic Conversion
The Case of Margaret Ebner

Leonard P. Hindsley O.P.

Conversion as treated in the majority of the essays in this volume concerns, for example, a change in religion from pagan to Christian or Muslim to Catholic, whether by force or free will. However, the ideal of conversion in the Middle Ages had more to do with the establishment of a setting that disposed the Christian to a deeper life in Christ, which in turn would bring about the interior conversion of the individual. To convert to Christ implied not only receiving the sacrament of baptism or learning the Lord's prayer and the Creed by heart but also knowing the love of Christ and living by his law of love. This interior conversion demands repentance, true belief in the Gospel of Jesus Christ, and the establishment of a personal relationship with Christ himself. It entails a "new life in Christ," which implies a process of growth in holiness.[1] In the case of Margaret Ebner and of many other such individuals, this process led to mystical experiences. The ideal (although not the only) setting for this deeper conversion to Christ in the Middle Ages and throughout Christian history is the monastery. In order to demonstrate this monastic ideal of conversion I shall refer to the *Rule* of St. Augustine and the *Constitutions* of the Dominican nuns and also use the autobiographical *Revelations* of the Dominican nun and mystic Margaret Ebner (ca. 1291–1351) to show that ideal as a lived experience. Margaret recorded the events of her life at the request of her spiritual director, Henry of Nördlingen. The *Revelations* is not a didactic text to teach others how to progress in conversion of life; rather and more importantly, it presents the events in the course of Margaret Ebner's life over almost her entire adulthood from 1311 to 1348. In this, the text gains its value for it records a life which can then be observed to see what "conversion of life" entailed in the story of a fourteenth-century woman. From that life we learn that there is an explicit connection between the ideal of monastic life and the perfection of Christian conversion. To illustrate this connection I shall discuss the monastic ideal of the Dominican nuns; show how that ideal was enfleshed by Margaret Ebner as recorded in the *Revelations;* and finally concentrate on three aspects of monastic conversion exemplified by Margaret Ebner—simplicity, patience, and compassion.

The Monastic Ideal of Conversion

The monastery provides the setting for living the monastic ideal of Christian life. Especially its rules and even its architecture foster conversion. Humbert of Romans, Master of the Order of Friars Preachers, imposed the *Constitutions* of the Sisters of the Order in 1259. He drew a direct connection between monastic life and conversion in the first paragraph of the *Constitutions.* "Since by precept of the Rule [of St. Augustine] the Sisters are commanded to have one heart and one mind in the Lord, it is fitting that since they live under the same Rule and under the vow of one profession, they should be uniform in the observance of the same Constitutions: for uniformity observed outwardly in our manners fosters and brings to mind that unity which ought to be preserved inwardly in our hearts."[2] The manner of life as observed externally should bring about an interior change in the individual sister. This interior conversion brings about unity of mind and heart with God/Christ and with neighbor. Because this process forms the core and very reason for living a monastic/Christian life, Humbert in the *Constitutions* pays careful attention to every possible aspect of life— how to pray in public, what to eat, how to dress, and even how to shampoo and cut hair (Const. I–XII). Everything done from singing in chapel to working in the monastery provides the external means for interior conversion. Having recognized this monastic ideal of conversion in a Dominican context, one should note that more than the setting is required for conversion of life. Not all monastics are converted to deeper union with Christ and neighbor. Not all achieve Christian perfection, yet many do. One such is Margaret Ebner.

To be open to the converting power of the Holy Spirit, the nun was asked to adhere strictly to the regimen of the monastery. Certain observances, as we shall see, fostered conversion even to the degree of mystical experience. Each of these activities prescribed by the *Rule* and *Constitutions*—silence, reading, and psalmody—will reappear in mystical guise: binding silence (*gebundene swigen*), uncontrollable speaking (*rede*), and loud outcries (*lute ruefen*).

Monastic life valued the use of silence as an aid to prayer and contemplation. Sisters had to keep silence in the "oratory, in the cloister, in the dormitory, and in the refectory" (*Const.* XIII). Permission had to be given to speak, even in the *locutorium.* Any sister who broke silence suffered progressively more severe penalties: to recite the *Miserere* (Psalm 50), to receive the discipline, to eat sitting on the floor (*Const.* XIII). The early Dominicans considered silence to be the guardian of all observances. It was a *sine qua non* in the monastery inasmuch as it fostered the interior life (conversion), prayer, and peace. St. Dominic emphasized the need and value of silence in his *Letter* to the nuns at Madrid (May 1220), who had just moved into their own monastery. "From now on I want you to keep the silence in the prescribed places, namely, the refectory, the dormitory, and the oratory, and to observe your Rule fully in everything else too."[3] Lest the point be missed he added, "Do not chatter with each other, or waste your time gossiping."[4]

Reading and *lectio divina,* an ancient method of becoming familiar with Christ by memorizing Scripture, held an important place in monastic life precisely because to be ignorant of the Scriptures is not to know Christ. In the *Constitutions,* disturbing reading was a light fault (XVII). Unlike most medieval women, nuns were taught to read precisely so that they could participate in the worship of the Divine Office and read Scripture, Commentaries, and other spiritual works. Especially in the fourteenth century, it is clear that the nuns valued books and actively sought to obtain copies of important texts for their libraries. Henry of Nördlingen sent texts to Margaret Ebner and the nuns of Maria Medingen. There also seems to have been a lively exchange of manuscripts between Medingen and the Cistercian monks of Kaisheim. Henry of Nördlingen refers to various important texts in his letters to Margaret Ebner and recommends reading them: the *Summa Theologiae* of St. Thomas, his *Summa contra Gentes,* Henry Suso's *Little Book of Eternal Wisdom.*[5] Henry also sent Margaret a copy of Mechthild of Magdeburg's *The Flowing Light of the Godhead.*[6] Further, in her own works Margaret demonstrates knowledge of the writings of St. Bernard of Clairvaux, especially his sermons on the Song of Songs, when she speaks of her desire for the "kiss of love."[7] Of course, Margaret's favorite reading was the passion narrative (ME 136). Especially during her periods of illness, she desired to hear of Christ's suffering. In her *Pater Noster* she prayed that she might take delight in nothing but Christ's passion (ME 175). In the *Revelations* she quotes or alludes to many scriptural verses, particularly from the Gospel of St. John or the Letters of St. Paul.[8]

The solemn singing of the psalms is probably the most recognizable characteristic of monastics. The canonical hours of worship (matins, lauds, prime, terce, sext, none, vespers, and compline) gathered the entire community together to worship God. The very first chapter of the *Constitutions* of 1259 gives direction on the office of the Church, thus emphasizing its importance for the community. "The Sisters assist all together at Matins and at all the canonical hours, unless some are dispensed for a reasonable cause. All the canonical hours must be recited in the church, distinctly and without precipitation, so that the Sisters will not lose devotion" (*Const.* I). After admission into the monastery, novices are to be trained "to diligently study psalmody and the Divine Office" (*Const.* XV). Any sister who sang inattentively, disturbed the choir, or offended by "singing badly" incurred a light fault (*Const.* XVII). More serious infractions such as lateness to choir, levity, acting in an unbecoming manner during office, singing anything that was not prescribed, or laughing and causing others to laugh during the canonical hour incurred the punishment of a medium fault (*Const.* XVIII). The various penalties imposed underscore the importance of the celebration of the canonical hours as acts of worship. For monastics it is the most important work of the community and the most important event in the horarium after the celebration of the Eucharist.

The observance of silence, reading, and singing the psalms in obedience to the *Constitutions* fostered intense private prayer and conversion of life for both the individual nun and for the community as a whole. It is important to note that Humbert of Romans intended this to be the case even if his *Constitutions* might appear to be simply a set of arbitrary rules. "He (Humbert) is at pains to make clear that mere external legalistic obedience for the sake of conforming to some human-made regulation is not what he means. That kind of conduct, lacking heart, is a mere shell. He is dealing with the whole-hearted generous dedication of one's self to God, expressed in the Dominican formula of profession."[9] Only such interior, whole-hearted dedication makes true conversion for the individual and for the whole community possible.

Into just such a community Margaret entered when she was accepted by the nuns of Maria Medingen around the year 1305. Presumably she took the veil of her own volition, but by her own admission she did not seem to have been as particularly fervent as she might have been (ME 85). This admission does not imply that she neglected the external observances of the Dominican monastic life; it merely asserts that her observance did not yet have any particular interior quality to it. After all, the observances should dispose the nun to conversion. It should be no surprise that Margaret should be converted after living as a nun in the monastery. At the beginning of the *Revelations* Margaret wrote unambiguously of her time in the monastery and at home prior to the initial conversion experience. "How I had lived during the previous twenty years I cannot describe because I had not been attentive to myself" (ME 10). By contrast, after the beginning of her conversion she wrote, "I took careful note of all that I did, in eating and drinking and sleeping" (ME 87). One of the petitions of her *Pater Noster* also emphasized her desire for self-awareness. "Give us, my Lord, constant attentiveness to ourselves in your heartfelt love and a powerful sign of victory over all evil" (ME 175). She had come to understand that such self-scrutiny was necessary to make progress in the spiritual life. This document of Margaret's awareness of herself, of the power of evil, and of the ways of God is her *Revelations*.

The Revelations: Documentary of Conversion

Remarkably, the *Revelations* of Margaret Ebner cover almost the entire length of her earthly life. Margaret began to write her "little book" at the insistence of her spiritual director and friend, Henry of Nördlingen, during the Advent of 1344. However, the time frame of the *Revelations* began with her initial conversion experience of 1312 and concluded with the year 1348. The fact that Margaret was careful to note the events of her life, her experiences in prayer, her insights into reality, and her relationships with saints in heaven, souls in purgatory, sisters in her monastery, and with Henry, and especially her mystical encounters with God, offers a rich field for research into the topic of conversion.

Margaret understood conversion of life not as a once for all, immediate event but rather as a lengthy process, which although initiated by some deep insight, nevertheless called for acquiescence of the will at every turn in the spiritual life. "In this sense . . . purification is a perpetual process. That which mystical writers mean, however, when they speak of the Way of Purgation, is rather the slow and painful completion of conversion."[10] This gradual process transformed Margaret by the action of God's grace such that she became by grace what Christ is by nature. Through meditation her life became a perfect imitation of the Savior in his acts of redemption. Margaret delighted in meditations on the mystery of the incarnation, the hidden life of Christ at Nazareth, the public ministry of healing and preaching, the passion, resurrection, and even Christ's continuing presence in the Church through the Eucharist and the sacraments. This process of conversion is the "putting on" of Christ in the fullest sense, and she wished that such a conversion might be brought to completion in all who believe. Her continuing conversion can be characterized not so much as a turning away from evil but rather primarily as a turning toward something good— toward Jesus, whom she understood as Truth and Beloved. Her conversion process then continued with her increasingly great desire for union with her Beloved Savior.

Although Margaret related that she was rather nonreflective during her first twenty years of life, she also intimated that she had a greater desire to live according to the will of God in 1311, having practiced the round of religious life, duties, and prayer as a Dominican nun at the monastery of Maria Medingen for approximately six years. This daily and seasonal cycle of choral and private prayer was meant to induce a spirit of conversion in the individual nun. These means by the grace of God acted to effect a conversion of heart or an interiorization of the Gospel Law of Love. The cloistered regimen provided a basis of faith by which the nun could interpret all the events of life in the light of the salvific mission of Jesus Christ so that she would be able to grow deeper by grace into the mystery of redemption and eternal life. For Margaret this gradual process was spurred on by means of a catalyst—her initial conversion experience in 1312. Margaret's conversion progressed over the years, but instead of speaking of the process of conversion in terms of the traditional "ways"—purgation, illumination, and union, which have already been discussed elsewhere—I shall speak of the characteristics of Margaret's conversion: simplicity, patience, and compassion.[11]

Simplicity

One of the necessary prerequisites for the monastic ideal of conversion to Christ is simplicity of life. Popular thought frequently associates simplicity with the vow of poverty understood as a rejection of material things, especially of money. However, simplicity of life covers many more aspects of life than money. For Margaret Ebner simplicity entailed new priorities in daily life. In view of the goal of union with Christ, the ideal of simplicity demanded the renunciation of attachment to all things, especially to others and to self-will. Even before Margaret's conversion insight she had secretly wished for union with the will of God. "Already during the previous year [1311] I had received continual exhortations to direct my whole life according to His will" (ME 85). Despite her desire to live by God's will, the struggle to do so was both difficult and protracted. Margaret's severe initial illness of thirteen years constantly reminded her of the change that she desired to make. She sought counsel from another nun whom she trusted. "She told me I should give myself over to God completely" (ME 85). During her illness Margaret gradually came to her conversion insight. Having been "abandoned" by her sisters in the monastery, she came to realize the source and depth of conversion. "Then I understood that God alone remains faithful. He would never abandon me" (ME 86). For her God is the "Faithful One" upon whom all else in life and in eternity rests. This insight inaugurated Margaret's conversion, her personal relationship with a living and true God. With this realization she was able to write: "So I gave myself over to the will of God and desired that He not let me recover my health, but then He restored me to health both in body and soul" (ME 86). The renunciation of her own will and the acceptance of God's will in her life had only begun. The contest of wills would continue even though Margaret desired to surrender to God. She worried about this:

> I was greatly concerned that I myself was not so well disposed to God with interior desire as I should have been, and also did not yet live according to His will. This bothered me especially because I did not have the necessary love and desire for the Eucharist and because I was not adequately prepared whenever I should receive Him in communion. I blamed myself and thought this was so because I had not withdrawn myself definitively from all earthly things. (ME 87)

Margaret viewed withdrawal from all earthly things as a necessary part of conversion. She adamantly pursued a course of action to focus her attention on her goal. She was reserved toward all and refrained from talking and visiting others. She did not consult her friends because she believed that "no one could help me except God alone" (ME 87). She attested that the struggle continued. "As much as I was able, I withdrew myself from all thoughts that disturbed me or hindered my prayer and devotions" (ME 87). Again and again she resolved to withdraw from all people and to spurn conversation, especially gossip. She, like St. Dominic, desired to hear talk only of God. In addition she devoted herself more fervently to private prayer by using her own *Pater Noster*, which helped to alleviate her sufferings. One of the petitions of Margaret's prayer expressed her desire and the reason for living by the will of God. "I ask you, my Lord, Jesus Christ, by your perfect grace, to help us always to be guided by your will, be good or ill done to us, so that your powerful might may bind us and your sweet love compel us such that we might have no mere natural life in us, but may you, Jesus Christ, live in us with all your grace; and may we live for you alone in truth" (ME 175). Eventually, this process of conversion would entail even a renunciation of self as she prayed here. However, the renunciation of self served not to negate the self but to prepare the self to take on the life of Christ to the fullest. Margaret paraphrased Gal. 2:20, "If I live, it is not I who live, Jesus Christ lives in me" (ME 159). This Pauline kenosis makes union with Christ possible. This withdrawal was not a disappointed reaction, as Zoepf claims.[12] The life of the contemplative requires withdrawal. As Evelyn Underhill points out, it is a natural and even necessary step in the mystical life.[13] Withdrawal was a method whereby Margaret wished to extricate herself from anything that would hinder prayer, her contact with God.

For Margaret, simplicity entailed withdrawal from all that was not of

God, so that she might be filled with all that was of God. In the *Pater Noster*, Margaret prayed to be delivered from all evil and concluded, "What is evil? All, my Lord, that is not you" (ME 177).

Likewise she simplified her prayer, reciting only vigils and the psalter, and simplified her intentions (ME 86). Later, she would adopt her own *Pater Noster* as her usual prayer and ultimately even that would be "taken away" from her, leaving only her favorite prayer, "Jesus Christus," recited as a mantra. Her final testament concludes the *Revelations* with a moving account of the simplicity of this prayer. "The Name *Jesus Christus* . . . blossoms within me during the season of Advent with especially sweet grace and I can do nothing except what is given me with Jesus and from Jesus and in Jesus" (ME 172). In its simplicity, this prayer not only stripped away anything that would hinder contact with God but focused Margaret's entire spirituality on Jesus. The simplicity of the prayer simplified Margaret's spiritual life and made it powerfully effective due to the focus on the God/Man. Every aspect of her life and spirituality was gradually simplified: one prayer—"Jesus Christus"; one guide—Henry of Nördlingen; one desire—union with the Beloved; one way—the path of suffering.

Patience

"Conformity to God's will is a bitter prescription for all of us, especially when it presents itself in the form of suffering."[14] When writing of Margaret's patience, I write not only of the practice of a virtue by which one demonstrates patience but of a patience that refers to any sort of suffering (*passio*) she had to endure during her spiritual journey. Her suffering included physical illness which was both severe and lengthy. She lay bedridden for over thirteen years and throughout her life she reported numerous incidents of illness that were so severe that those who witnessed her suffering often believed that she would die. Margaret described her initial "conversion" illness in detail.

> My illness began strangely with a great, unbearable pain which gripped my heart so that I could not easily breathe. My breathing could be heard from very far away. The pain then went to my eyes so that I could not see, and this continued throughout the illness. Then it went to my hands, and I could not move them. It affected my whole body, except for my hearing, which I never lost. I endured this pain for three years and, during that time, had no control over myself. (ME 85)

This suffering aided the process of conversion by withdrawing much of Margaret's capability to sense her surroundings. That her pain began around her heart already foreshadows the ultimate joy that she will experience in the exchange of hearts (*minnegriff*) in 1344. As we know, Margaret did not like this illness and sought a cure by human means, but with its continuation she realized that she had to give interior consent to the will of God in her life. She had come to the conclusion that God alone would always remain faithful and it was to him and to nothing else that she owed her will. This initial illness benefited Margaret by teaching her to withdraw from the ways of the world and to advance in the ways of God. This same lesson would be repeated again and again. Margaret's response to suffering gradually took on a more positive hue. Although she lamented her inability to follow the discipline of the monastery in her illness, she came to realize that the illness was for her spiritual welfare.

Margaret also suffered emotionally. Abandonment was her greatest fear. This may have been caused by the "abandonment" of her father dying. Nothing is known of him. He is not mentioned on the one occasion when Margaret was forced to return to her mother's home during the siege of Burgau in December 1324. Margaret never mentioned her father under any circumstances. However, there is clear evidence that "abandonment," from whatever deep psychological cause, was a major concern for Margaret. This sort of suffering manifested itself in the death of loved ones. The deaths of three consecutive laysister-companions caused her great grief. Her mourning for the first to die had been so intense that she seemed to be depressed beyond help. Even visions of her beloved laysister did nothing to alleviate her sorrow. Margaret related the whole process of this (unnamed) laysister's death. "I knelt before the altar after compline, and the grace was given me to realize that I must suffer, but that God would help me in this suffering" (ME 91). After reciting the psalms in choir for the repose of the soul of the deceased laysister, Margaret stated: "As I lay there my heart was flooded with a very strong, great light, with many graces and with much joy. I felt great joy in the thought that I should be suffering for God" (ME 92). Even though Margaret accepted this suffering, she continued to lament beyond the limit. In a vision, she beheld the deceased laysister, who chastised her. "How can you carry on about me in this way? If you could have me as I am now, you would prefer to have me so! You should cease to mourn for me as I once was" (ME 92). Even the promise that a throne awaited Margaret in heaven did not ameliorate her grief. Ultimately, Henry of Nördlingen, a spiritual director of some renown, was summoned to come to her aid. Progressively with the deaths of other laysisters, Margaret's suffering diminished in direct relationship to her detachment from the things of the world and her attachment to and trust in the One who would always remain faithful. Even the deaths of dearest friends became an instrument of conversion for Margaret. Her suffering had value for her own spiritual welfare.

Her attitude toward the Emperor, Louis IV (the Bavarian), also caused her sorrow. She considered him to be a special assignment of prayer for her. Why this is so is a subject of some speculation. She followed his political career throughout his life and remained faithful to him even after he had been killed. In a letter Henry chided her for speaking of the new emperor, Charles IV, as "his" king and admonished her to accept Charles as the "Christian" king, now that Louis was dead.[15]

Louis was also the cause of suffering in matters of conscience for Margaret. Because of the quarrel over the legitimacy of the various claimants to the imperial throne, Pope John XXII had excommunicated Louis and placed all his subject peoples under the ban of interdict. For Margaret and for all the nuns this caused untold suffering due to the prohibition on celebrating the sacraments. Ultimately, she and her whole monastery would view it as a matter of conscience and continue receiving Holy Communion. Margaret had revelations in this regard that strengthened her resolve to receive the Eucharist.

Also because of the interdict, Henry chose to leave his homeland and to exercise his priestly ministry outside the lands under the bann. His absence caused suffering for Margaret, because she had come to trust him and depend upon his advice. His absence had the positive effect of making necessary the first exchange of letters in German.

Most importantly, Margaret viewed the patient endurance of suffering as something positive and beneficial, not only to herself but to others such as the souls in purgatory. In fact, Margaret could understand no other sort of spirituality than the way of suffering. She wrote, "When I heard about someone who led a great and perfect life, but did not follow the way of the sufferings of Our Lord, I could not understand" (ME 107).

Compassion

Just as with the use of the word *patience,* the definition of the term *compassion* also has an extended sense for it refers to the virtue of compassion for the sufferings of others as well as to Margaret's commiseration with the passion of Christ. Both senses of the word apply to the spirituality of Margaret Ebner. Both indicate entrance into the highest degrees of spiritual progress.

In the *Revelations* Margaret acts with compassion for all manner of persons. For her first laysister companion she showed the depth of her love and appreciation for that nun in her own suffering. It is worth quoting an extended passage from the *Revelations* to demonstrate the relationship between the two nuns.

> I had a sister, whom God had given me for consolation in body and soul and who was very faithful to me. By divine design she served me joyfully throughout the years and protected me from all things that could disturb me. When, in my illness, I was sometimes unkind to her when she served me, she did not hold that against me. This sister became very ill by God's design. Then we were both sick and in suffering and patiently endured much pain. Because of that I was greatly distressed out of concern for my sister. I slept little every night due to sorrow, and still I desired to see her even in her suffering up to my own death. We were both weak and sick and suffering from the Assumption until St. Matthias Day of the next year. Then she died. (ME 90–91)

The importance of this relationship for Margaret seems evident in this passage even without reference to later events. In this sister, Margaret had found in a human being the very godlike quality that she so much desired— faithfulness. Margaret's compassion for this sister arose from her need for sororal companionship. Her concern was so great that she stated unequivocally, "I would gladly have died for her" (ME 91). That Margaret's "compassion" here had more to do with her own need than with compassion for the sufferings of the sister is clear from Margaret's intense and protracted period of grieving following the death of the laysister. "There were times when I thought I could not be without my sister and could not live without her" (ME 92). Further, despite revelations from a vision of this sister by which Margaret was assured of her heavenly happiness, Margaret refused to give up her grief. Her reaction to this death was so extreme that a well-known spiritual director, Henry of Nördlingen, had to be summoned to give her advice in overcoming her depression. He first met her on October 29, 1332, and his successful advice and care furthered the process of Margaret's conversion. Subsequently, other laysister companions whom she loved also suffered death, but for Margaret the suffering was not the same for her compassion became more genuine in that her primary concern was not her own loss but the suffering of the other sister.

Early in her spiritual journey, Margaret had the desire to pray for the souls in purgatory. She wrote in her *Revelations*: "I had a great yearning to pray for the souls. In turn, they were very comforting to me in all my affairs and revealed to me the things that I wanted to know about myself and also about the Souls" (ME 97). Here too, her compassion for the souls was well intentioned but also useful to her. She was also praised by the souls. "Sometimes they sent a Soul to me, who had been a sister of our monastery, and she thanked me for what I had done for them" (ME 88). With time her compassion extended even to souls who were of no immediate use to her. "Many Souls whom I did not know also visited me. They revealed their lives to me and asked me to keep them in mind" (ME 88). So great was her compassion for them that she often promised to pray a thousand vigils for their benefit and continued to pray for them diligently despite the ridicule of her companion during her visit home with her family while the monastery was in danger because of the Battle of Burgau. It should not seem strange for Margaret to turn first to the souls in purgatory and to adopt them as one of her primary prayer intentions. The practice of praying for the dead was very important among Dominicans. The deceased sisters were remembered every year on their anniversary of death. Each time a sister walked over the graves in the cloister corridor, she recited the *De Profundis* (Psalm 130) for the repose of their souls. Dominicans regularly offered special prayers for the dead and followed elaborate rituals for burial, even more so than those practiced by other orders. Chapter III of the *Constitutions* required suffrages for the dead from each sister. From the feast of St. Denis (October 9) until Advent, literate sisters had to pray the psalter while the illiterate sisters recited five hundred paters for the deceased.

Margaret showed sympathy for her contemporaries as well. In showing sympathy for the serving girls, Margaret used the opportunity to reflect upon the goodness of God despite her own unworthiness. "When I heard that some one was angry with our serving girls and had said to them, 'You are not worthy to serve us,' heartfelt sorrow overcame me so that I cried and thought, 'God has never said that I was unworthy to serve Him'" (ME 90). She made a clear connection between the perfect action and attitude of God and the attitude and actions that the Christian must imitate in order to fulfill the commands "You, therefore, must be perfect as your heavenly Father is perfect" and "You shall be holy for I am holy" (ME 90; Matt. 5:48; 1 Pet. 1:16).

Also, early on Margaret began to pray for the emperor—Louis the Bavarian. "I had great pity especially for one man who was in great sorrow and I prayed much for him. It was made known to me by God and by the Holy Souls how it would turn out with him in his difficulties. In a dream I saw how our Lord grasped this same man beneath his arms and spoke to him saying He would never forsake him, neither here nor in the life to come. At the same time I was told by my dear Souls that this man would not have lived so long without my prayers" (ME 87–88). Scholars speculate as to the reason Margaret became so attached to Louis the Bavarian. She recognized that Louis was in part to blame for the sorrowful state of Christianity at that time. Louis had been excommunicated by Pope John XXII because of their disagreement in the perennial problem of imperial/ papal authority. Eventually Louis would use the Franciscan spiritualist teachings of Marsilius of Padua and Michael of Cesena to assert imperial authority over papal claims with regard to the confirmation of the imperial dignity. Because of Louis, his subject lands suffered the disciplinary punishment of interdiction, which caused a crisis of conscience for Margaret and the other nuns at Maria Medingen who wished to receive Holy Communion. And yet Margaret clearly saw Louis as her special prayer concern throughout his life. "I considered him to have been given me by God. Then I received special grace and the inclination to pray for all his affairs and desires" (ME 88). Margaret's ardent attachment to Louis as a man, rather than to his cause, may have stemmed from personal friendship or acquaintance with him. The Ebner family of Donauwörth formed part of the imperial party that restored the city to the control of Louis the Bavarian. It is certain that Louis frequently visited Donauwörth, and Ludwig Zoepf concluded that Margaret's attachment to him may have arisen from unknown personal reasons.[16] From her own testimony this may be the case. At one time she was told in a revelation that she should convey a message to Louis. "I did not do that. I failed to do it out of fear that he would know that it was I" (ME 165). She firmly believed the revelation that he would not have lived so long without her prayers. She did not wish him to know that she was his spiritual benefactress, perhaps because he knew her from her time before admission into the monastery. This hesitancy also shows a progression in her compassion for Louis. There is no hint of political gain or obligation; she interceded for him simply because she believed the revelation that Louis bore love for God, "unknown to any but himself and me (God)" (ME 165). Her attachment to the emperor provided another moment of conversion and insight when she desired to view the imperial regalia consisting of the crown, scepter, orb, and coronation mantle, which were hidden within the cloister for protection. These instruments were considered to be almost sacral and were understood to be necessary for a valid coronation. In a revelation she was asked to choose between the desire to see the crown and scepter and other accoutrements and her desire for God. She was told, "They [the imperial regalia] are nothing to you! Go, instead, to the tabernacle in choir! There and nowhere else will you find my Holy Body as truly as in heaven!" (ME 89). Earthly pomp was nothing by comparison to the presence of God in the chapel. Having made the choice for the things of God, Margaret found that the reception of Christ in the Eu-

compassion with Christ's suffering caused her to weep and cry out in sympathy, thus disrupting the service (ME 137). Meditation upon the passion led to mystical experiences of the Passion. She received the invisible stigmata. She swooned while witnessing the horrors of Christ's suffering as if before her very eyes. Margaret's commiseration with him was complete in the constant and uncontrollable repetition of the sacred Name—Jesus Christus. In sympathy she cried out, "Oh no! My beloved Lord Jesus Christ!" (ME 157). She beheld him hanging upon the cross (ME 169). She understood no other way of growth in holiness than through the way of suffering and compassion for Christ in his martyrdom. Margaret understood this pattern of "putting on Christ" to be the normal course of the life of any Christian. It was not simply a part of "conversion" to Christ but was in fact conversion to Christ by imitating his experiences as well as following his teachings.

Conclusion

Conversion as exemplified in the life of Margaret Ebner, recorded and interpreted in her autobiographical *Revelations,* is a gradual process of conforming the will of the nun or of any believer to the will of a faithful and benevolent God. For Margaret this process of conversion began with her own interior desire for deeper conversion to Christ and intensified with her illness, which led to the profound insight that God alone is faithful in the deepest sense of that term. Upon this insight rests the remarkable and amazing growth in holiness that Margaret exhibits gradually during the course of her life. The monastery provided the setting for this process of conversion and the monastic observances furthered Margaret's progress by helping her to prioritize correctly all the details of life and faith always directed toward the goal of union with Christ. Progress toward that union is demonstrated by the gradual assumption of the qualities of simplicity, patience, and compassion, the fulfillment of which likens Margaret to Christ himself. Ultimately, Margaret entered into the highest levels of mystical life, entry into which, she believed, stands open to all who follow the path of joyful endurance of suffering by believing in Christ, living as he did, and loving him even unto death.

Notes

1. 2 Cor. 5:17.

2. *Early Documents of the Dominican Sisters,* vol. 2 (Summit, N.J.: Dominican Nuns of Summit, 1969), 5. This includes the *Constitutions* of the order and is henceforth cited in text as *Const.*

3. Simon Tugwell O.P., ed., *Early Dominicans* (New York and Mahwah: Paulist Press, 1982), 394.

4. Ibid.

5. Philipp Strauch, *Margaretha Ebner und Heinrich von Nördlingen* (Freiburg in Breisgau and Tübingen: Akademisches Verlagsbuchhandlung von J.C.B. Mohr, 1882; reprint, Amsterdam: Verlag P. Schippers, N.V., 1966), letters LXV, XL, XLIII, XXIX, XXX, LI.

6. Strauch, *Ebner und Nördlingen,* letter XLIII.

7. Leonard P. Hindsley, ed., *Margaret Ebner: Major Works* (New York and Mahwah: Paulist Press, 1993), 122.

8. John 4:14; 1 Cor. 2:9; 2 Cor. 4:16; Gal. 2:20; Rom. 14:8.

9. Mary Bede Kearns O.P., "An Introduction to the Thought and Writings of Humbert of Romans," *Dominican Ashram* 4, no. 2 (June 1985): 69.

10. Evelyn Underhill, *Mysticism: A Study in the Nature and Development of Man's Spiritual Consciousness* (New York: E. P. Dutton, 1961), 204.

11. See H. Wilms, *Das Tugendstreben der Mystikerinnen* (Vechta in Oldenburg: Albertus Magnus Verlag, 1927).

12. Ludwig Zoepf, *Die Mystikerin Margaretha Ebner* (Leipzig and Berlin: Verlag B.G. Teubner, 1914), 32.

13. Underhill, *Mysticism,* 204.

14. Hyacinth F. Roth O.P., "Venerable Margaret Ebner: A possible Dominican *Beata,*" *Torch* 20, no. 6 (March 1936): 18.

15. Strauch, *Ebner und Nördlingen,* letter LI, 263.

16. Zoepf, *Mystikerin,* 141.

Conversion, Christianization, Acculturation

3

✠

"For Force Is Not of God"?
Compulsion and Conversion from Yahweh to Charlemagne

Lawrence G. Duggan

The Hymnal of the Episcopal Church contains a hymn entitled "The Great Creator of the Worlds," the words of which are drawn from the anonymous *Epistle to Diognetus* of the second or early third century. The fifth verse of the hymn ends with the words, "For force is not of God."[1] Although actually the *Epistle* does not quite put it this way ("for compulsion is not God's way of working," according to one translation), the sentiment is the same: God does not force humankind to accept Him or to obey His will.[2] Yet by 785 the Frankish king Charlemagne stipulated for the Saxons a policy of forcible conversion to Christianity, with infractions punishable by death: "If there is anyone of the Saxon people lurking among them unbaptized, and if he scorns to come to baptism and wishes to absent himself and stay a pagan, let him die."[3] Even earlier, the reviser of the *Royal Frankish Annals* entered the following sentence under the year 775: "While the king spent the winter at the villa of Quierzy, he decided to attack the treacherous and treaty-breaking tribe of the Saxons and to persist in this war until they were either defeated and forced to accept the Christian religion or entirely exterminated."[4] How, when, and why did such a policy of conversion by compulsion to the religion of Yahweh come about after such a pacific one undertaken by the deity Himself? Was this a specifically "medieval" development, yet another perversion of "true" Christianity wrought during the long centuries of Germanic barbarism?

Surprisingly, one will search in vain in the literature to find an adequate treatment and explanation of these momentous developments. The relevant clauses of the "terror capitulary" of 785 have received surprisingly little attention, the dreadful royal decision of 775 even less. In his monumental *History of the Expansion of Christianity*, Kenneth Scott Latourette noted that this was "the first but not the last instance in which acceptance of baptism and of the Christian name was induced by a liberal application of the sword" — but then suggested without further elaboration that "[t]he methods employed in the conversion of the Saxons were so natural and logical an outgrowth of the policies of Charlemagne's predecessors that few seem to have been shocked."[5] It is easy and probably unfair to fault Latourette, given his ambitious attempt to cover the whole history of Christianity. It is harder to comprehend why Richard Sullivan, who devoted his scholarly energies to studying these kinds of issues in precisely this period, provides no toeholds to speak of in a half-dozen or so articles published over several decades.[6] In their detailed studies of the Franks and the Saxons, Albert Hauck and Heinrich Wiedemann offer many helpful clues, such as the particularly fierce opposition of the Saxons to Christianity, exacerbated by the participation of militant late Merovingian bishops in the military campaigns against the Saxons. Both scholars also underscore the events of 775–76 as a turning point, when the Saxons were decisively defeated; they submitted, many underwent baptism, and thereafter Charlemagne no longer viewed them as outsiders but as subjects of the Frankish kingdom. But neither Hauck nor Wiedemann addresses fully the fateful decision of 775 or the chilling decree issued at Paderborn; nor do most other scholars.[7]

Donald Bullough has argued that the reviser of the *Annals* assigned too early a date to Charlemagne's decision,[8] while the editor of the most recent edition of the *Annals* simply suppresses the passage without offering an adequate explanation for doing so.[9] This will not do for a number of reasons. Several other Carolingian sources corroborate the centrality of the events of 775–76. Although the poet Saxo (writing between 888 and 891) undoubtedly depended on the revised *Annals*,[10] the author of the annals of St. Gall perhaps did not, and he too connects the conversion and killing of the Saxons at that time.[11] Besides, the mass baptisms of the Saxons recorded for the following two years otherwise make little sense, especially in view of their previously implacable hostility to Christianity. In a different way, it does not matter whether the reviser is wrong about the date. What is telling is that he does give such an early date, provides no explanation for Charlemagne's new policy, and felt no inclination to disguise or minimize it, much less to pass over it in silence. Had the writer had any reason to feel embarrassed on his own or Charlemagne's behalf, he might well have done any of these things. If Einhard was indeed the reviser of the *Annals,* as scholars used to think, this argument is all the more compelling in view of both Einhard's intimate knowledge of Charlemagne and the artful way in which he crafted his life of the great king. Finally, Charlemagne is remembered in a similar way by the most important chronicler of the reign of Charlemagne's son, Louis the Pious—a learned soldier, Nithard, who also happened to be Charlemagne's grandson. Of Charlemagne's accomplishment he wrote: "Emperor Charles, deservedly called the Great by all peoples, converted the Saxons by much effort, as is known to everyone in Europe. He won them over from the vain adoration of idols to the true Christian religion of God."[12]

This view suggests that Charlemagne deserved all the credit, if one can call it that, for this initiative. Was Charlemagne capable of such a bold undertaking as to link conversion and killing in an unprecedented way as early as 775? Very likely, but in this paper I would like to explore the possibility that there was a long period of development leading up to Charlemagne's decision and that Charlemagne was simply pushing on to the next stage. I take my initial cue here from Erasmus of Rotterdam. Although he would probably have liked to assent heartily to the earlier proposition that these developments represented yet another perversion of true Christianity during the Dark Ages, he also formulated a more subtle and penetrating key to the solution of this puzzle in one sentence in his *Adage* of 1515, "Dulce bellum inexpertis [War is sweet to those who know nothing about it]": "Every bad thing either finds its way into human life by imperceptible degrees, or else insinuates itself under the pretext of the good."[13] Elsewhere in the same text he put it slightly differently: "The greatest evils have always found their way into the life of men under the semblance of good."[14] Although Erasmus was seeking to account for the long descent from the manifestly pacificistic teachings of Christ to the war-addicted Christian Europe of Pope Julius II, this observation has tremendous power and persuasiveness as an explanatory model of many historical phenomena. I shall argue that Erasmus was absolutely right in emphasizing "imperceptible degrees" in the slow linking of Christianity and force, and that, as often as not, "force" in the spread of Christianity came about as an inadvertent consequence of decisions taken in the pursuit of other "goods," especially divinely prescribed ones. Finally, we shall see that a good deal of pressure to apply force in spreading Christianity came from churchmen, especially bishops and including some popes.

To begin with, the appalling contrast between the tolerant ways of God and the intolerant ways of His creatures implied above is not quite so stark as it at first seems. Usually, when human beings have chosen a particular course of action and defend it in religious terms, they have received (or at least believe they have received) some kind of encouragement, justification, or even command from God or the gods. Although the Judaeo-Christian tradition has habitually emphasized that God endowed human beings with free will and holds us accountable for our deeds, He has not been above applying a certain amount of pressure on humankind. In recent times, a less publicized dimension of the Judaeo-Christian Godhead is His intolerance. It is clearly recorded in the Decalogue that Yahweh will allow His People to worship no other gods; and in the rest of the Old Testament one story after another recounts what kinds of pressures and inducements He applied to His chosen people to believe in Him alone and to obey His Commandments. Again and again the Psalms assure the faithful of peace and prosperity; again and again these and the other books remind unbelievers and the recalcitrant that condign punishments await them if they do not submit. While Yahweh has so created us in His image that, strictly speaking, no one can be *made* to do something (as the list of striking "superhuman" acts of defiance in the history of our species attests), He has certainly offered many "incentives," positive and negative, to urge us toward compliance. "Force," in short, is not all of a piece and certainly not a diametrically polar opposite of "freedom." Just as freedom is not absolute, force is not without gradation. There is a continuum from one to the other. It was by the application of various levels of force, as well as by miracle and gifts, that Yahweh eventually converted His chosen people into exclusive monotheists obedient to His will. Furthermore, in certain books of the Old Testament, God is recorded as having led His people in righteous wars, even to the extent of ordering the priests into battle, setting precedents which would be invoked repeatedly by various kinds of later crusaders.[15] Finally, as Roland Bainton astutely observed, as the *one* true God, Yahweh inevitably was both bestower of peace *and* author of war, joining religion and violence in a novel and potentially ominous way.[16]

Force also appears in the life of Jesus, if in subtler forms. Having been commanded by His Father to undergo death, He sweated blood out of fear; but His Father would not relent. Jesus in turn imposed a series of commandments on His followers, culminating in the "great commission" with which Matthew's Gospel ends: "Go therefore and *make disciples* of all nations, baptizing them in the name of the Father and of the Son and of the Holy Spirit, teaching them to observe all that I have commanded you" (Matt. 28:19–20). This was not an option but a requirement, one which Jehovah's Witnesses and other evangelicals continue to discharge, however much it may unsettle tasteful mainline Christians. Finally, Jesus held out the threat of hellfire more often than most modern Christians care to notice—a form of pressure buttressed by repeated warnings that while many were called, few would be chosen.

While Jesus did not specify the means His disciples were to employ in spreading the Gospel, the Acts of the Apostles and other documents reveal that they took a leaf from His book and through example, preaching, and the performance of miracles gradually persuaded others to follow Him. The preaching was not always mellifluous, however, nor were the miracles always healing ones. Like Jesus, His disciples often upbraided others and threatened them with punishments, especially if they refused to undergo conversion of life and moral reformation. Those still outside the fold could be persuaded by negative as well as positive miracles—by acts of destruction demonstrating that their idols had no power. Even if these deeds did not compel acceptance, they embodied applications of force designed to persuade unbelievers to come over to right belief and the one true faith.

A truly decisive step was taken in the fourth century, when the Emperor Constantine (306–37) was inspired to adopt Christianity. The prayers of his mother Helena notwithstanding, what moved him was the sign he was given on the eve of the battle of Milvian Bridge in 312. The context was crucial, for he was assured by a heavenly voice of victory that if he affixed the letters "Chi Rho" (the first two letters of "Christ" in Greek, the so-called "Labarum") to the shields of his soldiers, "In this sign you will conquer." Religion was now associated in a fateful way not only with the realm of politics but with the ultimate realm of force, the battlefield.[17]

As for forcing Christianity upon his subjects, Constantine had some understandable reservations, dictated partly by his traditional, nonexclusivist polytheism but partly also by prudence in the face of inevitable opposition. Even so, he openly espoused and promoted Christianity, his stance culminating in the dedication of the new, Christian capital of Constantinople in 330; and those who wished to gain and remain in imperial favor and enjoy its largesse knew what they had to do to succeed in the new regime. Nevertheless, neither he nor his successors for several generations made any attempt to impose their new religion on their subjects as a whole.

It was St. Ambrose, bishop of Milan (374–92), who changed all that. In a dramatic confrontation with Symmachus, advocate of the old Roman religion, Ambrose argued for the suppression of paganism and the establishment of Christianity as the sole official religion of the empire. Since Ambrose was able to cite the first commandment of the Decalogue in support of his arguments, the Emperor Gratian agreed and in 382 moved seriously against the pagan establishment in the direction of making Christianity the only imperial religion. This process eventually led to a decree in 416 barring all pagans from imperial service.[18] The result was that, from a legal point of view, Christianity was no longer a matter of choice for the citizens and subjects of the empire. They were effectively forced to accept it. It is important to stress, however, that the emperors probably did not view it that way, but rather as a matter of their own obedience to divine command as well as of the exercise of their responsibility to assuage the divine powers and keep them on the side of the empire. "Forcible conversion" may have been the de facto consequence but was probably not the intention behind imperial decisions producing that effect.

Once the established Christian Church had at its potential disposal the coercive power of the state, the temptation was bound to arise to use that power to settle disputes within the Church. It was only a question of when and whether the impulse would come from the emperors in their role of peace givers or from the bishops out of their concern that right religion prevail, since on right belief depended the salvation of human beings. (The assertion that outside the Church there is no salvation derives from this period, not from the popes of the High Middle Ages.)[19] Rightly or wrongly, much of the credit or blame is assigned to St. Augustine (354–430), who in his long and frustrating struggle with the Donatists in Africa eventually called upon the secular authorities to apply pressures to the Donatists for their own good and as a form of paternal correction.[20] In fact, on this as on so many other matters, Augustine was taking his cue from Ambrose.[21]

Force reached a new level of conspicuousness in this period in less obvious ways as well. Adult baptism, previously freely chosen, gave way to infant baptism, the rite of passage into the empire as well as the Church. In a rather different way, although within the Christian community from the later second century cultural pressures prompted more ardent Christians, clerical and lay, to observe chastity even within marriage, the imposition of the requirement of celibacy on various parts of the clerical world from the later fourth century onward moved from the realm of freely chosen option to binding obligation—at least in law. Finally, the appearance of the practice of oblation in the monastic world around the same time signified the triumph of a major force of traditional secular society in Christianity—parental decisions governing the fate of children offered as living sacrifices to God, now twice-blessed as innovative forms of the *imitatio Christi*.[22]

This raises the question of the policy of the newly Christianized Romans with respect to the polytheists beyond and now within their borders. While the connection between politics and religion forged by Constantine was a relatively new one to Christians, it was not so to the Romans or most other peoples of antiquity, for whom the declaration, conduct, and conclusion of war had long been associated with religious rites and even with acceptance of the religion of the conqueror by the conquered as part of the peacemaking process. For the polytheists of antiquity, this was an easy and logical step. They had been shown in battle the power of the victor's deity or deities, who therefore deserved worship, but without necessarily requiring repudiation of the gods of old. Thus, when the Anglo-Saxon King Alfred defeated the Danes at Edington in 878, "the enemy gave him preliminary hostages and great oaths that they would leave his kingdom, and promised also that their king should receive baptism, and they kept their promise. Three weeks later King Guthrum with thirty of the men who were the most important in the army came [to Alfred] at Aller, which is near Athelney, and the king stood sponsor to him at his baptism there."[23] Nor was it even necessary to have been defeated for polytheists to offer to become Christians. In his *History of the Goths* Jordanes tells us that, out of fear of the Huns, the Visigoths in the 370s negotiated with the Emperor Valens, stipulating that "if he would give them part of Thrace or Moesia to keep, they would submit themselves to his laws and commands. That he might have greater confidence in them, they promised to become Christians, if he would give them teachers who spoke their language. When Valens learned this, he gladly and promptly granted what he had himself intended to ask."[24]

Not all polytheists came over to Christianity quite this readily. Like Constantine, Clovis (ca. 466–511), king of the Franks, required a sign of God's power, even though Clovis, like Constantine, had a Christian female member of his house praying for him. "Nothing could persuade him to accept Christianity," Gregory of Tours tells us, until his troops were being annihilated in battle by the Alamanni in 496. In desperation, Clovis called upon the name of Christ, promising to be baptized if only Christ would grant him victory over his enemies. Even though Jesus obliged, thereby reaffirming the link between religion and the realm of force, Clovis apparently still held back. When Bishop Remigius of Rheims urged him to undergo baptism, Clovis announced, "There remains one obstacle. The people under my command will not agree to forsake their gods. I will go and put to them what you have just said to me." But "God in his power had preceded" Clovis and miraculously converted the hearts of his people before he could address them. What exactly would have happened if God had not intervened is not at all clear.[25]

Gregory of Tours tells a similar story a few pages later, however, which is full of relevant significance. King Gundobad, an Arian, came to realize the error of his beliefs and sought out the bishop of Vienne to be anointed in secret. The bishop upbraided him for his cowardice and cited Christ himself: "Whosoever therefore shall confess me before men, him I will confess also before my Father which is in heaven" (Matt. 10:32–33). The bishop also accused Gundobad of being afraid of his people and marshaled a variety of further arguments: "Do you not realize that it is better that the people should accept your belief, rather than that you, a king, should pander to their every whim? You are the leader of your people; your people is not there to lord it over you. When you go to war, you yourself march at the head of the squadrons of your army and they follow where you lead. It is therefore preferable that they should learn the truth under your direction, rather than that they should continue in their errors."[26] King Gundobad nevertheless refused to take such a step. He would not give in to a bishop who had tried to persuade him with nearly every conceivable argument not only to confess his faith before his people but to lead his people to the true Trinitarian faith.

A hundred years later, according to Bede, a somewhat similar episode took place in Anglo-Saxon England. There King Ethelbert of Kent (560–616) had graciously received monks, led by Augustine and sent by Pope Gregory I, and had allowed them to proselytize. Ethelbert initially declined to "forsake those beliefs which I and the whole English race have held so long."[27] Eventually, however,

> the king, as well as others, believed and was baptized, being attracted by the pure life of the saints and by their most precious promises, whose truth they confirmed by performing many miracles. Every day more and more began to flock to hear the Word, to forsake their heathen worship, and, through faith, to join the unity of Christ's holy Church. It is related that the king, although he rejoiced at their conversion and faith, compelled no one to accept Christianity; though none the less he showed greater affection for believers since they were his fellow-citizens in the kingdom of heaven. But he had learned from his teachers and guides in the way of salvation that the service of Christ was voluntary and ought not to be compulsory.[28]

When Pope Gregory heard of this outlook, he was evidently not at all pleased. He sent to Ethelbert both gifts and a long letter in which he exhorted the king to

> hasten to extend the Christian faith among the people who are subject to you. Increase your righteous zeal for their conversion; *suppress the worship of idols; overthrow their buildings and shrines;* strengthen the morals of your subjects by outstanding purity of life, by exhorting them, terrifying, enticing, and correcting them, and by showing them an example of good works; so that you may be rewarded in heaven by the One whose Name and knowledge you have spread upon the earth. For He whose honor you seek and maintain among the nations will also make your glorious name still more glorious even to posterity.[29]

Although Gregory clearly stressed here reliance on the traditional tactics of persuasion, he also in passing encouraged the king to employ calculated violence against the shrines and worship of the traditional gods. Gregory modified this position in a far more famous letter meant to provide Augustine, by now Archbishop of Canterbury, with advice about missionary tactics: "tell him what I have decided after long deliberation about the English people, namely that the idol temples of that race should by no means be destroyed, but only the idols in them. Take holy water and sprinkle it in these shrines, build altars and place relics in them. For if the shrines are well built, it is essential that they should be changed from the worship of devils to the service of the true God."[30] Gregory then went on to dispense the advice which seems largely to have shaped the missionary policy of the western, Latin church for the next thousand years: be flexible, adapt when possible, insisting only on observance of the essentials. Whether Gregory was here retreating from the counsel given to Ethelbert or modifying it in light of the recipient—a bishop, not a king—is unclear.

What is astonishing is that a bit over a century later the Anglo-Saxon monk Boniface (680–754), working on the Continent among the Germanic peoples and destined to be remembered as the "Apostle to the Germans," followed Pope Gregory's advice to King Ethelbert, not to Archbishop Augustine. Both before and after his consecration as bishop by the pope, Boniface destroyed sacred trees and shrines during his missions among the Frisians, while the Hessians watched him begin to cut down the mighty Oak of Jupiter at Geismar.[31] According to Boniface's biographer, God miraculously completed this task, causing many of the Hessians who had been cursing Boniface "to believe and bless the Lord."[32]

It is not surprising, therefore, that but a few decades later Charlemagne (771–814) also heeded the advice sent to Ethelbert. The *Royal Frankish Annals* recounts Charlemagne's first expedition against the Saxons 772 in this fashion:

> From Worms he marched first into Saxony. Capturing the castle of Eresburg, he proceeded as far as the Irminsul, destroyed this idol and carried away the gold and silver which he found. . . . The glorious king wished to remain there two or three days in order to destroy the temple completely, but they had no water. Suddenly at noon, through the grace of God, while the army rested and nobody knew what was happening, so much water poured forth in a stream that the whole army had enough. Then the great king came to the River Weser. Here he held a parley with the Saxons, obtained twelve hostages, and returned to Francia.[33]

Why Charlemagne attacked the temple at Irminsul is not illuminated by the official *Annals* at this point or by reference to earlier entries. Charlemagne's father Pepin had conducted retaliatory raids against Saxon tribes for their incursions into Frankish lands, but the most recent had been in 758, and none of them had evidently involved religion.[34] And while Charles's determination to destroy the temple was aided by God's miraculous provision of water to his parched soldiers, the terse terms of the truce allude to religion in no way. It may well be that, aside from the tempting store of immense riches at the shrine, Charles simply wanted to conduct frightening psychological warfare.[35] Hauck, in fact, rightly calls this simply a *Verwüstungszug*.[36]

Although the entries for the next two years indicate that God was on the side of the Franks in the deadly struggle with the Saxons, there is still nothing to prepare us for the opening words of the entry for 775 in the revised version of the *Annals*. Was there something that had happened in the interim? In 774 Charlemagne went to Rome and met with Pope Hadrian I (772–95). Although one German scholar long ago suggested that the pope may have exhorted the young king to do his utmost to convert the Saxons, he also had to admit that no evidence corroborated this speculation, and certainly there is none in the *Liber Pontificalis*.[37] In 773, however, Abbot Eanwulf wrote to Charlemagne a letter in which he quoted at length, but without acknowledgement, from Gregory the Great's letter to Ethelbert, urging him to "hasten to extend the Christian faith among the people who are subject to you . . . suppress the worship of idols; overthrow their buildings and shrines; strengthen the morals of your subjects by outstanding purity of life, by exhorting them, terrifying, enticing, and correcting them."[38] It is essential to note here the ambiguous legacy of Gregory the Great. Although he had authorized destruction of things, Charlemagne was now preparing for the killing of people. On the other hand, Gregory had legitimized, even commanded, forms of destruction in the name of right religion.

Other clerics, however, had sanctioned killing and contributed to the formation of that moral universe in which Charlemagne grew up. As the heir of several centuries of Christian contempt for the body, Augustine of Hippo put it this way: "What is it about war, after all, that is blameworthy? Is it that people who will someday die anyway are killed in order that the victors might live in peace? That kind of objection is appropriate to a timid man, not a religious one. What rightly deserves censure in war is the desire to do harm, cruel vengeance, a disposition that remains unappeased and implacable, a savage spirit of rebellion, a lust for domination and other such things."[39] Three hundred years later Bede (+735), who died only a few years before Charlemagne was born, wrote about Augustine of Canterbury's confrontation with the Celtic Christians of Britain. Having failed to convince them of the errors of their ways in the dating of Easter and other practices, "Augustine, the man of God, warned them with threats that, if they refused to accept peace from their brethren, they would have to accept war from their enemies; and if they would not preach the way of life to the English nation, they would one day suffer the vengeance of death at their hands. This, through the workings of divine judgment, came to pass in every particular as he had foretold." It was King Ethelfrith who brought this about at the battle of Caerlegion or Chester, where, in Bede's words, he "made a great slaughter of that nation of heretics" and "wicked host," including twelve hundred monks and priests who were there praying for Celtic victory. "Thus the prophecy of the holy Bishop Augustine was fulfilled, although he had long been translated to the heavenly kingdom, namely that those heretics would also suffer the vengeance of temporal death because they had despised the offer of everlasting salvation."[40]

If the monk Bede could set down such sentiments in writing about the slaughter of Christian "heretics," monks, and priests, why should Charlemagne—a layman born to be a king and raised to be a killer for the sake of law and order—have flinched at the thought of exterminating heathen Saxons if they did not submit to his will and be baptized? Perhaps Charlemagne, but certainly the men of the royal court who later recorded his great deeds, would have preferred that he monopolize all the honors for introducing this new policy. Whether Yahweh, Jesus, Ambrose, Augustine of Hippo, Remigius of Rheims, Gregory the Great, Augustine of Canterbury, Bede, Boniface, or Eanwulf would have been willing to acknowledge any role in contributing to this outcome is open to speculation; but, as in his *Praise of Folly, Dulce bellum inexpertis,* and other writings, Erasmus would have had no reservation whatever about assigning a high degree of responsibility to men of intelligence and faith for encouraging and justifying the result.

NOTES

1. *The Hymnal 1982 According to the Use of the Episcopal Church* (New York: Church Hymnal Corporation, 1985), no. 489.

2. "The So-called Letter to Diognetus," in *Early Christian Fathers,* ed. and trans. C. C. Richardson et al., Library of Christian Classics 1 (Philadelphia: Westminster Press, 1970), 219. On the authorship and date of the letter, see 206–10.

3. H. R. Loyn and John Percival, trans., *The Reign of Charlemagne: Documents on Carolingian Government and Administration* (New York: St. Martin's Press, 1975), 52.

4. Friedrich Kurze, ed., *Annales regni Francorum,* in *Monumenta Germaniae*

Historica, Scriptores in usum scholarum 6 (Hannover: Impensis Bibliopolii Hahniani, 1895; reprint 1950), 41: "Cum rex in villa Carisiaco hiemaret, consilium iniit, ut perfidam et foedifragam Saxonum gentem bello adgrederetur et eo usque perseveraret, dum aut victi christianae religioni subicerentur aut omnino tollerentur." The translation used is that in *Carolingian Chronicles*, trans. Bernhard Scholz with Barbara Rogers (Ann Arbor: University of Michigan Press, 1970), 51.

5. Kenneth Scott Latourette, *A History of the Expansion of Christianity*, 7 vols. (New York: Harper & Bros., 1937–45), 2:105–6.

6. These have now been gathered in Richard E. Sullivan, *Christian Missionary Activity in the Early Middle Ages* (Aldershot: Variorum, 1994).

7. Albert Hauck, *Kirchengeschichte Deutschlands* (Leipzig: J. C. Hinrichs, 1896–1920), 2:360–418; Heinrich Wiedemann, *Die Sachsenbekehrung*, Missionswissenschaftliche Studien 5 (Münster i.W.: Verlag Missionshaus Hiltrup, 1932), 36, 45–49, and *Karl der Grosse, Widukind und die Sachsenbekehrung* (Münster i.W.: Aschendorff, 1949), 15, 19. As for other scholars, see, for example, Sigurd Abel and Bernhard Simson, *Jahrbücher des fränkischen Reiches unter Karl dem Grossen* (Leipzig: Duncker & Humblot, 1866–83), 1:175; Louis Halphen, "La conquête de la Saxe," in *Etudes critiques sur l'histoire de Charlemagne*, ed. Halphen (Paris: F. C. Alcan, 1921), 145–218, esp. 149, and *Charlemagne et l'empire carolingien* (Paris: Editions Albin Michel, 1947; reprint, 1995), 63–70; Heinrich Fichtenau, *The Carolingian Empire*, trans. Peter Munz (New York: Blackwell, 1964), 21–22; Walther Lammers, ed., *Die Eingliederung der Sachsen in das Frankenreich*, Wege der Forschung 185 (Darmstadt: Wissenschaftliche Buchgesellschaft, 1970); Friedrich Prinz, *Grundlagen und Anfänge, Deutschland bis 1056* (Munich: Verlag C. H. Beck, 1985), 95–96; P. D. King, *Charlemagne: Translated Sources* (Lancaster: P. D. King, 1987), 44–45; Rudolf Schieffer, *Die Karolinger* (Stuttgart: Verlag W. Kohlhammer, 1992), 76–77; Pierre Riché, *The Carolingians: A Family Who Forged Europe*, trans. M. I. Allen (Philadelphia: University of Pennsylvania Press, 1993), 103. Curiously, there is no chapter at all on the conquest of the Saxons in the five-volume *Karl der Grosse: Lebenswerk und Nachleben*, ed. Wolfgang Braunfels et al. (Düsseldorf: Verlag L. Schwann, 1965).

8. Donald Bullough, *The Age of Charlemagne* (New York: Putnam, 1980), 51.

9. Reinhold Rau, ed. and trans., *Quellen zur karolingischen Reichsgeschichte* (Darmstadt: Wissenschaftliche Buchgesellschaft, 1968–87), 1:3, 31.

10. *Monumenta Germaniae Historica, Poetae Latini aevi Carolini*, pt. 1, vol. 4, ed. P. von Winterfeld (Berlin: Apud Weidmannos, 1899; reprint, 1978), 11 (lib. 1, ll.177–88). On this author and his dates, see Peter Godman, ed. and trans., *Poetry of the Carolingian Renaissance* (Norman: University of Oklahoma Press, 1985), 342n.62.

11. *Monumenta Germaniae Historica, Scriptores*, 1, ed. G. H. Pertz (1826; reprint, Stuttgart: Anton Hiersemann, 1963), 63: "in ipso anno [775] perrexit Karolus super Saxones, et plurimos ex ipsis ad baptismi gratiam perduxit, et multos pluriores interfecit."

12. Nithard, "Histories," 4.2, in *Carolingian Chronicles,* 166–67. For other instances of contemporary praise of the forcible conversion of the Saxons, see Richard E. Sullivan, "Carolingian Missionary Theories," *Catholic Historical Review* 42 (1956–57): 277–78.

13. *Erasmus on His Times: A Shortened Version of the "Adages" of Erasmus,* trans. M. M. Phillips (Cambridge: Cambridge University Press, 1967), 123.

14. Ibid., 113.

15. See, most recently, Susan Niditch, *War in the Hebrew Bible: A Study in the Ethics of Violence* (New York: Oxford University Press, 1993), with a rich bibliography on this complex issue.

16. Roland Bainton, *Christian Attitudes toward War and Peace* (Nashville: Abingdon Press, 1960), 47.

17. For useful recent introductions, with extensive bibliography, see the entries in the *Oxford Dictionary of the Christian Church,* ed. F. L. Cross and E. A. Livingstone, 2d ed. (Oxford: Oxford University Press, 1983), and *Encyclopedia of Early Christianity,* ed. E. Ferguson et al. (New York: Garland Publishers, 1990), s.v. "Constantine the Great," "Labarum," and "Milvian Bridge, Battle of the."

18. For a brief synopsis, see W. H. C. Frend, *The Rise of Christianity* (Philadelphia: Fortress Press, 1984), 701–4.

19. See ibid., 346–48, 354–57, 653–57.

20. Of the large body of literature on this subject, see, for example, Louis J. Swift, *The Early Fathers on War and Military Service* (Wilmington, Del.: Michael Glazier, 1983), 141–49, and Peter Brown, "St Augustine's Attitude to Religious Coercion," *Journal of Roman Studies* 54 (1964):107–16.

21. See Swift, *Early Fathers,* 106, and, more fully, idem. "St. Ambrose on Violence and War," *Transactions of the American Philological Association* 101 (1970): 533–43.

22. See M.-P. Deroux, *Les origines de l'oblature bénédictine,* Les éditions de la Revue Mabillon 1 (Vienne: Abbaye de Saint Martin de Ligugé, 1927).

23. *Anglo-Saxon Chronicle,* rev., trans., and ed. D. Whitelock et al. (New Brunswick: Rutgers University Press, 1961), 49, s.a. 878.

24. Charles C. Mierow, trans., *The Gothic History of Jordanes* (Princeton: Princeton University Press, 1915), chap. 25, p. 88.

25. Gregory of Tours, *History of the Franks,* trans. L. Thorpe (Harmondsworth: Penguin Books, 1974), 2.29–31, pp. 141–45.

26. Ibid., 2.34, pp. 148–49.

27. *Bede's Ecclesiastical History of the English People,* ed. and trans. Bertram Colgrave and R. A. B. Mynors, Oxford Medieval Texts (Oxford: Clarendon Press, 1969), 1.25, p. 75.

28. Ibid., 1.26, pp. 77–79.

29. Ibid., 1.32, pp. 112–13. The Latin of the words which I have italicized is "idolorum cultus insequere; fanorum aedificia euerte."

30. Ibid., 1.30, pp. 106–7. Scholars habitually treat the letter to Mellitus (and Augustine) at length while ignoring that to Ethelbert. For a typical instance, see

Valerie I. J. Flint, *The Rise of Magic in Early Medieval Europe* (Princeton: Princeton University Press, 1991), 75–77. One of the few who have discussed the differences is Wiedemann, *Karl der Grosse,* 32n.30.

31. Willibald, "Life of St Boniface," chaps. 5 and 8, in *The Anglo-Saxon Missionaries in Germany,* ed. and trans. C. H. Talbot (New York: Sheed & Ward, 1954), 41, 55.

32. Ibid., chap. 6, 45–46. Interestingly, in the numerous letters sent by Pope Gregory II (715–31) and Bishop Daniel of Winchester, Boniface did not receive advice to destroy idols (*The Letters of St Boniface,* trans. E. Emerton [New York: W. W. Norton, 1940], 32–33, 42–56). *After* the incident of the Oak of Jupiter, however, it may be that Pope Gregory III wrote to him in 740 or 741, approving of Boniface's action and urging him to deal in similar fashion with other sacred trees: "Ceterum dilectissime arbores illas, quas incole colunt, monemus, ut succidantur, sicut subvertisti arborem, que Jovis appellabatur, que ab incolis venerabatur" (Klemens Honselmann, "Der Brief Gregors III. an Bonifatius über die Sachsenmission," *Historisches Jahrbuch* 76 [1957]:83–84, reprint in Lammers, *Eingliederung der Sachsen,* 307–8). The authenticity of this letter, however, has long been doubted and continues to be: Franz Flaskamp, "Der Bonifatiusbrief von Herford: Ein angebliches Zeugnis zur Sachsenmission," *Archiv für Kulturgeschichte* 44 (1962): 315–34 (reprint in Lammers, *Eingliederung der Sachsen,* 365–88). In any event, Boniface is not recorded as having been exhorted before the fact by any contemporary prelate to undertake such destructive measures.

33. *Carolingian Chronicles,* 48–49.

34. Ibid., s.a. 743, 744, 747, 753, 758, pp. 38–39, 42.

35. Riché, *The Carolingians,* 103, offers no specific explanation for this choice of target.

36. Hauck, *Kirchengeschichte,* 2:371.

37. W. Kentzler, "Karl des Grossen Sachsenzüge, 772–775," *Forschungen zur deutschen Geschichte* 11 (1871):88–89.

38. *S. Bonifatii et Lulli epistolae,* ed. E. Dümmler, in *Monumenta Germaniae Historica, Epistolarum tomus III Merowingici et Karolini aevi* (Munich: Monumenta Germaniae Historica, 1978), 409, no. 120.

39. *Questions on the Heptateuch* 6.10, quoted in Swift, *Early Fathers,* 120. On the matter of the flesh and Christianity, see Peter Brown, *The Body and Society: Men, Women, and Sexual Renunciation in Early Christianity* (New York: Columbia University Press, 1988).

40. Bede, *Ecclesiastical History,* II.2, 140–43.

4

✠

The Conversion of the Physical World
The Creation of a Christian Landscape

John M. Howe

"My Kingdom is not of this world." Christ's disavowal to Pilate evokes cognitive dissonance in anyone who has ever traveled through a traditional European landscape where Christian territory is proclaimed by steepled churches, imposing religious houses, monumental crosses, ornate cemeteries, votive plaques, and even crosses with plastic flowers marking the sites of traffic accidents. In the Middle Ages such omnipresent *tropaea* established hegemony. This is apparent, for example, in the account of Saladin's conquest of Jerusalem, written by the Muslim historian Ibn al-Athir (d. 1233), which climaxes with a symbolic reversal: "When the Muslims entered the city . . . some of them climbed to the top of the cupola [of the Dome of the Rock] to take down the cross. When they reached the top a great cry went up from the city and from outside the walls, the Muslims crying the *Alläh akbar* in their joy, the Franks groaning in consternation and grief. So loud and piercing was the cry that the earth shook."[1]

Although religious conversion is normally thought of as a personal process involving a reorientation of soul, it also transforms the surrounding world. Conversion of large numbers of people requires conversion of their cult centers. It may lead to the reinterpretation of geography itself. Historians of religion describe natural "heirophanies," revelations of the divine through numinous natural features.[2] Because religious traditions mediate these perceptions, changes in belief require interpretive changes. Thus an understanding of Christian conversion in the Middle Ages would not be complete without a look at Christian landscape. How was it created? In what ways did it develop? How was it important to medieval religion? A brief survey of Christian religious geography may help to correct such common beliefs as that it appeared late, suddenly, or only in the context of the initial evangelizing of a region. Sacred space in the medieval Latin West continued to develop as internal and external frontiers were converted into Christian territory.

Christianity always had sacred geography. This assertion contradicts scholars such as Robert Markus, who champions Christianity's "indifference to place" and maintains that it occupied "a spatial universe spiritually largely undifferentiated" until it gradually created a new sacred geography through the cult of the martyrs.[3] In fact, Christianity began as a Jewish heresy, part of a tradition that saw God acting in history, preserving a special land for a special people, centering his sacrificial cult on a single temple. Although local Jewish religious life was based on synagogues, people also worshipped at the tombs of patriarchs, prophets, and would-be messiahs.[4] Christ, who was said to have fulfilled and transcended this old order, inevitably created new sacred space by his earthly presence. The Mount of Calvary, for example, was symbolically transfigured to such an extent that even Hadrian's superimposition of a temple to the Capitoline Venus could not reclaim it.[5] Informed traditions about Christ's tomb circulated in the second century.[6] An elaborate Christian sacred geography in the Holy Land emerged just as soon as Christian pilgrimage became publicly acceptable.[7]

Like Judaism, Christianity had its sacred tombs. One wall underlying the *memoria* for Peter in Rome has been claimed to be as early as about 90 A.D., although the evidence of mid–second-century construction is clearer.[8] Avoidance of such burial honors may underlie the request to the Romans made by Ignatius of Antioch (d. ca. 107), who asked them to pray that the wild beasts "may become a sepulchre for me; let them leave not the smallest scrap of my flesh" so that "there is no trace of my body for the world to see."[9] It was allegedly the Jews who attempted to secure the destruction of the body of Polycarp (d. ca. 155), but they were unable to stop the Christians of Smyrna from gathering his bones, laying them to rest "in a spot suitable for the purpose," and assembling there regularly to celebrate the day of his martyrdom.[10] It is hard to resist the conclusion that these early geographical elements represent an ongoing tradition appropriated from Judaism.[11] The tombs of martyrs would have become more prominent after the middle of the third century, once more general persecutions had mass-produced them. Nevertheless, the resulting geography was somewhat arbitrary: the persecutors, not the Christians, determined the places where the martyrs were executed (normally the larger cities where officials were empowered to judge capital crimes); the burial customs of antiquity required that their tombs be located outside city walls, at some distance from largely urban early Christian communities.[12]

Another sort of sacred geography centered on churches. Like the Jews, Christians clustered into their own neighborhoods. Their meeting places, such as the "upper room" (Acts 1:13), were Christian forums where a new type of assembly (*ecclesia*) replaced the old loyalties of the citizen assemblies of the *poleis*. In such assembly rooms, wandering apostles and prophets gradually became less important than bishops, geographically defined overseers whose *cathedrae* on raised platforms in front of congregations clearly marked ecclesiastical power. Since the geography of the churches differed from the geography of the martyrs, there could be tension between them, as is hinted at, for example, in Origen's description of the Alexandrian Church. He describes how during the Severan persecution (shortly after 200), Christians living and martyred could assemble together spiritually but not physically:

> That was when one really was a believer, when one used to go to martyrdom with courage in the Church, when returning from the cemeteries whither we had accompanied the bodies of the martyrs, we came back to our meetings, and the whole church would be assembled there, unbreakable. Then the catechumens were catechized in the midst of the martyrdoms, and in turn the catechumens overcame tortures and confessed the living God without fear.[13]

With Constantine's triumphs came churches fit for an emperor, including some basilicas with incomes like those of small provinces. Equally important, however, was the merging of sacred geographies. In the post-Constantinian Church, imperial support overcame any popular reluctance about mingling the living and the dead and made feasible the translations of holy bodies into urban churches.[14] Translations allowed persecuting cities to showcase their treasuries of relics in places other than suburban sanctuaries. They allowed newer cities such as Constantinople to achieve higher status by importing the remains of saints on a massive scale. They enabled bishops to enhance their own power through the cult of relics.[15] The sacred geographies did not always merge successfully: the network of rural shrines to the martyrs in Donatist northern Africa resisted elite attempts to impose order.[16] In the eastern countryside, especially in Egypt and Syria, holy men emerged as successors of the martyrs and established their cells and pillars as new decentralized loci of the sacred.[17] In the West, however, the usual effect of translations of the saints was to create coherent patterns of sacred geography, a process codified by canon laws requiring that every altar contain relics.[18] This shift strengthened ecclesiastical organization. Without it, Christian cult in the West might have been privatized like almost all other parts of the public sphere; with it churches retained some independence, since each had a heavenly owner, the saint "residing" in the altar, whom potential oppressors would often hesitate to make angry.

The system of churches backed by relics was spread in many ways. Powerful men established private churches on great estates. Bishops counterbalanced them with strong baptismal churches. These initiatives provided a basis for a fully articulated parish structure, even though in some regions it was not complete until the twelfth century.[19] Interrelated systems of churches were carefully and deliberately established by missionary efforts, some of which are described in other chapters of this volume. Translations of saints reinforced bonds between old and new Christian regions.[20] The great monasteries favored by the Carolingians and rejuvenated by the monastic reforms of the tenth and eleventh centuries did much to enhance the cult of relics and popular pilgrimage.[21]

Beneath and beyond the sacred grid of saints and their churches existed a sacred geography based upon nature. Christians did not start with a *tabula rasa*. The religious geography of the ancient Mediterranean and Transalpine worlds had been powerful. According to Robin Lane Fox, "Prophetic places were as abundant as ever in the Imperial period. . . . From Gaul to Palmyra, gods and heroes gave guidance . . . at their shrines and sacred springs. . . . Wherever there was water, indeed, there was a possible source of prophesy. . . . Uncanny places were everywhere."[22] Celtic and Germanic religion also relied heavily on groves, caves, mountains, and other numinous sites.[23] Mountain peaks had sacred resonances.[24] Fountains were major sites for worship—and for miracles.[25] Forests were awesome.[26] When these natural features occurred together, their power was enhanced.

From the beginning, Christians saw non-Christian sacred space as potentially or actually demonic. In Mark's Gospel, Christ proclaims, "The Kingdom of God is at hand" and then exorcizes a possessed man, commanding the unclean spirit who had cried out, "Jesus of Nazareth, Art thou come to destroy us?" to "Speak no more and go" (Mark 1:15–26). Mark describes sixteen more exorcisms. As territory is reclaimed from the spirits of evil, the Kingdom of God becomes immanent. Little wonder then that the desert fathers fought monstrous demons who looked suspiciously like Egyptian gods.[27] In eastern Rome, rioting Christians destroyed temples, dismaying the pagan Libanius, who held that shrines were "the very soul of the countryside."[28] Sts. Martin of Tours, Benedict, and Boniface chopped down sacred trees in the West; John of Ephesus did so in the East. In fact, the destruction of sacred groves became so common in the Carolingian world that synods legislated the appropriate procedures.[29] As Christianity expanded, demonic territory contracted. According to Walafrid Strabo, when St. Gall built his hermit hut at Lake Constance, the fleeing demons moaned that they would soon have no place left to them on earth.[30]

Unless wilderness springs, wells, forests, and mountains were specifically claimed for Christ, their pagan resonances remained. The canons of local councils and the penitentials, all the way up through the time of

Burchard of Worms in the early eleventh century, repeat injunctions against going "to temples, to fountains, to trees, or to cells"; they forbid leaving offerings, candles, "little houses," etc.[31] Bishop Atto of Vercelli (d. 964) had to admonish even his priests against visiting groves and springs.[32] The chronicler Rodulfus Glaber (d. ca. 1047) made no secret of his own belief in the demons who inhabited such places.[33] Miracle stories tell how people encountered evil spirits associated with certain plants or geographical features.[34]

Pagan geography had to be converted into Christian geography. Here I would take issue with Robert Markus's thesis that there was "no simple substitution of a Christian for a pagan religious topography"; that "between the two lies a slow attrition of Christian belief in the unholiness of pagan holy places, and the emergence, only slightly faster, of a readiness to envisage the possibility of holiness attached to particular spots."[35] Although a reductionist identification of the cults of saints with those of pagan gods oversimplifies, Christian sacred geography was linked to older sacralities.[36] In the fourth and fifth centuries, "countershrines" had begun to arise on or near old pagan sites.[37] In central Italy, temple sites were converted into the two greatest monasteries, Farfa and Monte Cassino. The most famous instruction on such recycling is the letter sent by Pope Gregory I to Abbot Melitus:

> The idol temples of that race [the English people] should by no means be destroyed, but only the idols in them. Take holy water and sprinkle it in these shrines, build altars and place relics in them. For if the shrines are well built, it is essential that they should be changed from the worship of devils to the service of the true God. When this people see that their shrines are not destroyed they will be able to banish error from their hearts and be more ready to come to the places they are familiar with, but now recognizing and worshipping the true God.

Gregory goes on to encourage the missionaries to substitute picnics for sacrificial meals, so that people can continue their old habits but "with changed hearts."[38] Adam of Bremen in the eleventh century described churches established in Scandinavian sacred groves.[39] The extent of this process is suggested in recent work by Mary and Sidney Nolan, who attempted to catalogue all the major current western European pilgrimage sites: most are associated with features that have some aura of traditional natural sanctity, especially mountains and water sources.[40]

The conversion of temples and awesome natural sites was not completed during the first phases of missionary activity. In his profile of medieval Rome, Richard Krautheimer shows that even in the very center of western

Christendom, it was well into the 600s before Christians routinely dared to turn pagan temples into churches.[41] The Tiber island with its healing fountain of Aesclepius was not fully converted to Christian use until around the turn of the millennium when Otto III constructed the church of San Bartolomeo.[42] Although in France the vast majority of the more than six thousand sacred springs that have been identified are now dedicated to saints, most of these Christian dedications are apparently Carolingian or later.[43] To convert the landscape completely took centuries.

One way to see the process in action is to study geographical references in hagiography. *Lives, miracles,* and other texts provide a series of snapshots witnessing cultic developments over time. A few examples taken from them illustrate how sacred geography expanded:

Bishop Germanus of Auxerre (d. 450), who, his biographer Constantius specifies, had *no* hermitage ("he . . . inhabited the desert while dwelling in the world"), had acquired one before Auxerre's *Gesta Episcoporum* was written in the ninth century.[44]

The young Wandregisilus (d. ca. 668) retreated to a hermitage known to the author of the *Gesta Abbatum Fontanellensium,* in a section written prior to 830, only as "quodam in loco" but which the so-called *Vita Secunda,* written just a few years later, identified as Saint-Ursanne.[45]

In the *Life* of Gerald of Aurillac (d. 909) written by Abbot Odo of Cluny (d. 942), Gerald was a monkish count not associated with any special geographical sites. However, once the monastery that Gerald had attempted to found during his lifetime finally prospered, amassed property, and needed his sacrality, he came to be honored at the hill where he is said to have died; at three fountains where he allegedly worked miracles; and even at a tree, the "arbre de Saint Géraud."[46]

In the first surviving *Life* of the seventh-century hermit Rodingus, written by Richard of Saint-Vannes (d. 1046), he is said to have dwelt in an unknown "place of horror and vast solitude" about a half a mile from the monastery; in the closely related but slightly later second *Life,* the hermitage is located and is announced as available for tours.[47]

In the hagiography associated with the seventh-century hermit Bavo of Ghent, no hermitage site is specified until the fourth edition of the *Life,* ca. 1100, when he became a forest dweller in a hollow tree, a place of popular veneration "where now Mass is frequently offered."[48]

In most of the above examples, hermits could Christianize wilderness by dwelling within it. It may be more than coincidence that the wave of popularity of hermit saints in tenth–eleventh-century Italy and late eleventh–early twelfth-century northern Europe correlates with expanding population moving into former wilderness areas. In central and southern Italy, for example, the era of encastellation seems to have witnessed a new wave of cave christenings. This is a region where cave sanctuaries such as those at Subiaco, Monte Tancia, and Monte Gargano had been important foci of early medieval spirituality. Now, however, Dominic of Sora (d. 1032), who founded a dozen monasteries in the high Appennines, took up eremitical residence in three different caves, which, except for two sites that claimed his relics, became his most important cult centers (his monasteries without relics or caves relatively quickly disappeared).[49] Amicus of Monte Cassino (d. ca. 1045) lived on Monte Torano in a cave that was later opened up for tours.[50] The Christianization of forests also seems to have accelerated in the eleventh century. Forest sites in Italy were donated to Romuald of Ravenna and Dominic of Sora. The forest of Craon between Brittany and Normandy was filled with hermits. The Cistercians happily acquired such "deserts." Also impressive are the oak trees in which hermit saints such as Bavo of Ghent or Gerardus of Falkenburg (12th century) were supposed to have lived. Oaks, pines, beeches and other trees of the ancient forests appear in sacral contexts. For example, it was while sitting on an oak log that Columbanus (and many imitators) had prophetic visions.[51]

Awesome places were Christianized not only to neutralize their pagan associations but also to appropriate their power. Romuald of Ravenna (d. ca. 1027), out hunting before he became a hermit, exclaimed, "O how well hermits would be able to dwell in the recesses of the woods, how nicely they could meditate here away from all the disturbances of secular strife."[52] St. Bruno (d. 1101), after founding the Carthusian order, abandoned it for a Calabrian hermitage, about which he rhapsodized, "Where can I find the words to describe its charms, its healthy climate, or the wide and beautiful plain that stretches into the mountains where there are green pastures and meadows filled with flowers?"[53] Bernard of Clairvaux, in his letter to Henry Murdoch, exhorted, "Believe me, you will find more in forests than in books. The trees and the rocks will teach you what you cannot hear from teachers."[54] Places relevatory for the ancient world were relevatory for Christians too—so long as they could be presented in a Christian context and carefully surrounded by Christian symbols.

This rapid survey of Christian geography has thus far, for the sake of convenience, treated churches, shrines, relics, caves, and so forth as though they had meaning in themselves. In reality, sacred space requires audience interaction—human beings to comprehend, explain, and animate it. A space can only be numinous *to someone*. Interrelated churches, relics, and natural sites had to be manifested by and through people.

Geographical foci usually made crowds part of the pageant. Churches drew multitudes on their saints' days.[55] Even the most inaccessible, awesome natural sites could attract annual crowds.[56] Relics brought pilgrims.[57] All participants became symbols themselves, part of the entourage of the saints. Since Late Antiquity such symbolic roles had been easy for the clergy, who had clerical garments, tonsures, and other distinctives. Although in his *Rule* Benedict seems to have envisioned simple monks dressed in modest local costume, even his monks had become rather elegant by Carolingian times. Reformers worked to put penitents, pilgrims, and hermits into recognizable uniforms. Simple lay people could wear special "church clothes," although it is unclear how far down the social ladder this would be customary or even possible. They could at least carry scarves, banners, medals, and staffs for pilgrimages and other special occasions. Guilds and confraternities used their insignia in festival roles.

Processions expanded sacred space outward. Christian processions had many precedents, including Christ's entry into Jerusalem with hosannas and palm branches. From Late Antiquity onward, individual cities such as Jerusalem, Rome, and Constantinople developed elaborate annual liturgical parades.[58] Translations of relics came to be choreographed like imperial *adventus* ceremonies.[59] Statue reliquaries, which began to appear in the late Carolingian period, became popular in the last half of the tenth century and in the eleventh.[60] These "majesties," which were excellent for processions, proliferated just when the proponents of the Peace of God movement began bringing collections of relics to regional meetings.[61] Processional activity was associated with all ecclesiastical rites that could be carried on out of doors, including blessings, penitential rituals, exorcisms, and ordeals. In the later Middle Ages, the great Corpus Christi parades show that these traditions could still be adapted to new forms of piety.[62]

Processions brought monastic sacred space into the world. At Saint-Riquier in the ninth century, and at Cluny in the tenth, monks traveled from one church to another during certain offices.[63] Although detailed liturgical information is lacking for the vast majority of houses, it seems reasonable to suppose that similar processions graced megamonasteries such as ninth-century Farfa, which contained six churches in its monastic precincts, or ninth-century San Vincenzo al Volturno, which had eight. Monks sang psalms on their way to formalized, sometimes *pro forma,* manual labors.[64] Those traveling on business might sing the monastic hours on the way, either on foot or on horseback.[65] Traveling Cluniac monks were even supposed to stop at the appropriate hours, prostrate themselves, and ritually beg pardon.[66]

Western medieval church architecture also extended the sphere of the sacred outward. Suffice it to note that bell towers are a western innovation, appearing early at St. Martin's and St. Peter's, and soon becoming widespread. In Italy dozens of older churches had added campaniles during the tenth, eleventh, and twelfth centuries. Both Romanesque and Gothic architecture tried for extraordinary height effects, including elaborate entrances and bell towers, the only functions of which were to dominate the world visually and audially. Monumental crosses, rural shrines, and other structures proclaimed Christian territory.

The Christianization of landscape has significance far beyond medieval Europe. Lionel Rothkrug has drawn attention to the role of sacred geography in the Reformation—to the way German regions with many shrines and saints, such as Bavaria, remained loyal to the traditional church, while less favored regions rejected it.[67] Eamon Duffy emphasizes the dynamic role that ecclesiastical furniture, imagery, and ceremony played in the piety of England's "old religion."[68] Terrence Ranger's study of the creation of a Christian landscape in twentieth-century Zimbabwe deals with these patterns from a contemporary anthropological standpoint.[69] Cross-cultural comparative studies show promise.[70] Perhaps there are more edifying ways to view the Church than to see it as a body firmly rooted in the earth, extending itself outward like a patch of crabgrass on a lawn. But the message the Church conveyed was not always sophisticated. Medieval people expressed ideas concretely in gestures, images, and physical structures. In churches, shrines, and sacred places, western European churchmen made the kingdom of God immanent to their congregations—and to themselves.

NOTES

1. Francesco Gabrielli, *Arab Historians of the Crusades* (Berkeley: University of California Press, 1969), 144.

2. The standard discussion of hierophanies is in Mircea Eliade, *Patterns in Comparative Religion,* trans. Rosemary Sheed (New York: Sheed & Ward, 1958). Clarifying reflections include Jonathan Z. Smith, *Map Is Not Territory: Studies in the History of Religions,* Studies in Judaism in Late Antiquity, vol. 23 (Leiden: Brill, 1978), 88–89. For a brief supplement, see Laurence E. Sullivan, "Nature," *The Encyclopedia of Religion,* 16 vols. (New York: Collier Macmillan, 1987), 10:326. Note also Bryan S. Rennie, *Reconstructing Eliade: Making Sense of Religion* (Albany: State University of New York Press, 1996).

3. Robert Markus, *The End of Ancient Christianity* (New York: Cambridge University Press, 1990), 139–55; "How on Earth Could Places Become Holy? Origins of the Christian Idea of Holy Places," *Journal of Early Christian History,* 2 (1994): 258–71.

4. John Wilkinson, "Jewish Holy Places and the Origins of Christian Pilgrimage," in *The Blessings of Pilgrimage,* ed. Robert Ousterhout, Illinois Byzantine Studies 1 (Urbana: University of Illinois Press, 1990), 41–53.

5. David Golan, "Hadrian's Decision to Supplant 'Jerusalem' by 'Aelia Capi-

tolina,'" *Historia* 35 (1986): 226–39. Note, however, the problems highlighted in Annabel Jane Wharton, "The Baptistery of the Holy Sepulcher in Jerusalem and the Politics of Sacred Landscape," *Dumbarton Oaks Papers* 46 (1992): 321–22.

6. John Wilkinson with Joyce Hill and W. F.Ryan, *Jerusalem Pilgrimage, 1099–1185*, Hakluyt Society, 2d ser., 167 (London: Hakluyt Society, 1988), 34.

7. Because the evidence for Christian pilgrimage is sketchy prior to the fourth century, the extent and even the existence of earlier traditions are fiercely debated. Continuity with earlier Jewish-Christian traditions is argued by Günter Stemberger, *Juden und Christen im Heiligen Land: Palästina unter Konstantin und Theodosius* (Munich: C. H. Beck, 1987), esp. 61–73; Wilkinson, "Jewish Holy Places," 41–53; and Robert L. Wilken, *The Land Called Holy: Palestine in Christian History and Thought* (New Haven: Yale University Press, 1992), esp. 46–64. Origin *de novo* in the fourth century—a thesis that, however elegantly stated, ultimately struggles to establish an *argumentum ex silentio*—is championed by Peter Walker, *Holy City, Holy Places? Christian Attitudes to Jerusalem and the Holy Land in the Fourth Century*, Oxford Early Christian Studies (Oxford: Clarendon Press, 1990), 7–15; Wharton, "The Baptistery of the Holy Sepulcher," 313–25; Kenneth G. Holum, "Hadrian and St. Helena: Imperial Travel and the Origins of Christian Holy Land Pilgrimage," in *Blessings of Pilgrimage*, ed. Ousterhout, 66–81; and Joan E. Taylor, *Christians and the Holy Places: The Myth of Jewish-Christian Origins* (Oxford: Clarendon Press, 1993), esp. 314–20.

8. References to the archaeological literature are noted in Joseph D. Alchermes, "Petrine Politics: Pope Symmachus and the Rotunda of St. Andrew at Old Saint Peters," *Catholic Historical Review* 81 (1995): 3–5.

9. Ignatius of Antioch, *Epistle to the Romans* 4, trans. Maxwell Staniforth, in *Early Christian Writings: The Apostolic Fathers*, rev. ed. (Baltimore: Penguin, 1987), 86.

10. *Martyrdom of Polycarp* 18, trans. Staniforth, in *Early Christian Writings*, 131.

11. On Jewish glorification of martyrdom, see W. H. C. Frend, *Martyrdom and Persecution in the Early Church: A Study of a Conflict from the Maccabees to Donatus* (Garden City: New York University Press, 1967), 22–63. Details on Christian developments are given in Hyppolyte Delehaye, *Les Origines du culte des martyrs*, 2d ed., Subsidia hagiographica 20 (Brussels: Société des Bollandistes, 1933).

12. Letizia Pani Ermini, "Santuario e città fra tarda antichità e altomedioevo," *Santi e demoni nell'alto medioevo occidentale (secoli V–XI), 7–13 aprile 1988*, 2 vols., Settimane di studio del Centro italiano di studi sull'alto medioevo 36 (Spoleto: Il Centro, 1989), 2:837–81.

13. Origen, *Homily on Jeremiah* 4.3, trans. in Frend, *Martyrdom and Persecution*, 241.

14. John McCulloh, "The Cult of Relics in the Letters and 'Dialogues' of Pope Gregory the Great: A Lexicographical Study," *Traditio* 32 (l976): 145–46; Martin Heinzelmann, *Translationsberichte und andere Quellen des Reliquienkultes*,

Typologie des sources du moyen âge occidental 33 (Turnhout: Brepols, 1979), 17–27; Hunt, "The Traffic in Relics: Some Late Roman Evidence," in *The Byzantine Saint: University of Birmingham Fourteenth Spring Symposium of Byzantine Studies*, ed. Sergei Hackel, Studies Supplementary to *Sobornost* 5 (London: Fellowship of St. Alban and St. Sergius, 1981), 171–80.

15. Peter Brown, *The Cult of the Saints: Its Rise and Function in Latin Christianity* (Chicago: University of Chicago Press, 1981).

16. W. H. C. Frend, *The Donatist Church: A Movement of Protest in Roman North Africa* (Oxford: Clarendon Press, 1952), 52–56; "Donatist and Catholic: The Organization of Christian Communities in the North African Countryside," *Cristianizzazione ed organizzazione ecclesiastica delle campagne nell'alto medioevo: espansione e resistenze, 10–16 aprile 1980*, 2 vols., Settimane di studio del Centro italiano di studi sull'alto medioevo 28 (Spoleto: Il Centro, 1982), 2:616–20, 632–34.

17. Peter Brown, "The Rise and Function of the Holy Man in Late Antiquity," *Journal of Roman Studies* 61 (1971): 80–101, reprint in *Society and the Holy in Late Antiquity* (Berkeley, 1982), 103–52. His later reflections are in "The Saint as Exemplar in Late Antiquity," *Representations* 1 (1983): 1–25, and "Arbiters of the Holy: The Christian Holy Man in Late Antiquity," in his *Authority and the Sacred: Aspects of the Christianization of the Roman World* (Cambridge: Cambridge University Press, 1995), 55–78.

18. On altar relics, see Cyril E. Pocknee, *The Christian Altar in History and Today* (London: A. B. Mowbray, 1963), 37–41; Heinzelmann, *Translationsberichte*, 27–28; and McCulloh, "Cult of Relics," 178–79. North African canon law seems to have been the earliest to insist that all altars have relics: see *Registri Ecclesiae Carthaginensis excerpta 73*, ed. C. Munier, *Concilia Africae a. 345–a. 525*, Corpus Christianorum: Series Latina 149 (Turnhout: Brepols, 1974), 204–5. The continued force of such legislation is demonstrated by, for example, *Capitulare Aquisgranense*, ed. *Monumenta Germaniae Historica: Leges 2/1: 170.*

19. For a brief English survey, see George W. O. Addleshaw, *The Development of the Parochial System from Charlemagne (768–814) to Urban II (1088–1099)*, 2d ed., St. Anthony's Hall Publications 6 (York: St. Anthony's Press, 1970). On the importance of the Carolingian contribution, see also John J. Contreni, "From Polis to Parish," *Religion, Culture, and Society in the Early Middle Ages: Studies in Honor of Richard E. Sullivan*, Studies in Medieval Culture 23 (Kalamazoo: Medieval Institute Publications, 1987), 155–64. Studies on the particular patterns of parish development found in Italy, France, England, Germany, and Eastern Europe are in *Cristianizzazione ed organizzazione*. Note also Joseph Avril, "La paroisse médiévale: Bilan et perspectives d'après quelques travaux récents," *Revue d'histoire de l'église de France* 74 (1988): 91–113.

20. Heinzelmann, *Translationsberichte*, 43–66. On particular problems involved in relic acquisition, see Patrick Geary, *Furta Sacra: Thefts of Relics in the Central Middle Ages*, rev. ed. (Princeton: Princeton University Press, 1990), and John McCulloh, "From Antiquity to the Middle Ages: Continuity and Change in Papal

Relic Policy from the 6th to the 8th Century," in *Pietas: Festschrift für Bernhard Kötting*, ed. Ernst Dassmann and K. Suso Frank, Jahrbuch für Antike und Christentum Ergänzungsband 8 (Münster: Aschendorff, 1980), 313–24.

21. Bernhard Töpfer, "The Cult of Relics and Pilgrimage in Burgundy and Aquitaine at the Time of the Monastic Reform," in *The Peace of God: Social Violence and Religious Response in France around the Year 1000*, ed. Thomas Head and Richard Landes (Ithaca: Cornell University Press, 1992), 41–57.

22. Robin Lane Fox, *Pagans and Christians* (New York: Knopf, 1987), 204–7. For further development of these ideas, see Sabine MacCormack, "*Loca Sancta:* The Organization of Sacred Topography in Late Antiquity," in Ousterhout, *Blessings of Pilgrimage*, 7–40.

23. H. R. Ellis Davidson, *Myths and Symbols in Pagan Europe: Early Scandinavian and Celtic Religions* (Syracuse: Syracuse University Press, 1988), 26, 115.

24. Diana Eck, "Mountains," *Encyclopedia of Religion* 10:130–34.

25. Aline Rousselle, *Croire et Guérir: La foi en Gaule dans l'Antiquité tardive* (Paris: Librarie Arthème Fayard, 1990), 31–49, 181–86, solidly surveys pagan Gallo-Roman fountain lore. The flood of pertinent material, too extensive to cite here, is not always so critically analyzed or analyzable.

26. For recent survey introductions to sacrality of forests, see Réginald Grégoire, "La foresta come esperienza religiosa," *L'ambiente vegetale nell'alto medioevo, 30 marzo–5 aprile 1989,* 2 vols., Settimane di studio del Centro italiano di studi sull'alto medioevo 37 (Spoleto: Il Centro, 1990), 2:663–703, and Roland Bechmann, *Trees and Man: The Forest in the Middle Ages,* trans. Katharyn Dunham (New York: Paragon House, 1990), 276–82.

27. Violet MacDermot, *The Cult of the Seer in the Ancient Near East: A Contribution to Current Research on Hallucinations Drawn from Coptic and Other Texts* (Berkeley: University of California Press, 1971), 76–80.

28. Libanius, *Declamation* 30, ed. Richard Foerster, *Libanii Opera,* 12 vols. (Leipzig: B. G. Teubner, 1903–23), 6:623.

29. *Concilium Francofurtense* 43, ed. *Monumenta Germaniae Historica: Concilia* 2 (1):170. On the destruction of sacred groves, see Richard E. Sullivan, "The Carolingian Missionary and the Pagan," *Speculum* 28 (1953): 720–21, 736, reprint in *Christian Missionary Activity in the Early Middle Ages,* Variorum Collected Studies (London: Variorum, 1994).

30. Walafrid Strabo, *Vita Galli* 1.12, ed. *Monumenta Germaniae Historica: Scriptores Rerum Merovingicarum* 4:293–94.

31. John T. McNeill and Helena M. Gamer introduce the relevant penitential literature in their *Medieval Handbooks of Penance: A Translation of the Principal 'Libri Poenitentiales' and Selections from Related Documents,* Columbia University Records of Civilization Sources and Studies 29 (1938; reprint ed., New York: Octagon Books, Inc., 1965), 276, 331, 390, 419–21. An attempt at listing all the surviving citations and penitentials is Dieter Harmening, *Superstitio Uberlieferungs- und theoriegeschichtliche Untersuchungen zur kirchlich-theologischen Aberglaubensliteratur des Mittelalters* (Berlin: E. Schmidt, 1979), 320–24. On how

to evaluate them, see Heinrich Fichtenau, *Lebensordnungen des 10. Jahrhunderts: Studien über Denkart und Existenz im einstigen Karolingerreich,* 2 vols., Monographien zur Geschichte des Mittelalters 30 (1–2) (Stuttgart: A. Hiersemann, 1984), 2:412–15, trans. (without notes) by Patrick Geary as *Living in the Tenth Century: Mentality and Social Orders* (Chicago: University of Chicago Press, 1991), 314–16.

32. Atto of Vercelli, *Capitulare* 48, in Jean-Paul Migne, ed., *Patrologiae Cursus Completus: Series Latina* 134:38 (later cited as *PL*).

33. Rodulfus Glaber, *Historiae* 4.8, ed. John France (Oxford: Clarendon Press, 1989), 185.

34. For example, note the demon who inhabited the thermal baths at Aachen before Pepin III and Charlemagne developed the place, who is mentioned in Notker the Stammerer, *Charlemagne* 15, trans. Lewis Thorpe in *Two Lives of Charlemagne* (Baltimore: Penguin Books, 1969), 160–61, or the demons in the Vienne who had to be banished by St. Martial, who are described in his *vita* 15, ed. Laurentius Surius, *De Probatis Sanctorum Vitis*, 4th ed., 12 vols. (Cologne, 1618), 6:369.

35. Markus, *End of Ancient Christianity,* 139–55, and "How on Earth?" esp. 259, 263–64.

36. On the saints as successors of the gods, see Raoul Manselli, "Resistenze dei culti antichi nella pratica religiosa dei laici nelle campagne," in *Cristianizzazione ed organizzazione,* 2:65.

37. Fox, *Pagans and Christians,* 206; Clare E. Stancliffe, "From Town to Country: The Christianization of the Touraine, 370–600," in *The Church in Town and Countryside: Papers Read at the Seventeenth Summer Meeting and the Eighteenth Winter Meeting of the Ecclesiastical History Society,* ed. Derek Baker, Studies in Church History (Oxford: Basil Blackwell, 1979), 47–49, 56; Ian N. Wood, "Early Merovingian Devotion in Town and Country," ibid., 74.

38. *Bede's Ecclesiastical History of the English People* 1.30, ed. and trans. Bertram Colgrave and R. A. B. Mynors, Oxford Medieval Texts (Oxford: Clarendon Press, 1969), 106–9.

39. Adam of Bremen, *Historia* 2:48, trans. Francis J. Tschan, *History of the Archbishops of Hamburg-Bremen,* Columbia University Records of Civilization Sources and Studies 53 (New York: Columbia University Press, 1959), 87.

40. Mary Lee Nolan and Sidney Nolan, *Christian Pilgrimage in Modern Western Europe,* Studies in Religion (Chapel Hill: University of North Carolina Press, 1989), 82, 290–338, esp. 301–3, 306; M. L. Nolan, "Shrine Locations: Ideals and Realities in Continental Europe," *Luoghi sacri e spazi della santità,* ed. Sofia Boesch Gajano and Lucretta Scaraffia (Torino: Rosenberg & Sellier, 1990), 23–35.

41. Richard Krautheimer, *Rome: Profile of a City, 312–1308* (Princeton: Princeton University Press, 1980), 107–8, 114–15, 141.

42. Francesco Gandolfo, "Luoghi dei santi e luoghi dei demoni: il riuso dei templi nel medio evo," in *Santi e demoni,* 1:913–15.

43. Jean Hubert, "Sources sacrées et sources saintes" (1967), reprint *Arts et vie sociale de la fin du Moyen Age: Études d'archéologie et d'histoire. Recueil offert à*

l'auteur par ses élèves et ses amis, Mémoires et documents publiés par la Société de l'École des Chartes 24 (Geneva: Droz, 1977), 3–9, esp. 6–7. For a detailed example, see Michel Roblin, "Fontaines sacrées et nécropoles antiques, deux sites fréquents d'églises paroissiales rurales dans les sept anciens diocèses de l'Oise," *La Christianisation des pays entre Loire et Rhin, IVe–VIIe siècles: Actes du Colloque de Nanterre publiés avec le concours de l'Université de Paris X, = Revue d'histoire de l'église de France* 62 (1975): 235–51.

44. Constantius, *Vita Germani* 6, trans. from F. R. Hoare, *The Western Fathers* (1954; reprint New York: Harper & Row, 1965), 290; Louis Maximilien Duru, *Bibliothèque historique de l'Yonne, ou collection de légendes, chroniques et documents divers pour servir à l'histoire des différentes contrées qui forment aujourd'hui ce département,* 2 vols. (Auxerre: Perriquet, 1850–63), 1:318.

45. Compare the *Gesta Sanctorum Patrum Fontanellensis Coenobii,* ed. Fernand Lohier and Jean Laporte, Société de l'histoire de Normandie publication 55 (Rouen: A. Lestringant, 1936), 38, to *Acta Sanctorum Ordinis Sancti Benedicti* 2:537 (later cited as *ASOSB*). An analysis of the texts in question will appear in *Francia,* in John Howe, "*Sources hagiographiques de la Gaule (SHG):* The Hagiography of Fontenelle (Province of Haute-Normandy)."

46. E. Joubert, *Les saints de la Haute-Auvergne* (Aurillac: U.S.H.A., 1973), 26–27.

47. Compare Richard of Saint-Vannes, *Vita Rodingi* 2, ed. *Acta Sanctorum: Sept.* 5:516 with the later version in 5:509.

48. For an illustration of Bavo in his oak tree, see Albert D'Haenens, "Bavone di Gand, santo," *Bibliotheca Sanctorum,* 13 vols. (Rome: Istituto Giovanni XXIII della Pontificia università Lateranense, 1961–70), 2:981–86. Bavo's cult is discussed in Adriaan Verhulst, "Saint Bavon et les origines de Gand," *Saint Géry et la christianisation dans la nord de la Gaule, V^e–IXe siècles: Actes du Colloque de Cambrai, 5–7 octobre 1984,* ed. Michel Rouche = *Revue du nord* 68 (1986): 455–70.

49. John Howe, *Church Reform and Social Change in Eleventh-Century Italy: Dominic of Sora and His Patrons* (forthcoming, University of Pennsylvania Press).

50. *Acta Sanctorum Nov.* 2 (1): 94.

51. Some eleventh-century illustrations of forest sacrality are described in John Howe, "Greek Influence on the Eleventh-Century Western Revival of Hermitism" (Ph.D. diss., University of California at Los Angeles, 1979), 1:53.

52. Peter Damian, *Vita Romualdi* 1, ed. Giovanni Tabacco, Fonti per la storia d'Italia 94 (Rome: Istituto storico italiano per il medio evo, 1957), 14.

53. Bruno, *Letter to Radulphus,* ed. Anselme Hoste, in *Lettres des premiers chartreux I,* Sources Chrétiennes 88 (Paris: Editions du Cerf, 1962), 68.

54. Bernard, *Letter* 106, ed. *PL* 182:242.

55. Ian N. Wood, "Early Merovingian Devotion in Town and Country," in Baker, *The Church in Town and Countryside,* 65–68; Benedicta Ward, *Miracles and the Medieval Mind: Theory, Record and Event, 1000–1215* (Philadelphia: University of Pennsylvania Press, 1987), 34. For Greek areas, see Speros Vryonis,

Jr., "The *Panēgyris* of the Byzantine Saint: A Study in the Nature of a Medieval Institution, Its Origins, and Fate," in Hackel, *Byzantine Saint,* 196–226.

56. E.g., Robert Hertz, "St. Besse: A Study of an Alpine Cult," and Pierre Sanchis, "The Portuguese *Romarias,*" in *Saints and Their Cults: Studies in Religious Sociology, Folklore and History,* ed. Stephen Wilson (Cambridge: Cambridge University Press, 1983), 55–100, 261–89.

57. Franco Cardini, "Reliquie e pellegrinaggi," in *Santi e demoni,* 2:981–1041.

58. Processions are surveyed in John Francis Baldovin, *The Urban Character of Christian Worship: The Origins, Development, and Meaning of Stational Liturgy,* Orientalia Christiana Analecta 228 (Rome: Pont. Institutum Studiorum Orientalium, 1987). For the most-articulated and best-studied example, see Victor Saxer, "L'Utilisation par la liturgie de l'espace urbain et suburbain: L'exemple de Rome dans l'antiquité et le haut moyen âge," *Actes du XIe Congrès international d'archéologie chrétienne: Lyon, Vienne, Grenoble, Genève et Aoste (21–28 septembre 1986),* Collection de l'École française de Rome 123, Studi de Antichità cristiana 41 (Rome: École française de Rome, 1989), 917–1033. Elaborate festal processions for Centula and its associated monastery of Saint-Riquier, described by Angilbert (d. 814), are discussed in Rosamond McKitterick, "Town and Monastery in the Carolingian Period," in Baker, *The Church in Town and Countryside,* 99–102. On the Roman-style stational liturgy developed at Metz in the late eighth century, see Roger E. Reynolds, "Metz, use of," *Dictionary of the Middle Ages,* 8:301–2.

59. On the *adventus,* see Michael McCormick, *Eternal Victory: Triumphal Rulership in Late Antiquity, Byzantium, and the Early Medieval West,* Past and Present Publications (Cambridge: Cambridge University Press, 1986). For an example of its application to saints, see Kenneth G. Holum and Gary Vikan, "The Trier Ivory, *Adventus* Ceremonial, and the Relics of St. Stephen," *Dumbarton Oaks Papers* 33 (1979): 113–33.

60. Jean Hubert and Marie-Clothilde Hubert, "Piété chrétienne ou paganisme? Les statues-reliquaires de l'europe carolingienne," *Cristianizzazione ed organizzazione,* 1:234–75; Claire Wheeler Solt, "Romanesque French Reliquaries," *Studies in Medieval and Renaissance History* 9 (1987): 165–236.

61. Geoffrey Koziol, "Monks, Feuds, and the Making of Peace in Eleventh-Century Flanders," in Head and Landes, *Peace of God,* 253–54, and *Begging Pardon and Favor: Ritual and Political Order in Early Medieval France* (Ithaca: Cornell University Press, 1992), 297, 304, 313–14.

62. Miri Rubin, *Corpus Christi: The Eucharist in Late Medieval Culture* (Cambridge: Cambridge University Press, 1991), 243–71.

63. André Vauchez, *La Spiritualité du moyen âge occidental, VIIIe–XIe siècles* (Paris: Presses Universitaires de France, 1975), 40–41.

64. Udalrich, *Consuetudines Cluniacenses,* ed. PL 149:675–77.

65. Examples of public psalming include the hermits Marinus (fl. 10th century) and Bruno of Querfurt (d. 1009) in Peter Damian, *Vita Romualdi* 4 and 27, pp. 20–21 and 57; Odo of Cluny in John of Salerno, *Vita Odonis* 2.5, ed. ASOSB

5:165, trans. Gerard Sittwell, *St. Odo of Cluny: Being the Life of St. Odo of Cluny by John of Salerno and the Life of St. Gerard of Aurillac by St. Odo* (London: Sheed & Ward, 1958), 47; and Wulfstan of Worcester in William of Malmsbury, *Vita Vulstani* 2.10 and 3.5, ed. Reginald R. Darlington, Camden Society Publications, 3d ser., 40 (London: Royal Historical Society, 1928), 33, 49 (cf. 96), trans. Michael Swanton, *Three Lives of the Last Englishmen,* Garland Library of Medieval Literature, Ser. B., 10 (New York: Garland Pub., 1984), 117, 131–32.

66. Udalrich, *Consuetudines Cluniacenses,* ed. *PL* 149:739. For context see Koziol, *Begging Pardon and Favor,* 183 and passim.

67. Lionel Rothkrug, "Popular Religion and Holy Shrines: Their Influence on the Origins of the German Reformation and Their Role in German Cultural Development," in *Religion and the People, 800–1700,* ed. James Obelkevich (Chapel Hill: University of North Carolina Press, 1979), 20–86.

68. Eamon Duffy, *The Stripping of the Altars: Traditional Religion in England c. 1400–c. 1580* (New Haven: Yale University Press, 1992).

69. Terrence Ranger, "Taking Hold of the Land: Holy Places and Pilgrimages in Twentieth-Century Zimbabwe," *Past & Present,* 117 (1987): 158–94.

70. For example, Boesch Gajano and Scaraffia, *Luoghi sacri*; Jean Holm, ed., *Sacred Place* (London: Pinter Press, 1994); Ann Grodzins Gold, "Magical Landscapes and Moral Orders: New Readings in Religion and Ecology," *Religious Studies Review* 21 (1995): 71–77.

Women in Conversion History

5

✠

Gender and Conversion in the Merovingian Era

Cordula Nolte

"The language of conversion can be abrupt." With these words Karl F. Morrison approaches an account by Snorri Sturluson (1178/9–1241) of the Christian king of Norway, Olav Tryggvason (969–1000) and the non-Christian Queen Sigrid of Sweden, whom the king wished to marry. "Marriage negotiations progressed well until the queen refused to abandon the religion that she held, as her kinsmen before her had done. Olav, she said, could, without hindrance or reproach, worship whatever god pleased him.

"King Olav was very wroth and answered hastily, 'Why should I wed you, you heathen bitch?', and he struck her in the face with the glove he was holding in his hand." This was no way to win the heart of Queen Sigrid the Strong-minded. Her response was instant: "This may be your death," she said. Turned into Olav's staunchest enemy, she married the king of Denmark, whom she incited to the battle in which Olav died (1000 C.E.)."[1]

From the Merovingian era an account by Gregory of Tours (538–594) has come down in which the "language of conversion" is no less "abrupt." The Visigothic King Amalarich (+531), an Arian Christian, married Chlotchilde, a Merovingian princess who was a Catholic Christian. As Chlotchilde held fast to her Catholic faith instead of converting to Arianism at the Visigothic court in Spain, far from her Frankish homeland, Amalarich had her pelted with muck and foul-smelling rubbish on her way to church and he struck her violently. Thereupon Chlotchilde sent to her brother, the Frankish King Childebert I, a piece of cloth stained with her own blood. "Exceedingly angry," Childebert launched a war against Spain. Amalarich was killed while fleeing.[2]

The parallels between the texts of Snorri Sturluson and Gregory of Tours are obvious at a glance. In both narratives, a woman's refusal to give up her ancestral religion at her marriage brings on an insulting and violent reaction. This is followed by an initiative of the woman to take revenge, assisted by her relations, and finally by the violent death of the frustrated "convert-maker." Each text opens questions about the relationship of the historical event and its literary representation, about the author's perspective and intention and the public he is aiming at, and "about the information concerning the relative status of men and women, converted and unconverted," which is contained in the description of male and female behavior.[3]

The very similarity of the texts also raises questions. Snorri Sturluson wrote his narrative about the marriage negotiations and the conversion efforts of King Olav at a distance of over two hundred years. For Gregory of Tours, on the other hand, there lay only a few decades between the events and their recording. Besides, Procopius confirms his description of the events. In the case of King Olav, he is treated as an orthodox Christian from Snorri's perspective, while the Arian Amalarich is, in the eyes of the Catholic bishop Gregory, an abominable heretic. King Olav's behavior toward Sigrid conforms with his earlier representation as a brutal and ruthless "converting king," according to Snorri.[4] On the other hand, besides the actions taken against his wife, the Arian Visigothic King Amalarich engaged in no anti-Catholic measures. Rather like his predecessors, he appears to have been tolerant toward Catholics in the Visigothic kingdom. His violent attempt to force Chlotchilde to abandon Catholicism did not have consequences for other Catholics.[5] With all of these differences, how can we explain the similarities of the two texts with regard to the description of female and male behavior?

Obviously Snorri and Gregory had similar ideas of the actions and reactions of men and women in the context of marriage and conversion. On whatever information both narratives might rest, in the eyes of the authors the behavior of Olav and Sigrid, Amalarich and Chlotchilde as depicted in the texts must have been plausible for their public. One can ask whether these narratives illustrate current gender-specific behavior patterns in a specific conversion situation. Generalizing from the two texts, shall we conclude that in the early Middle Ages men quite often attempted to convince their (future) wives to accept their own religion? Were their efforts frequently accompanied by insults and attacks, while women resisted forced conversion and mobilized all available powers (e.g. kinship group, later husband) in order to take revenge? At the same time the question arises whether the state of affairs described can be attributed exclusively to men and women of royal status, whose religious position was decisive for the entire people (*gens*).

The two narratives leave us with a multitude of considerations, not only generally on the theme of conversion but also addressing the special link between gender and conversion. In this study I wish to concentrate on the following questions: What do the early medieval sources tell us about women as "objects" of missionary work, Christianization, and conversion? What do these texts tell us about the conversion of women themselves, and in what context is this discussed? With regard to men and women, can one speak of conversion in broadly the same terms or is it necessary to point out that conversion was something different for men and women?[6] Do the sources portray women as convert-makers of men in a manner different from men who converted women? Questions of this kind are rarely discussed in the numerous works that have been published on early medieval Christianization. The few studies so far examining the presence of women in the process of Christianization are primarily concerned with the active role of women as convert-makers (in particular with regard to royal husbands) rather than with the conversion of the women themselves.[7]

I will examine the aforementioned questions for the period from the fifth to the eighth century. This period includes the first phase of the Christianization of the Frankish kingdom, beginning with the conversion of King Clovis I to the Catholic Christianity of his wife Clotilda at the end of the fifth century.[8] In the course of this same era, the neighbors of the Frankish kingdom—Anglo-Saxons, Visigoths, Lombards—also accepted Christianity or else passed from Arianism to Catholicism. The texts dealing with the Christianization of the peoples (*gentes*) of early medieval Europe often use the terms *conversio, converti,* or *conversari* in order to identify the reception of Christianity or the change from Arianism to Catholicism by particular persons or groups.[9] In this context, the term *conversio* does not refer to a process of an inner reorientation, as it does for example in Nock's classic definition of conversion.[10] Rather, in many instances conversio must be identical with baptism or, in the case of the change from Arianism to Catholicism, with the anointing, without these acts of institutional incorporation necessarily being preceded by an inner conversion.[11] I shall refrain then from laying out the problematics of applying the term *conversion* to the early Middle Ages and from discussing its different meanings.[12] Suffice it to say that I use the term *conversion* here exclusively to mean "reception of Christianity by a particular individual" or "change of a particular individual from Arianism to Catholicism or the reverse," and that thereby I intend to make no judgment about the degree of inner conversion. In this connection I would also like to point to Karl F. Morrison's statement "that what can be discussed is not conversion but writings about conversion."[13] This differentiation between historical experience and text, it appears to me, is fundamental for the examination of written sources.

Turning now to the early medieval texts, we have to begin by noting that the material supplies few references to women as objects of missionary work and as converts. Only rarely is it knowable in what way and under what circumstances women became Christians or converted from one Christian denomination to another. The nearly complete silence of the sources is traceable above all to two factors: on the one hand it results from lack of interest on the part of early medieval authors in writing expressly about the conversion and baptism of women and girls, and on the other hand it is connected with the collective nature of early medieval conversion and baptism. The tendency of the writers to discuss only the conversion of men is apparent above all in relation to the famous conversions of kings, resulting in an incomplete picture of the conversion of the royal families to Catholic Christianity. This is especially true for the Anglo-Saxon region, which in itself offers rich materials for considering missionary endeavor, Christianization, and conversion in the early Middle Ages.[14] It is difficult to discern from the texts women's participation in the collective decision about a change of religion and the collective act of receiving baptism, which were the characteristic form of conversion in early medieval societies.[15] At the head of the *gentes,* the ruler and his great men—that is, the political leadership—decided about the reception of Christianity. At the head of the *domus* the *pater familias,* as the possessor of the right of guardianship over the family and the domestic servants, stepped forward and had himself baptized along with his household. In the texts the members of the household are not expressly mentioned but are put together in collective terms: the head of the household converts "together with his house" or "together with his entire family."[16] Beyond such references to the conversion and baptism of entire households, however, evidence also appears in the texts that within a family—at least temporarily—different religions or denominations could exist. This point will be discussed further.

The bulk of the surviving materials dealing with the conversion of men and women refers to the members of royal families. In spite of the lack of information regarding female family members, still we find in the sphere of kingship a starting point for the answer to the questions initially posed. Beyond the ruling families the conversion of a woman is scarcely ever mentioned, as for example in the lives of missionaries and of bishops. The *Life* of Bishop Eucherius of Orléans (+738) reports that the saint snatched a woman *"de gentilitatis errore"* (from the false teachings of the gentiles) by his exhortations and became the godfather of her son.[17] The husband and father is not named in this context. According to the *Life* of Amandus, at the command of the saint (+ about 676) a woman destroyed a pagan shrine, a tree.[18] This woman knew that she had been blinded as punishment for her earlier "idol worship." Obviously she was already Christian, but only Amandus made her give up her old gods. As Amandus worked as a missionary in the Schelde region, he encountered strong opposition there from men and women. The women (*mulieres*) and the country folk (*rustici*) blocked his missionary work and physically abused him.[19] Although it is not out of question that here the paired concepts of "women" and "country men" serve merely as a comprehensive derogatory designation for Amandus's enemies, this information appears to indicate that Amandus's missionary efforts actually aimed at both sexes and that women engaged in the same way as men in the defense of their ancestral religion against him. On the other hand, the *Life* of Amandus states clearly that during his missionary work he was supported by both pious men and women.[20]

The *Life* of Liudger also contains a reference, although veiled, to women as the objects of the missionary work. According to the *vita*, Liudger (+809) looked upon women in their capacity as mothers of future Christians. As he was driven away from his mission field because of a Saxon invasion, he ordered a native layman to baptize seriously ill children during his absence, "after he had persuaded the married women (*matronae*) about it."[21] Apparently the women's consent was necessary for baptism of the children; this suggests that the decision about baptism was not entirely the concern of the *pater familias* but was perhaps a special responsibility of women as well.[22] Liudger counted on the cooperation of these women when he tried to rescue endangered souls and to provide for the continuation of the mission. Unquestionably, the long-term success of each Christian mission depends on the subsequent growth of new generations which have been baptized and brought up in the Christian faith from childhood. Therefore, it is conceivable that, like Liudger, other missionaries referred to women as (potential) mothers, yet the early medieval sources pay no further attention to this.[23]

As noted in connection with the early medieval practice of collective conversion and baptism, the members of a family could adhere to different religions or denominations. The texts repeatedly attest to this situation in regard to the Germanic royal families in the course of (Catholic) Christianization. In most cases such a religious division was the result of marriage between adherents of different religions or denominations.[24] A difference of religion could also emerge between parents (or one parent) and children, as for example when Germanic rulers such as the Frankish King Clovis I (+511) and King Edwin of Northumbria (+633/34) allowed some of their children to be baptized without themselves first converting to Christianity, or when an Arian such as the Lombard King Agilulf (+616) allowed his son to be baptized a Catholic without himself becoming a Catholic.[25] The three kings mentioned were married to Catholic Christian wives: Clovis to the Burgundian princess Clotilda; Edwin to Ethelberga, the daughter of the King of Kent; and Agilulf to Theodelinde, a member of the Bavarian ruling family. Other kings, as was the case with Ethelbert of Kent (+616/18), who was married to the Catholic Merovingian Bertha, were themselves converted to Christianity but left their male heirs unbaptized.[26] In Spain, during the lifetime of King Leovigild, Prince Hermenegild (+585) was the first member of the Visigothic royal family to convert from Arianism to Catholicism; he was married to the Merovingian Ingunde.[27]

Compared with the information on the Germanic ruling families, there is little evidence of the coexistence of different religions and denominations in families of other social strata. However, we may assume that in the early Merovingian era a significant number of families had both Christian and non-Christian members. Since the Franks from the beginning—in contrast to the Burgundians, Visigoths, and Ostrogoths—did not prohibit *conubium* (legal marriage) between Germanic and Gallo-Roman persons, numerous marriages between Christian Gallo-Romans and non-Christian Franks must have been contracted. Likewise in the border regions of the Frankish kingdom, there presumably often occurred religiously mixed marriages between Franks and their non-Christian or Arian Germanic neighbors.

These ethnic and religious processes of amalgamation may be proven concretely from the sources only with difficulty.[28] Gregory of Tours reports on a married couple apparently living in the Visigothic area of southern Gaul. The wife was a Catholic Christian; the husband, identified as a heretic (*vir hereticus*), was obviously an Arian Christian. Eventually he was converted to Catholicism "along with his household."[29] Bishop Medardus of Noyon (ca. 480–after 550/561) had a Frankish father and a Roman mother. The special emphasis on the mother in the *Life* of Medardus may indicate that only she was Christian.[30] The *Life* of Bishop Bibianus or Vivianus of Saintes (+ mid-fifth century) says of his father that he was "ensnared in the error of the heathens" and remained unbaptized until the end of his life. Bibian's mother, Maurella, on the other hand, was a Christian. This, according to the *vita*, ought to have been of great advantage with regard to the religious instruction of the saint.[31] It appears that this couple's religious differences already existed when they married; at least, it is not indicated whether Maurella first converted to Christianity after her marriage.

It was also possible during the process of Christianization that from a non-Christian couple, only one partner would accept the Christian faith in the course of the marriage. About 700, the *Discipulus Umbrensium* in his version of the penitential statutes passed down under the name of Theodore of Canterbury, discussed the possibility of only one partner converting to Christianity. In such a case, the *Discipulus Umbrensium* allowed divorce or, more precisely, the dismissal of the woman by the man.[32] The *Discipulus Umbrensium* referred in this matter to the Apostle Paul (1 Cor. 7:15) who, however, does not recommend that a man who converts to Christianity might leave his wife in the event that she does not convert as well (see 1 Cor. 7:12).

For the Merovingian era there is no definite case known to me in which a husband or wife accepted Christianity while the other partner remained in the old religion. Sulpicius Severus tells us in his life of St. Martin of Tours about one such case of individual conversion in the fourth century, a case that concerned Martin's own parents. According to Sulpicius, Martin received the divine mandate to undertake his first missionary journey from Poitiers to his Pannonian homeland, to his parents, "who were still caught in the errors of the heathens."[33] His goal, to convert his parents, he achieved only in part. While he won his mother to Christianity, he was unable to move his father to a change of religion.[34] It would be interesting to know why Martin was successful in his attempt at conversion with his mother and not with his father, but the *Life* here offers no clue. Sulpicius rushes to assure us that Martin converted many other people in his homeland. According to J. Fontaine, this could suggest that Martin remained there for a longer time in hopes of moving his father to convert eventually. At the same time Fontaine considers the reference to Martin's success as an attempt by the author to eradicate the disagreeable impression the public might form from the news of Martin's failure in the case of his father.[35] In our context it is worth remarking that the father nevertheless does not appear to have stood in the way of his wife's conversion, although by her step the religious unity of the marriage and of the household was broken. As for the consequences of her conversion for the life of this couple, nothing is known for certain.

We now turn to the Merovingian kingdom and its neighbors and search the texts discussing the Christianization and "Catholicizing" of Germanic ruling families for information about the conversion of royal women. The information that has been transmitted leads us to conclude that in several cases male and female family members, mostly brothers and sisters, jointly converted to (Catholic) Christianity in accordance with the collective character of early medieval conversion. The most complete description of such a family and brother-sister conversion is found in the narrative of Gregory of Tours concerning the baptism of King Clovis I at the end of the fifth century. We learn that along with Clovis (and over 3,000 members of his army) his sister Alboflede was baptized and that his sister Lantechilde, "who had fallen into the Arian heresy," was converted to Catholic Christianity and, as was customary in the cases of converted Arians, was anointed.[36] On the occasion of Lantechilde's conversion, Bishop Avitus of Vienne wrote a sermon, the text of which has not survived.[37] It is not known how and when Lantechilde had become Arian. Possibly there was a connection between her conversion to Arian Christianity and the marriage of her sister Audofleda to the Arian Ostrogoth Theodoric the Great at the beginning of the last decade of the fifth century.[38] Clovis himself, before his baptism, was obviously courted by the Arians and seems to have felt more or less inclined toward Arianism.[39] As the head of the family, was he concerned that Lantechilde first accepted Arian Christianity and that she later became a Catholic along with him? Did Alboflede and Lantechilde decide for themselves about their conversion, or did they at least participate in the decision? Gregory's text does not give us any answer. While it fully describes how Clovis, after long hesitation, decided to be baptized, the intimate details of the conversion of the women remain obscure.

A few years after Clovis and his sisters, Sigerich, the son of the Burgundian king, and his sister Suavegotho converted one after the other to Catholic Christianity.[40] The brother and sister previously had been Arians. Soon after the beginning of his reign in the Anglo-Saxon kingdom of Kent, King Eadbald, son of King Ethelbert and the Merovingian Bertha, was baptized, according to Bede.[41] It was on this occasion in all probability that Eadbald's sister Ethelberga was baptized as well, although Bede does not mention her baptism. Only in connection with Ethelberga's marriage do we learn that she was a Christian. The newly converted Eadbald explained to the pagan King Edwin of Northumbria who was wooing Ethelberga his doubts about giving Edwin his Christian sister in marriage, whereupon Edwin promised the bride and her retinue free exercise of their Christian faith.[42] Although it is conceivable that in contrast to her brother, Ethelberga had already been baptized as a child, a letter of Pope Boniface V contains a clear reference to her not having been a Christian from childhood but having converted only at a later date.[43] Thus there is every reason to assume that Ethelberga and Eadbald, like the Merovingian and Burgundian brothers and sisters, underwent conversion together. Bede's silence on the baptism of Ethelberga can be explained by the fact that the baptism of a king's daughter usually did not have the same significance as the baptism of a king's son with regard to the Christianization. The conversion of kings and their male heirs formed the first step of the (Catholic) Christianization of their *gentes* and therefore warranted mention.[44] The baptism of royal women and girls, however, proved only in the long run to have important consequences when the girls in question, like Ethelberga, were married to men who in the course of the marriage were won over to (Catholic) Christianity and thereupon allowed or even promoted the Christianization of their people.

It is likely that just as royal brothers and sisters were inclined to convert together, so also in many instances a royal married couple was converted and baptized together. The *Annales regni Francorum* tell of such a family baptism in the ninth century. The Danish King Harold, his wife, and his son were baptized together at Mainz in 826.[45] For the previous centuries we lack evidence that kings and their spouses converted together to Christianity—that is, to Catholicism. We are here forced to guess about the conversion of royal wives. In Burgundy, for example, Sigismund (+523), the father of the previously mentioned brother and sister Sigerich and Suavegotho, converted from Arianism to Catholicism before 516.[46] It is not known whether his Arian wife Ostrogotho (Ariagne), a daughter of Theodoric the Great, converted as well. In the conversion of Anglo-Saxon kings it is likewise not clear whether the queens were baptized along with their husbands.[47] There is a reference to this only in the case of King Raedwald of East Anglia. He was baptized in Kent as a result of the influence of King Ethelbert, but upon his return home, "led astray by his wife and some false teachers," he offered sacrifice to his old gods along with Christ. Apparently Raedwald's wife had not been converted to Christianity together with him.[48] Combined with the obviously considerable influence of Raedwald's wife in political and religious matters, this account indicates that the process of a people's Christianization could turn out unfavorably when the queen was not converted to Christianity together with the king.

Turning to the conversion of royal women in connection with entering into marriage, the Merovingian Chlotchilde who got pelted with muck was not the only princess who was expected to give up her own religious tradition and accept the religion, that is, the denomination, of her husband. About fifty years after the frustrated attempt of the Visigoth Amalarich to convert his wife to Arian Christianity, another Merovingian princess, Ingunde, was sent to the Arian Visigothic court. At most twelve or thirteen years old, Ingunde was the daughter of the Frankish King Sigibert I and Queen Brunichilde and was married to Hermenegild, the son of the Visigothic King Leovigild. Again the court of Toledo anticipated the conversion of the Catholic Merovingian to Arianism. According to Gregory of Tours, Ingunde's husband Hermenegild did not concern himself about her conversion. This fell to Ingunde's mother-in-law, Queen Gosuintha, who was at the same time her grandmother.[49] Gosuintha attempted "to entice" her granddaughter "with flattering words" to submit herself to being baptized again, something that the Arians demanded of converted Catholics.[50] When this was not effective, she mistreated Ingunde in unpleasant ways, if we are to believe Gregory's dramatic description.[51] Ingunde, however, was as little dissuaded from her Catholic faith even by the use of violent methods as Chlotchilde had been previously. Rather, according to Gregory of Tours, she began to work for the conversion of Hermenegild to Catholicism and finally achieved this.[52]

The conflict between Gosuintha and Ingunde is also noteworthy in light of Gregory's announcement that about thirteen years previously, Gosuintha's daughter Brunichilde, the mother of Ingunde, at her marriage to the Merovingian Sigibert, had given up her Arian denomination. According to Gregory of Tours, Brunichilde "was converted through the preaching of the bishops and the admonition of the king himself." She confessed and believed in the Holy Trinity "in unitate," was anointed, and remained firm in the Catholic faith.[53] Sigibert did not leave the conversion work entirely to the bishops but personally urged conversion upon his wife. His "admonition" possibly had a more or less forceful form, even though Gregory does not say so. Gregory's assurance that Brunichilde remained firmly Catholic may aim at praising Brunichilde, but perhaps it also hints at the danger of a relapse into Arianism. Gregory reports from the perspective of a Catholic bishop on the conversion of Brunichilde; besides, he had obtained his bishopric in 573 under the aegis of the royal couple Brunichilde and Sigibert. For that reason he certainly was not inclined to admit the use of pressure on the part of the king or to discuss any kind of difficulties in the conversion of Brunichilde. Only a short time after Brunichilde's entering into marriage, her sister Galsuintha married Sigibert's brother Chilperich I and converted to Catholicism. She was murdered by her husband soon afterward.[54]

Was there a connection between the conversion of Brunichilde and her sister Galsuintha and the later behavior of their mother Gosuintha toward Ingunde? According to the opinion of K. Schäferdiek, Gosuintha's unrelenting pressure for the conversion of her grandchild to Arianism may have been brought about by the bitterness she felt because of her daughters' conversion to Catholicism under Frankish influence or perhaps even under Frankish pressure and because of Galsuintha having been murdered by her husband.[55] Along with this plausible psychological explanation, there remains the question of to what extent we can trust the narrative of the Catholic Bishop Gregory of Tours. Gregory confronts "Christian-persecuting" Arians (such as Amalarich and Gosuintha) with Catholics who remain firm in their belief (as Chlotchilde and Ingunde). He shows on the other hand Arians (such as Brunichilde and Galsuintha) as willingly giving up their denomination and being won over to the "true faith" (*vera fides*). Nevertheless, apart from this stylization, it is established that both Merovingian women outside of the Merovingian kingdom remained firmly committed to Catholicism, while the Visigothic women at their entry into the Merovingian royal family converted from Arianism to Catholicism.

Other Catholic women already mentioned who did not convert to the religion of their husbands after marriage to non-Christian or Arian kings were Clotilda, the wife of Clovis I; Bertha, married to Ethelbert of Kent; Theodelinde, the wife of the Lombard King Agilulf; and Ethelberga, who was married to Edwin of Northumbria. This list of women can be extended.[56] Apparently under specific political circumstances or promises on the occasion of marriage, the non-Christian and Arian rulers were ready to tolerate their wives' continued adherence to Catholicism.[57] On the other hand, the conversion of Brunichilde and Galsuintha seems to indicate that the Catholic Merovingians in the sixth century did not allow any deviation from orthodoxy on the part of royal wives. One can draw from this that other "foreign" princesses who were married to Merovingian rulers became Catholic as well. However, we lack evidence on the presumed conversion of those Arian or non-Christian princesses. Among them there were the Burgundian Suavegotho, who married Theuderich I in 511 (?); the Thuringian Radegunde, married to Chlothar I about 540; the Lombard Wisigarde, who was engaged to Theudebert I about 530 and some years later was married to him; and Wisigarde's sister Walderada (Vuldetrada), who married Theudebald, the son of Theudebert I, about 540.[58] Between 711 and 714 Theudesinde, a daughter of the non-Christian Frisian *dux* Radbod, married Grimoald, the mayor of the palace in Neustria.[59] In this case too, nothing is known about the baptism of the bride, but it may be supposed that Theudesinde became a Christian, at the latest when getting married.

Above all in the case of Radegunde, who shortly after her death in 587 was revered as a saint, it would be interesting to know how she came to accept Christianity. In 531 as a result of the conquest of Thuringia by the Franks, she was taken to the Frankish kingdom as part of the war booty. Chlothar I decided on her as his latter wife and had her educated in the royal *villa* Athies.[60] Radegunde in all probability had not previously come into contact with Arian or Catholic Christianity in her homeland, Thuringia, so it may be supposed that the future queen became acquainted with Christian teachings and was baptized during her education in Athies.[61] Later, according to tradition, not only did she distinguish herself through personal piety and monastic commitment, but she also specifically worked on the Christianization of the Frankish kingdom. She is the only member of the Merovingian family of whom it is reported that on her own initiative she had a pagan religious shrine destroyed. In doing so she resisted intimidation by a number of armed men and her behavior caused everyone eventually to praise God.[62]

I would like to sum up some results with regard to the conversion of women, before passing on to how women appear in the role of convert-makers in early medieval texts. As we have seen, there are a few indications in hagiography that the missionaries turned to both men and women. Not only men, as possessors of patriarchal power over the household, but also women appear to have been the objects of missionary work. With reference to the conversion of royal women, the texts do not often mention the baptism of queens and princesses. In some cases these events can be deduced, particularly in the context of a marriage or of conversion of an entire family. I used the example of Clovis and his sisters to point out that nothing is known concerning the decision-making progress that preceded the women's conversion. Yet as regards whether "conversion" in the early Middle Ages meant the same for women and men, it would be important to find out more about the participation of women in the decision to convert. Here also the moment of force comes into play. Both the representation of events at the Visigothic royal court by Gregory of Tours and Bede's reference—that Ethelbert of Kent and Edwin of Northumbria at their marriages had to guarantee the free exercise of their spouses' religion—imply the danger of force being used. Women could possibly be put under great pressure to give up their ancestral religious practices. On the other hand, it is hard to imagine that a man could have been the object of an (attempted) forced conversion initiated by his wife and her family. This would have been prevented by the unilateral right of the husband to exercise over his wife the power secured by his guardianship (*munt*).[63] Moreover, at her marriage a woman left her home and her kin and went to live within the sphere of influence of her husband's family. Some women were largely cut off from the support of their own family by a long distance. In addition to this, a man was much freer than a woman to terminate the marriage and to get divorced. In short, we are obliged to consider that conditions applying to the conversion of men may have been very different from those for women.

We have encountered two men who sought the conversion of their wives:

Sigibert was successful by means of "admonition," but Amalarich failed, even with drastic measures. What do the early medieval texts tell us about women as converters of men? Once again the sources are productive only in reference to royal persons, while the story of the conversion of members of other social strata remains largely obscure.[64] The Christianization—that is, Catholicization—of several early medieval *gentes,* as is well known, began with the ruler being married to a Catholic wife.[65] The observation that several Arian or non-Christian rulers with Catholic wives accepted Catholic Christianity in the course of their marriages suggests that these women cooperated in the conversion of their husbands. However, in the texts we find only a few explicit references to women converting their husbands. Detailed descriptions of their conversion activities are rare.

Here once again Gregory of Tours proves informative. In connection with King Clovis's decision to be baptized, Gregory provides a detailed treatment of Clotilda's effort to bring her husband to accept Catholic Christianity. As W. von den Steinen has pointed out, the passages in which Clotilda and her activities are central go back to the accounts of the queen herself.[66] Certainly this does not mean that Clotilda's own narrative has been passed on by Gregory without any other literary stylization. According to Gregory, the queen sought to reach her goal above all by means of the "sermon": "She preached to her husband unceasingly" (*praedicabat assiduae viro*).[67] As an illustration of this activity, Gregory places a fictional sermon in Clotilda's mouth in which she allegedly attempts to point out to her husband the powerlessness of his gods. As the tireless preaching achieved nothing, the queen attempted to address the religious feelings of the king directly on the cult-ritual level, but this approach also remained unsuccessful.[68] It is not possible here to analyze Gregory's entire narrative; yet we can say that Clotilda's preaching, in spite of its apparent lack of success, nevertheless in the long run played a major part in Clovis's decision to embrace Christianity.[69] As noted, Gregory of Tours also portrays the Merovingian princess Ingunde as converting her husband, the Visigothic prince Hermenegild. According to Gregory, she caused Hermenegild's conversion to Catholicism by her "preaching."[70]

In the *Historia Langobardorum* of Paul the Deacon, Queen Theodelinde appears indirectly as the person who was responsible for the conversion of the Arian Agilulf. Paul the Deacon does not mention any conversion of Agilulf to Catholicism under Theodelinde's influence, but such an event seems to be tacitly assumed. He writes that the king, "moved by the salutary prayers" of his wife, held on to the Catholic faith and supported the Catholic Church.[71] This statement does not entirely conform to the historical record—during his life Agilulf did not convert to Catholicism. Yet it shows that Paul puts a high value on the queen's influence on Agilulf's religious attitude. It also reflects his idea of her conversion methods ("salutary prayers").

The preaching of Clotilda and Ingunde and the salutary prayers of Theodelinde: here in three cases the verbal work of conversion is assigned to women. The *Vita Balthildis,* in reference to Clotilda's conversion efforts, also speaks of "holy admonition."[72] The letters in which churchmen admonish royal wives to show commitment to the conversion of their husbands and to the Christianization of their people (gens) present the same picture: this mandate is always to be accomplished by verbal means. Bishop Nicetius of Trier, for instance, sometime in the sixth decade of the sixth century, wrote a letter to the Merovingian princess Chlodosinde (+ before 568), who was married to the Arian (or perhaps still non-Christian) King of the Lombards, Alboin. He impressed upon her to explain his letter carefully and frequently to her husband and to preach unceasingly the Word of God.[73] In 601, Pope Gregory the Great called upon Bertha of Kent to strengthen in his Christian faith King Ethelbert, who had been baptized presumably in 597, through "continuous admonitions" and to stimulate him to a greater commitment to the process of Christianizing the Anglo-Saxon people (gens).[74] Pope Boniface V commissioned Ethelberga shortly after her marriage to suggest piously to King Edwin the commandments of God and thereby to soften "the hardness of his heart." Concerning Edwin, she should bear witness of the secret and of the reward that had come to her with faith and baptism, proclaiming to him the Holy Spirit and thereby inflaming "the coldness of his heart." Through her numerous admonitions "the warmth of divine faith" should ignite his spirit, "the rigidity of the pernicious cults of idols" having been eliminated.[75]

With the prospect of incorporating entire *gentes* into the Catholic Church via the Germanic kings, the letter writers willingly allow the royal wives to speak—this is a "privilege" in view of women being prohibited from teaching in 1 Tim. 2:12, and at the same time it is a call to employ women for the goals of the churchmen.[76] The letter-writing churchmen do not consider women to act as convert-makers other than by means of language. None of them mentions the possibility that a woman could win over her husband to (Catholic) Christianity through exemplary conduct, good example (*exemplum*), good works (*bona opera*), or a Christian way of life (*conversatio,* see 1 Peter 3:1). Language—whether preaching or admonition—is clearly the most efficient means that women could use for the conversion of their husbands, in the opinion of the authors.[77] Perhaps this also reflects the experience that women could not employ more massive and pressurizing nonverbal means in order to make a husband change his religious attitude and practice. Such an attempt could endanger the wife, as is pointed out in the life of Bishop Barbatus of Benevento (+682). According to this text, a wife risked her life by secretly handing over to the bishop the "golden image of a snake" that her husband worshipped.[78]

Morrison's statement that "the language of conversion can be abrupt," stood at the beginning of this study. In the meantime we have again returned to the theme of language, now to the "language of conversion" that is associated in the early medieval texts with women as convert-makers. To conclude I wish to point out that this study is intended primarily as a survey of numerous and varied references to the appearances of men and women in the texts discussing conversion from the fifth century to the eighth. In the context of this survey it was possible to make only a first attempt at relating literary representations to historical events and the real lives of men and women. More intensive examination of the texts on the basis of philological, literary-historical, and source-critical analysis will provide fuller explanation of the patterns by which men and women are represented in the roles of converter and converted and of how the content of "historical reality" in a text is to be evaluated.

NOTES

I thank James Muldoon very much for the translation and for helpful suggestions.

1. Karl F. Morrison, *Understanding Conversion* (Charlottesville: University Press of Virginia, 1992), 1. See *Heimskringla or the Lives of the Norse Kings*, chaps. 61, 91, 108, ed. and trans. Erling Monsen and A. H. Smith (New York: Dover, 1990), 165, 184, 204 (here quoted according to Morrison).

2. Gregory of Tours, *Libri historiarum decem* (henceforth *Hist.*) III.10, ed. B. Krusch and W. Levison, Monumenta Germaniae Historica (MGH) Scriptores rerum Merovingicarum (SSrerMerov) 1.1 (Hannover: Impensis Bibliopolii Hahniani, 2d ed., 1951), 106 f. See also Procopius, *De bello Gothico* I.13, ed. Otto Veh (Munich: Heimeran, 1966), 107.

3. Morrison, *Understanding*, 1.

4. Birgit Sawyer, "Scandinavian Conversion Histories," in *The Christianization of Scandinavia*, report of a symposium held at Kungälv, Sweden, August 4–9, 1985, ed. Birgit Sawyer, Peter Sawyer, and Ian Wood (Alingsås: Viktoria Bokförlag, 1987), 88–110, here 109.

5. Dietrich Claude, *Geschichte der Westgoten* (Stuttgart e.a.: Kohlhammer, 1970), 64. See also Edward Arthur Thompson, *The Goths in Spain* (Oxford: Clarendon Press, 1969), 34 f.

6. See Morrison, *Understanding*, 50 f.

7. See *Frauen im Frühmittelalter: Eine ausgewählte, kommentierte Bibliographie*, ed. Werner Affeldt, Cordula Nolte, Sabine Reiter, and Ursula Vorwerk (Frankfurt e.a.: P. Lang, 1990), 642–46, and Cordula Nolte, *Conversio und Christianitas:*

Frauen in der Christianisierung vom 5. bis 8. Jahrhundert, Monographien zur Geschichte des Mittelalters (Stuttgart: Hiersemann, 1995), 5–7.

8. Nolte, *Conversio und Christianitas,* 1.

9. Gregory the Great, *Registrum epistularum,* letters XI.35 and XI.37, ed. Dag Norberg, Corpus Christianum, Series Latina (henceforth CCSL) 140A (Turnholt: Brepols, 1982), 924, 930; Gregory of Tours, *Hist.* IV.27, IV.28, V.38, IX.25, MGH SSrerMerov 1.1, 160 f., 244, 444; Gregory the Great, *Dialogues* III.31, ed. Adalbert de Vogüé, Sources chrétiennes (henceforth SC), 260 (Paris: Editions du Cerf, 1978–79), 384; *Bede's Ecclesiastical History of the English People,* ed. and trans. Bertram Colgrave and R. B. Mynors, Oxford Ecclesiastical Texts (Oxford: Clarendon Press, 1969), I.26, p. 76.

10. A. D. Nock, *Conversion: The Old and the New in Religion from Alexander the Great to Augustine of Hippo* (Oxford: Oxford University Press, 1933; reprint, 1961), 7.

11. Hans-Dietrich Kahl, "Die ersten Jahrhunderte des missionsgeschichtlichen Mittelalters: Bausteine für eine Phänomenologie bis ca. 1050," in *Kirchengeschichte als Missionsgeschichte,* vol. 2.1 = *Die Kirche des früheren Mittelalters,* ed. Knut Schäferdiek (Munich: Kaiser, 1978), 11–76, here 52; Knut Schäferdiek, "Missionary Methods," in Sawyer, Sawyer, and Wood, *Christianization of Scandinavia,* 24–26, here 24.

12. See the introduction by James Muldoon; see also Nolte, *Conversio und Christianitas,* 15 f., and Morrison, *Understanding,* 5, 10 ff., 50.

13. Morrison, *Understanding,* 23.

14. Nolte, *Conversio und Christianitas,* 56–58.

15. Arnold Angenendt, *Kaiserherrschaft und Königstaufe: Kaiser, Könige und Päpste als geistliche Patrone in der abendländischen Missionsgeschichte,* Arbeiten zur Frühmittelalterforschung 15 (Berlin and New York: W. de Gruyter, 1984), 66 ff.

16. Angenendt, *Kaiserherrschaft und Königstaufe,* 68n.18, provides examples.

17. *Vita Eucherii episcopi Aurelianensis,* chap. 11, ed. W. Levison, MGH SSrerMerov 7 (Hannover and Leipzig: Impensis Bibliopolii Hahniani, 1920), 52.

18. *Vita Amandi episcopi,* chap. 24, ed. B. Krusch, MGH SSrerMerov 5 (Hannover and Leipzig: Impensis Bibliopolii Hahniani, 1910), 447.

19. Ibid., chap. 13, 437.

20. Ibid., chap. 15, 439.

21. *Vita Liudgeri,* chap. I.26, ed. Wilhelm Diekamp, *Die Vitae sancti Liudgeri,* Die Geschichtsquellen des Bisthums Münster 4 (Münster: Theissing, 1881), 31.

22. Nolte, *Conversio und Christianitas,* 150 f.

23. On the efforts of Christian missionaries to convert Sioux girls in the nineteenth century, see Carol Devens, "'If We Get the Girls, We Get the Race': Missionary Education of Native American Girls," *Journal of World History* 3 (1992):219–37.

24. On mixed marriages see Nolte, *Conversio und Christianitas,* 21–68.

25. Gregory of Tours, *Hist.* II.29, MGH SSrerMerov 1.1, 74 f.; Bede, *Ecclesiastical History* II.9, 166; Paulus Diaconus, *Historia Langobardorum* IV.27, ed. G.

Waitz, MGH SSrerGerm in us. schol. 48 (Hannover, 1878; reprint, Hannover: Buchhandlung 1978), 156.

26. Angenendt, *Kaiserherrschaft und Königstaufe*, 68–72, 178.

27. Gregory of Tours, *Hist.* V.38, MGH SSrerMerov 1.1, 244; Gregory the Great, *Dialogues* III.31, SC 260, p. 384.

28. Nolte, *Conversio und Christianitas*, 21–23.

29. Gregory of Tours, *Liber in gloria martyrum* 79, ed. B. Krusch, MGH SSrerMerov 1.2 (Hannover: Impensis Bibliopolii Hahniani, 1885; reprint, 1969), 91 f.

30. *Vita sancti Medardi* adscr. Venantio Fortunato, chap. II.4, ed. B. Krusch, MGH Auctorum antiquissimorum (AA) 4.2 (Berlin: Weidemann, 1886), 68.

31. *Vita Bibiani vel Viviani episcopi Santonensis,* chap. 2, ed. B. Krusch, MGH SSrerMerov 3 (Hannover: Impensis Bibliopolii Hahniani, 1896), 95.

32. Canon. Theod. U II.XII.18 and 19, ed. Paul Willem Finsterwalder, *Die Canones Theodori Cantuariensis und ihre Überlieferungsformen,* Untersuchungen zu den Bussbüchern des 7., 8., und 9. Jahrhunderts (Weimar: H. Böhlau, 1929), 1:328.

33. Sulpicius Severus, *Vita sancti Martini episcopi et confissoria,* chap. 5.3, ed. Jacques Fontaine, SC 133 (Paris: Editions du Cerf, 1967), 262.

34. Ibid., chap. 6.3, 264.

35. Jacques Fontaine, "Commentaire," SC 134 (Paris: Editions du Cerf, 1968), 581.

36. Gregory of Tours, *Hist.* II.31, MGH SSrerMerov 1.1, 77 f. Gregory uses the terms *conversio* and *converti* with regard to the change from the Arian to the Catholic creed but not with regard to the change from a non-Christian religion to Christianity.

37. Avitus of Vienne, Homilia 31 "De conversione Lenteildis Chlodovaei sororis," *Alcimi Ecdicii Aviti Viennensis episcopi opera quae supersunt,* ed. R. Peiper, MGH AA 6.2 (Berlin: Weidemann, 1883; reprint, 1961), 152.

38. Nolte, *Conversio und Christianitas,* 30 f.

39. Avitus of Vienne, letter 46, MGH AA 6.2, p. 75; Knut Schäferdiek, "Die geschichtliche Stellung des sogenannten germanischen Arianismus," in *Kirchengeschichte als Missionsgeschichte,* vol. 2.1 = *Die Kirche des früheren Mittelalters,* ed. Schäferdiek, 79–90, here 81; Friedrich Prinz, *Grundlagen und Anfänge. Deutschland bis 1056,* Neue Deutsche Geschichte 1 (Munich: C. H. Beck, 1985), 63 f.; Ian Wood, "Gregory of Tours and Clovis," *Revue Belge de Philologie et d'Histoire* 63 (1985): 249–72, here 266 f.; Nolte, *Conversio und Christianitas,* 83 ff.

40. Avitus of Vienne, Homilia 26, MGH AA 6.2, p. 146. On Suavegotho see Eugen Ewig, "Studien zur merowingischen Dynastie," *Frühmittelalterliche Studien* 8 (1974): 15–59, here 37.

41. Bede, *Ecclesiastical History* II.6, 154.

42. Ibid. II.9, 162.

43. Boniface's letter has been transmitted by Bede, *Ecclesiastical History* II.11, esp. p. 172. See also *Councils and Ecclesiastical Documents Relating to Great*

Britain and Ireland, ed. Arthur West Haddan and William Stubbs (Oxford: Clarendon Press, 1870), 3:78. This edition of the letter has "confessione" instead of "conversione."

44. Accordingly Paul the Deacon relates the Catholic baptism of the prince Adaloald, the son of the Catholic Theodelinde and the Arian Agilulf, but he does not mention the baptism of Adaloald's sister Gundeperga. *Historia Langobardorum* IV.27, MGH SSrerGerm in us. schol. 48, p. 156.

45. *Annales regni Francorum inde ab a. 741 usque ad a. 829 qui dicuntur Annales Laurissenses maiores et Einhardi,* a. 826, ed. F. Kurze, MGH SSrerGerm in us. schol. 6 (Hannover, 1895; reprint, Impensis Bibliopolii Hahniani, 1950), 169 f.

46. Laetitia Boehm, *Geschichte Burgunds: Politik—Staatsbildungen—Kultur* (Stuttgart e.a.: Kohlhammer, 2d supplemented edition, 1979), 68.

47. Nolte, *Conversio und Christianitas,* 56 f.

48. Bede, *Ecclesiastical History* II.15, 190. See also Angenendt, *Kaiserherrschaft und Königstaufe,* 180.

49. Gosuintha had two daughters, Galsuintha and Brunichilde (Ingunde's mother), from her first marriage with the Visigothic King Athanagild. After Athanagild's death she married Leovigild and thus became the stepmother of Leovigild's sons, Reccared and Hermenegild.

50. Gregory of Tours, *Hist.* V.38, MGH SSrerMerov 1.1, 244.

51. Ibid. The scene seems to present a forced rebaptism; see also *Hist.* II.2, MGH SSrerMerov 1.1, 40.

52. See n. 70.

53. *Hist.* IV.27, MGH SSrerMerov 1.1, 160.

54. Gregory of Tours, *Hist.* IV.28, MGH SSrerMerov 1.1, 160 f.

55. Knut Schäferdiek, *Die Kirche in den Reichen der Westgoten und Suewen bis zur Errichtung der westgotischen katholischen Staatskirche,* Arbeiten zur Kirchengeschichte 39 (Berlin: de Gruyter, 1967), 141.

56. Nolte, *Conversio und Christianitas,* 62.

57. As mentioned, King Edwin of Northumbria, for instance, promised to allow his bride the free exercise of her faith. Likewise King Ethelbert of Kent, before marrying the Merovingian princess Bertha, had to guarantee that he would not prevent her from exercising her Christian religion. Bede, *Ecclesiastical History* I.25 and II.9, 74, 162.

58. Gregory of Tours, *Hist.* III.5, III.20, III.27, IV.9, MGH SSrerMerov 1.1, pp. 101, 121, 124, 140. A connection between Suavegotho's conversion (see above) and her marriage is not discernible. See Nolte, *Conversio und Christianitas,* 35 ff., on the marriages of these women and on their presumed conversion.

59. *Liber Historiae Francorum* 50, ed. B. Krusch, MGH SSrerMerov 2 (Hannover, 1888; reprint, Hannover: Impensis Bibliopolii Hahniani, 1956), 324f.

60. Venantius Fortunatus, *Vita Radegundis,* I, chap. 2, ed. B. Krusch, MGH SSrerMerov 2, 365.

61. On the christianization of Thuringia see Knut Schäferdiek, "Bekehrung und Bekehrungsgeschichte II: Deutschland und Nachbarländer," *Reallexikon der Germanischen Altertumskunde* 2 (1976): 180–88, here 183.

62. Baudonivia, *Vita Radegundis*, II, chap. 2, ed. B. Krusch, MGH SSrerMerov 2, 380. See Jacques Fontaine, "Hagiographie et politique, de Sulpice Sévère à Venance Fortunat," *Revue d'Histoire de l'Église de France* 62 (1976):113–40, here 133 f.

63. Paul Mikat, "Ehe," *Handwörterbuch zur deutschen Rechtsgeschichte* 1 (1971), cols. 809–33, here col. 828.

64. See Édouard Salin's remark on "la femme gallo-romaine que le barbare a voulu posséder mais qui le domine, par la religion chrétienne à laquelle il s'est converti," *La civilisation mérovingienne d'après les sépultures, les textes et le laboratoire* (Paris: A. et J. Picard, 1949), 1:409.

65. Kahl, "Die ersten Jahrhunderte," 63. On Catholic royal wives as convert-ers of their husbands see Nolte, *Conversio und Christianitas,* 69–134.

66. Wolfram von den Steinen, "Chlodwigs Übergang zum Christentum: Eine quellenkritische Studie," *Mitteilungen des Österreichischen Instituts für Geschichtsforschung,* suppl. vol. 12 (1933): 417–501, here 423 ff.

67. Gregory of Tours, *Hist.* II.29, MGH SSrerMerov 1.1, 74.

68. Ibid.

69. Gregory shows Clovis as expressly asking *Clotilda's* god for help in a hope-less situation on the battlefield: *Hist.* II.30, MGH SSrerMerov 1.1, 75.

70. Gregory of Tours, *Hist.* V.38, MGH SSrerMerov 1.1, 244. According to Gregory the Great, however, Hermenegild's conversion resulted from the preach-ing of Leander of Seville, *Dialogues* III.31, SC 260, p. 384.

71. *Historia Langobardorum* IV.6, MGH SSrerGerm in us. schol. 48, p. 146.

72. *Vita sanctae Balthildis,* A, chap. 18, ed. B. Krusch, MGH SSrerMerov 2, 505 f.

73. *Epistolae austrasicae,* letter 8, ed. W. Gundlach, CCSL 117 (Turnholt: Brepols, 1957), 419–23.

74. *Registrum epistularum,* letter XI.35, CCSL 140A, p. 924.

75. Bede, *Ecclesiastical History* II.11, 174.

76. See Janet L. Nelson, "Women and the Word in the Earlier Middle Ages," in *Women in the Church,* papers read at the 1989 summer meeting and the 1990 winter meeting of the Ecclesiastical History Society, ed. W. J. Sheils and Diana Wood (Oxford: B. Blackwell, 1990), 53–78, here 74 ff.

77. On the connection of women and language see Nelson, "Women and the Word," 60 ff., and Sharon Farmer, "Persuasive Voices: Clerical Images of Medi-eval Women," *Speculum* 63 (1986): 517–43, here 538 ff.

78. *Vita Barbati episcopi Beneventani,* chaps. 8–10, ed. G. Waitz, MGH SSrerLang (Hannover, 1878; reprint Hannover: Impensis Bibliopolii Hahniani, 1964), 561–63.

6

✠

God and Man in Medieval Scandinavia
Writing—and Gendering—the Conversion

Ruth Mazo Karras

Stories of individual conversions are usually written by the subjects themselves. Such accounts tell us what they experienced and how they interpreted that experience—at least as much of it as they choose to reveal.
Stories of the conversions of peoples, however, cannot be written by their
subjects. Even if one member of the group in question writes the story, that
one person is interpreting the experiences of others. More usually the writer
is a contemporary outsider—the missionary rather than the converted—or
a group member from a later generation, who has not personally undergone the conversion. These stories do not recount the experiences of their
subjects but rather their retellers' visions of those experiences. This pattern
is particularly apparent in the spread of Christianity across Europe. Many
of the converted peoples did not acquire writing until after their conversion and integration into the international community of Christendom.
Hence whatever stories they may have told about their own conversion,
the versions that have come down to us are either later or are written by
outsiders. What we have, then, are stories of the replacement of paganism
by Christianity, written by men who were Christians all their lives and who
never knew paganism at first hand.

The conversion of the Scandinavian countries—Denmark, Norway, Sweden, and Iceland—to Christianity took place over the course of the tenth
and early eleventh centuries (there were earlier efforts as well, but these
had little lasting effect).[1] While there are a few contemporary accounts, the
greatest literary monuments describing the process date from the thirteenth
century.[2] Scholars have attempted to use these late accounts to determine
the nature of pagan belief as well as the converts' understanding of the
Christianity they accepted.[3] What these accounts really tell us, however, is
how the thirteenth-century authors constructed their own version of early
Christianity and the paganism that preceded it.[4] I will explore this ques-

tion by examining three texts: Saxo Grammaticus's *Gesta Danorum*, Snorri Sturluson's *Heimskringla*, and *Njal's Saga*, an Icelandic family saga.[5]

These accounts create an image of the conversion as the choice by a small group of elite men of one set of beliefs over another. Christianity and paganism were more or less interchangeable: there was no major qualitative difference between the two sets of beliefs. Conversion represented a transfer of loyalty, not an inner transformation, and as such was a matter for men. Women were not significant as political actors in the texts describing the conversion, and therefore their allegiance did not matter to the same degree. I do not propose to discuss here how well this representation fits the actual circumstances of the conversion; rather, I shall focus on its meaning for the authors' own society.[6]

None of these authors was writing a story to stand alone as a conversion narrative. All the passages discussed are part of larger stories, and the authors all had larger purposes in writing. Saxo's account of early Christianity in Denmark, written in part as a reaction to Adam of Bremen, "tries to undermine the claims of the church of Hamburg-Bremen and to justify the superiority of the Danish over the Swedish church."[7] Snorri's *Heimskringla* is fundamentally concerned with royal power; his presentation of Olaf Tryggvason and Olaf Haraldsson as somewhat brutal in their methods may be a criticism of the kings of his own day and their centralizing tendencies.[8] He renders the changes in religious allegiance as being of the same kind and quality as changes in political allegiance.[9] The overall theme of *Njal's Saga* has been variously interpreted and it is not necessary to discuss it here; suffice it to say that even if we accept that the story is a Christian one, of the triumph of humility and of reconciliation over the pagan virtues, the conversion episode contributes to that theme mainly by setting the historical context and allowing Njal's virtue to be highlighted even before the conversion itself.[10] It also—though not as much as some other Icelandic sources—takes the emphasis off Olaf Tryggvason as converter of the Icelanders and places it on their own activities.[11] It is a collective decision they make for themselves, not one imposed on them from outside by a Norwegian bully.

All of the three sources discussed here treat conversion as a moment rather than a process. In Snorri's account of Norway, the conversion happens over the course of two reigns, little by little; but for each group that accepts Christ, it is still a moment. Conversion is equivalent to the granting of allegiance. Of course, the country could hardly be called fully Christian for a long time afterward; the customs and aspects of daily life related to paganism were only gradually supplanted, as an institutional church hierarchy was established and began educational efforts.[12] Nevertheless, for these authors it is the act of acceptance of Christianity that matters. It is always possible to present conversion as a single moment when it is the conversion of a nation through its leader. The principle of *cuius regio eius religio* was grasped, although not enunciated, in the Middle Ages. The extent to which Scandinavia was in fact converted from the top down may have been exaggerated by these writers.[13] Nevertheless that is clearly how they present it. Missionaries direct their efforts at nations, and when they do concentrate on individuals it is on kings, who can presumably bring their nations with them. Conversion of a country is undertaken through royal power (or in the case of Iceland through a collective decision, prompted perhaps by Norwegian royal power).[14]

The understanding of the conversion as presented in these texts in relation to royal power, I argue here, explains two important features of the Scandinavian conversion narratives: their relatively relaxed or noncondemnatory attitude toward pre-Christian religion (as compared to texts from other regions), and the lack of importance accorded to women in the conversion process.

Saxo Grammaticus's laconic account of the initial conversion of the Danes makes no reference to any inner process of spiritual change; conversion for Harald Gormsson involves joining the Christian community (*consortium catholicae religionis*).[15] Harald around 960 "came to an agreement with Caesar [the German emperor, who was threatening Jutland], embraced the fellowship of the Catholic religion and gave his kingdom peace by means of a spiritual and a secular concord."[16] Saxo implies that Harald's conversion entailed at least the nominal conversion of his people, though some opposed him "both because he favoured the worship of God, and also because he was imposing unprecedented burdens on the people."[17] Harald's son Svein returned the kingdom to paganism. The tenth-century Danes, to Saxo, were not basically good people eager for the Christian truth, nor were they devoted to paganism; they were fairly flexible, depending on the wishes of their king.

In contrast to his father, Svein Haraldsson seems to Saxo to have undergone a more personal conversion experience, but this did not apply to his people. After a defeat by the Swedish king Eirik and rejection by potential allies, Svein despaired and called to God out of the depths: "the veil of darkness was torn from his eyes, and he gazed upon the light of salvation." Svein was baptized and returned to his kingdom. He did not publicly reveal his conversion, however, fearing "the people's vindication of their religious practises." Eventually he called in a priest named Poppo, who by performing a miracle persuaded the Danes to accept baptism. Poppo placed his hand in a glove of red-hot iron and removed it unscathed.[18] The Danes accepted Christianity as the truth, but again Saxo fails to indicate what it was they were accepting: there is no reference to any doctrine being preached to them at all. They accepted the superior power of the Christian God without knowing anything about him or undergoing any spiritual transformation.

Although Saxo's description of the conversion of the Danes indicates merely a decision to assent to Christianity, as expressed through baptism, Saxo himself does not question the validity of this kind of conversion. In the case of Norway, by contrast, he calls into question the sincerity of the conversion, whether it amounted to "true holiness." Olaf Tryggvason, the Norwegian king, "was so given up to the taking of auspices and the noting of omens that, even after he had been immersed in the waters of baptism and had imbibed the rudiments of religious discipline, he could not be prevented either by pious example or by authoritative teaching from heeding the admonitions of augurs, and learning the future from wizards. Thus he was void of true holiness, and merely adopted its empty shadow, blighting his professed religion with a 'superstitious cast'."[19] Saxo is anti-Norwegian in this section; Icelandic sources give a very different picture of Olaf Tryggvason.[20]

The more detailed accounts of the conversion of Norway found in the sagas of Olaf Tryggvason and Olaf Haraldsson (St. Olaf) in the Icelander Snorri Sturluson's *Heimskringla* (History of the Norwegian Kings), highly literary reworkings of earlier accounts, present a similar vision of conversion as a deliberate choice rather than a spiritual experience.[21] In the failed conversion of the Norwegian Earl Hakon, the Dane Harald "forced the earl to accept baptism." Hakon, however, as soon as he was out of Harald's reach, made a great sacrifice to Odin for victory in battle in Sweden.[22] It is clear that Snorri does not consider baptism to be entirely the equivalent of conversion, though he does in some sense consider Hakon to have accepted Christianity at least temporarily, since he says that Hakon "renounced" it (*kastat*).[23] Snorri does not condemn the renunciation. When Hakon died, it was because it was time for the passing of the old ways.[24] His un-Christian life led to an evil end (in a pigsty with a slave), but Snorri finds much to admire in the earl and does not editorialize about his fall from grace; he became Christian as a political choice (or necessity).

Perhaps because Snorri, like other Icelanders, credited Olaf Tryggvason with the conversion of Iceland, he represents Olaf as coming to Christianity not through force or political calculation but because of true belief in its efficacy. While harrying in the Scilly Isles, Snorri recounts, Olaf met a wise hermit.[25] Olaf heard the hermit prophesy about his future and came to believe him because one part of the prophecy was immediately fulfilled.[26]

While Snorri presents Olaf's acceptance of Christianity as based on persuasion, knowledge, and understanding, not political advantage, his conversion of others is not as peaceful or as internalized. Snorri depicts him as apostle to the Orkneys: "And when the earl came it was not long before the king commanded him to accept baptism, together with all his people, or else suffer death at once; and the king said he would devastate the islands with fire and flame, and lay the land waste unless the people accepted baptism. And seeing the pinch he was in, the earl chose to be baptized."[27] Olaf's methods in Norway were not much different, beginning in 996 after he was accepted king over all of Norway. He called a council and asked his kinsmen to help him spread the Gospel. "Very soon King Óláf made it clear to all the people that he would proclaim Christianity in all his realm. . . . but those who spoke against it he punished severely, killing some, maiming others or driving them out of the country."[28] He pursued similar policies in other provinces, "and wherever he assembled with the farmers he ordered all to be baptized, and all accepted Christianity, because no one among the farmers dared to rebel against the king; so people were baptized wherever he came."[29]

Although Snorri makes clear that both the magnates and the farmers accepted Christianity (which he equates with accepting baptism) solely through force, he never doubts the thoroughness or efficacy of that acceptance. For Snorri, once the acceptance is made, they are Christian; they may relapse into paganism, but that does not mean they were not Christian for a time. Their religious affiliation is not a matter of interior belief but a matter of to whom they have given their loyalty at a particular moment.

In Snorri's account, God helps Olaf out with miracles, yet these miracles do not demonstrate the power or truth of the Christian faith but rather prevent anyone from opposing it. God's assistance to Olaf in this conversion process does not extend to changing hearts and minds but only to determining the political conditions. At an assembly of farmers in Rogaland, the farmers choose a representative to speak against the king, but he is taken with a coughing fit; a second stammers and a third becomes hoarse. The farmers agree to be baptized.[30]

In Snorri's rendering the conversion of Norway is an instrument of royal policy rather than a result of divine inspiration. His account of the conversion as an inexorable progress is much more systematic than that of the major source he used and reworked.[31] In another district Olaf persuaded one of the leading men to accept Christianity by giving the man his sister in marriage; the brother-in-law then convinced the rest of the men of the district. At Mærin he destroyed idols of Thor and other gods. Elsewhere the threat of force was sufficient, although sometimes the king did not succeed at first and had to call in reinforcements.[32]

To Snorri, placing one's faith in a god is a matter of choice, as can be seen in an account of one of Olaf's failed conversions. Olaf tortured Eyvind Kinnrifa by placing a basin full of hot coals on his belly. Eyvind eventually revealed that he was not human but an evil spirit conjured up by sorcery. Only such a one would be so unreasonable as to reject Olaf's wishes. As Eyvind was dying of a burst belly, Oláf asked him, "Will you now believe [*trúa*] in Christ?"[33] *Trúa* implies the placing of trust or the making of an alliance, not belief in the sense of being convinced something is true. In the saga of St. Olaf, Gauka-Thorir agreed to baptism in this way: "If I am to believe in some god, what difference is it to me whether I believe in the White Christ or some other god? So now it is my advice that we let ourselves be baptized if the king thinks that it is of such great importance."[34] As Snorri depicts conversion, it is a matter of shifting allegiance, not of internal faith.

Allegiance, in Snorri's writings, is a matter for men, which explains why his vision of conversion mentions women so little. Another failed convert was Queen Sigrid the Haughty of Sweden, with whom Olaf was negotiating a marriage treaty. He demanded that she "be baptized and accept the true faith." She declined "to abandon the faith I have had, and my kinsmen before me," although she did not object to her husband being a Christian. Olaf became angry, called her "dog of a heathen," and slapped her. She threatened that this might result in his death, a bit of foreshadowing typical of Snorri and other Icelandic writers.[35] As one of the few women to appear in these conversion narratives, Sigrid is cast in a clearly negative role: she was the enemy of the true faith. Her choice of paganism, however, arose not from a belief that the old religion was true and the new one false but rather from the traditions of her dynasty. For her too, the change of faith is a change of allegiance. As a queen, she is one of the few women who is involved in the system of loyalty and allegiance, and therefore one of the few for whom conversion appears as an issue.

Snorri describes circumstances following Olaf's Christianization of Norway that may make a modern reader question the depth of that conversion, but he himself does not cast doubt upon it. After Olaf's death, the earls governing Norway "were both baptized and accepted the true faith; but during the time they ruled over Norway they let everyone do as he pleased about the keeping of Christianity."[36] And in 1016 when Olaf Tryggvason's godson, King Olaf Haraldsson (later St. Olaf), began to tour the country, "in nearly all settlements along the seashore people were baptized, although most of them were ignorant of the Christian commandments; but in the remote valleys and the mountain settlements people were for the most part altogether heathen; because whenever people were allowed to do as they pleased, the faith which they had learned in childhood became fixed in their minds." St. Olaf held meetings at which "he had the Christian laws read and also the commandments that went with them," something Olaf Tryggvason is never depicted as doing.[37]

That Snorri describes such a superficial Christianization, yet still considers Olaf Tryggvason responsible for much of the conversion of Norway, means that he considers the acceptance of baptism, not a thorough program of education and of Christianization of daily life, to constitute that conversion. Many of his descriptions of Olaf Haraldsson's (St. Olaf's) conversion of different parts of the country follow the same pattern as Olaf Tryggvason's.[38]

Snorri's account of Olaf Haraldsson reveals that he sees the pagan reaction to conversion as a matter of loyalty rather than one of faith. In the Dales, Dala-Gudbrand (Gulbrasnd of the Dales) opposed Olaf, claiming that his god was more powerful than Olaf's, who could not be seen, and demanded that Olaf's god keep it from raining the following day. God obligingly produced weather miracles on two consecutive days. The pagans still worshipped their idol, until one of Olaf's men struck it and vermin ran out. Gudbrand then admitted, "Great damage have we suffered in our god. But, seeing that he was not able to help us, we shall now believe in the god you believe in."[39] The pagans are devoted to their gods not because of any deep belief system but because they have received benefits from them (or because the gods have desisted from punishing them). When their gods are shown to be ineffective, they accept the god who seems to grant his believers more power. This approach to conversion—demonstrating the power of Christianity by destroying idols with impunity—is hardly unique to St. Olaf or to the conversion of Scandinavia but is common in hagiography and conversion accounts throughout the history of Christianity. Snorri's use of it demonstrates that he views the pagans as making a choice on the grounds of efficaciousness, not logical or metaphysical truth. He does not see them as hypocrites; they simply recognize that the Christian god is strongest.

Snorri describes the conversion of Iceland as a similar process of political calculation. Olaf Tryggvason sent out the Saxon priest Thangbrand as a missionary because Thangbrand was making himself unwelcome at the Norwegian court. Thangbrand converted Sidu-Hall (Hall of Sida), a leading Icelander, by preaching but also became involved in violence, killing three men.[40] In addition, Olaf made use of native Icelanders who came to his court. Kjartan Olafsson had been favorably impressed with a church service, especially the singing and the bells. When Olaf urged him to become a Christian, Kjartan said that "he would not refuse to if thereby he could gain the friendship of the king."[41] Despite his personal inclination toward the religion, it was the practical advantage that governed his conversion. Kjartan expected the conversion of Iceland to be carried out in much the same way as was his own, through the calculation of personal advantage; he pointed out that "there are here [in Norway] many influential men's sons from Iceland, and their fathers are likely to afford us great help in this matter."[42]

Other Icelandic sources agree with Snorri in presenting conversion as a matter of practical advantage. The conversion of Iceland as described in *Njal's Saga* agrees in most of the factual details with that in *Heimskringla*. The five chapters in which it is retold, in the middle of the story, have sometimes been considered an interpolation, and whether or not they form an integral part of the saga, they rely on an earlier written source.[43] But this does not obviate their function in the story: the author uses the account of the conversion to enhance his portrait of the character of Njal. When the Icelanders heard of the conversion of Norway, Njal responded, "In my opinion the new faith is much better; happy the man who receives it. And if the men who spread this faith come out to Iceland, I shall do all I can to further it."[44] Njal spoke these prescient words before any missionaries arrived; he was presented as a good pagan with some mystical knowledge predisposing him to Christianity.

The saga describes Thangbrand's conversion of Sidu-Hall in terms of advantage, as with the conversions in Norway. Hall asked about the Angel Michael, whose feast Thangbrand was celebrating.

> "What power has this angel?" asked Hall. "Great power," said Thangbrand. "He weighs everything you do, both good and evil, and he is so merciful that the good weighs more heavily with him than the evil." "I would like to have him as my friend," said Hall. "You can do that easily," said Thangbrand. "Give yourself to him in God's name this very day." Hall said, "I want to stipulate that you pledge your word on his behalf that he shall become my guardian angel." "I give you my promise," said Thangbrand. After that, Hall and all his household were baptized.[45]

Thangbrand is persuading Hall not of the truth of Christian doctrine but to make an act of allegiance to a particular saint, just as he might earlier have done to a particular pagan god. He does not explicate the relationship between archangels and the deity or mention Christ at all. Hall, for his part, is clearly not being convinced either by divine inspiration or by reason but rather by an advantage for which he is willing to negotiate a detailed contract.

One person in the the saga who is presented as contesting the conversion as a matter of faith rather than allegiance is a woman: Steinunn, with whom Thangbrand got into a debate. "She lectured to him for a long time and tried to convert him to paganism. Thangbrand listened to her in silence, but when she had finished he spoke at length, turning all her own arguments against her."[46] She does not fit into the masculine world of decision making the saga writer constructs, but she competes on doctrinal grounds. More convincing to those watching the debate was that Thangbrand was able to hallow a fire that warded off a *berserkr* (an ecstatic warrior) more effectively than one hallowed by the pagans.[47] Thangbrand, as in Snorri's account, ultimately failed, largely because of his abrasive and violent personality, and the conversion of Iceland eventually came about because of a decision made at the Althing (the national assembly). That was a rational political decision, a change of allegiance.

The final conversion of Iceland was quite unusual. Like that of many European countries, it was a political decision, imposed from the top down. But Iceland had neither king nor state. Rather, the assembly of the free farmers decided that they needed to have one religion and appointed one man, a pagan, to make the decision for them:

> Thorgeir asked to be heard, and said, "It seems to me that an impossible situation arises if we do not all have one and the same law. If the laws are divided the peace will be divided, and we cannot tolerate that. Now, therefore, I want to ask heathens and Christians whether they will accept the law which I am going to proclaim." They all agreed. Thorgeir insisted on oaths and binding pledges from them; they all agreed to that, and gave him their pledge. "The first principle of our laws," declared Thorgeir, "is that all men in this land shall be Christian and believe in the one God— Father, Son, and Holy Ghost—and renounce all worship of idols." . . . The heathens felt they had been grossly betrayed, but despite that the new faith became law, and the whole land became Christian.[48]

Once again, conversion is presented not as the result of introspection or divine inspiration but rather as deliberate choice. Men will believe what Thorgeir decides they will believe—not just follow the teachings of a religion, or worship in a certain way, but believe. But this belief is not what we usually think of when we think of Christian faith; it is more like loyalty or fealty, a formal relationship rather than an emotion. For the Icelanders to believe in the Christian god becomes a quasi-contractual obligation.

When the Scandinavians in these accounts shift their allegiance from one or more of the pagan gods to Christ, they do so by assuming an equivalency in function and then comparing the gods' relative strengths. The Christian religion is "better" than the pagan (a formulation used in other places besides *Njal's Saga*). Christianity is not seen as absolutely true where the other is absolutely false; it is merely more powerful or more efficacious.

Christ is the most powerful of many gods, not the only god. These comments about Christianity being the better religion could be considered "antipagan sentiment"[49] in the simplest sense that the accounts were written by Christians who clearly did believe that Christianity was the better religion and that their ancestors had done the right thing by converting. On the other hand, if one views the sagas and Saxo's *Gesta* as the artifacts of a culture that by the thirteenth century was thoroughly Christian, what is striking is not the antipagan sentiment but the pro-pagan sympathy, the sense that paganism was not unremittingly evil but just another system that was not quite as good as the one they got later. The descriptions of pagan practices are not condemnatory but are rather matter-of-fact in tone: this is how we used to do things before we found a better way. The sagas are not pagan survivals; they are products of a Christian age, but it was an age that did not cast the pagan past as devilish, just as less fortunate in not having as good a deity to which to give allegiance. Those who persist in pagan practices after the coming of Christianity may be depicted as evil[50] but not those before the initial conversion. Snorri's concern elsewhere with preserving pagan myth (notably in his *Edda*) reflects antiquarian, perhaps nationalistic, interest in the pagan past, which keeps him from seeing the conversion as the triumph of total light over total darkness.

I do not want to suggest that there was little difference between paganism and the Christianity the Scandinavians came to accept. Although much of what we think we know about Scandinavian paganism is based on quite shaky evidence, it seems likely that it was not nearly as intellectually or doctrinally sophisticated as Christianity; nor did it have nearly as elaborate an ethical system (although there certainly was a pre-Christian ethos, it is not clear how directly tied it was to religion).

If we do accept that the belief systems were fundamentally different, however, we run into two questions. The first is methodological: if the sources present them as similar, on what basis do we say they are dissimilar?[51] If the sources water down the Christianity they present to make the religions look parallel, how are we to know they did not water down the paganism as well? This set of questions I do not propose to answer here; others have addressed it based on poetic sources that go back to pre-Christian oral traditions as well as on archeological material.[52]

The second question is, why do Saxo, Snorri, the author of *Njal's Saga*, and other authors present the religions as basically similar? We must first decide what we mean by *similar*. There were of course major differences that the texts recognize: one religion was new to the Scandinavians and the other was traditional, one was native and the other foreign, and the new religion had more demanding behavioral standards than the old. The similarity that the texts present is in the nature of belief. Belief is not in a system but in a particular deity or group of deities; it amounts to trust or allegiance. A change in belief involves merely switching the object of one's trust; it does not require divine revelation, although that could be a persuasive factor.

This picture of religious belief and the way it changed has a familiar ring to it. It resembles the ideals behind much of medieval government and military organization. A man gives his loyalty, fealty, allegiance to a lord. If he finds his lord is ineffective, or if coerced, he may switch to another. The authors in question were all writing at a time when these ideas were becoming important in Scandinavian aristocratic social organization. This is not to say that Scandinavia became an idealized feudal society—nowhere in Europe did—but the language was present there as in the rest of Europe, in charters and laws, in romances and allegories. Even kingless Iceland had great magnates who commanded the (sometimes shifting) allegiance of the yeomanry. If "feudal" is too far to go in describing Icelandic society, the model of "instrumental friendship," the deliberate formation of a relationship for mutual advantage, serves the same function.[53] The three authors examined here present Christianity's acceptance as the result of the realistic assessment that Christ would be a more powerful and effective overlord, patron, or instrumental friend than any of the other gods.

This model of the conversion put forward by thirteenth-century authors explains a curious silence in all the accounts: there are no women. There is an occasional pagan woman (Queen Sigrid the Haughty, Steinunn) but none who become Christian. In other Icelandic sagas one may find important Christian women, like Gudrun Osvifsdottir of *Laxdæla Saga*, who becomes a nun at the end of her life, but they do not participate in the conversion.[54] In earlier Scandinavian conversion accounts women may appear—in the life of St. Anskar, a widow at Birka and her daughter are important early converts[55]—and in other parts of Europe, even when missionaries aimed at converting kings and through them their people, they often aimed at royal wives as well or converted the kings through their wives.[56]

This does not happen in the thirteenth-century accounts of Scandinavia, because the choice of religion is a matter of allegiance, in which women did not participate. The construction of conversion in such a manner acted to exclude half the population, the half that likely had a great deal of say about the religion practiced in the home and taught to the children. In most cultures women are important as transmitters of cultural and religious tradition, and they may well have been important in the spread of Christianity in Scandinavia, but these texts present religion as a wholly masculine domain.

The suppression in these accounts of any role played by women in the conversion is all the more striking in light of the significant role these same texts attribute to women in pagan times. While there has been substantial scholarly debate over whether the power acccorded to women in the Icelandic family sagas and other sources represents reality or not, it is clear that these late sources do depict women as having been more powerful in pagan than in Christian times.[57] This is in large part a misogynistic, negative depiction. As Birgit Sawyer puts it, "Saxo sought to underline the point that female power, like pagan magic, belonged to a past and imperfect time: the victory of Christianity also meant the conquest of women's power."[58] A case like the argument between Steinunnr and Thangbrand, which presents the pagan woman against the Christian man, can thus represent the process of conversion. That process (or moment) meant the overcoming of the bad influence of women, whose power was often used for the stirring up of strife.[59]

The exclusion of women from the conversion narratives had multiple causes: the shift to Christianity was constructed as a question of allegiance and therefore a matter of a relationship between a masculine deity and a masculine worshipper, and at the same time it was constructed as an exclusion of women from positions of power within Scandinavian culture and therefore could not be presented as instigated by women. One may doubt whether the actual process experienced by the medieval Scandinavians was as simple, or as masculine, as the thirteenth-century sources indicate; but the erasure of women from the texts was an integral part of how those writers understood conversion.

NOTES

1. The most useful general work on the subject is *The Christianization of Scandinavia,* ed. Birgit Sawyer, Peter Sawyer, and Ian Wood (Alingsås: Viktoria Bokförlag, 1987). For a more concise account, see Peter Sawyer, *Kings and Vikings* (New York: Methuen, 1982), 131–43.

2. The most important accounts before that date are the *Vita Anskarii* by Rimbert, the *Gesta Hammaburgensis ecclesiae pontificum* by Adam of Bremen, and the *Íslendingabók* by Ari Þorgilsson.

3. For a critique of this approach, see Sawyer, Sawyer, and Wood, *Christianization of Scandinavia,* 18–20.

4. These sources do not go into much detail about the conversion of Sweden; the narratives on the conversion of Sweden have already been thoroughly discussed by Birgit Sawyer in "Scandinavian Conversion Histories," in Sawyer, Sawyer, and Wood, *Christianization of Scandinavia,* 88–110.

5. I have Anglicized Icelandic names in the text by removing diacritical marks and the nominative -r endings and by rendering thorn (þ) as *th* and eth (ð) as *d.*

6. Most scholars would agree that in the long run it does not fit the actual

circumstances at all well: conversion to Christianity, when it came to have some personal and not just external meaning, involved changing both people's daily customs and habits and their basic outlook on life. However, as I shall discuss, the authors in question here were looking at conversion as a moment, not as a long process.

7. Sawyer, "Conversion Histories," 96; see also Birgit Sawyer, "Valdemar, Absalon, and Saxo: Historiography and Politics in Medieval Denmark," *Revue Belge de philologie et d'histoire* 63 (1985): 685–705.

8. Sawyer, "Conversion Histories," 109.

9. Sverre Bagge, *Society and Politics in Snorri Sturluson's* Heimskringla (Berkeley: University of California Press, 1991), 105–7.

10. On the theme of the "noble pagan," who understands some of the Christian message even before the coming of Christianity, see Lars Lönnroth, "The Noble Heathen: A Theme in the Sagas," *Scandinavian Studies* 41 (1969): 1–29.

11. Sawyer, "Conversion Histories," 108.

12. See Peter Sawyer, "The Process of Scandinavian Christanization in the Tenth and Eleventh Centuries," in Sawyer, Sawyer, and Wood, *Christianization of Scandinavia,* 80, 83–84.

13. "The Discussions," in Sawyer, Sawyer, and Wood, *Christianization of Scandinavia,* 8–9.

14. See Joaquín Martínez Pizarro, "Conversion Narratives: Form and Utility," in *Sixth International Saga Conference Workship Papers* II (Copenhagen: Arnamagnæanske Institut, 1985), 813–32, for further discussion of how the sources present central authorities' attempts at conversion by force.

15. The notes in the first volume of Eric Christiansen's translation (Saxo Grammaticus, *Danorum Regum Heroumque Historia Books X–XVI,* vol. 1, British Archaeological Reports 84 [Oxford: British Archaeological Reports, 1980]) provide useful guidance as to the sources Saxo used for this part of his work. See also Sawyer, "Valdemar, Absalon, and Saxo," 687.

16. Saxo Grammaticus, *Gesta Danorum,* 10:4:1, ed. J. Olrik and H. Ræder (Copenhagen: Levin & Munksgaard, 1931), 1:272; trans. Christiansen, 7.

17. Ibid., 10:8:2, p. 276; trans. Christiansen, 12.

18. Saxo, *Gesta Danorum,* 10:11:1–4, pp. 280–82; trans. Christensen, 20–21. The Poppo story comes originally from Widukind of Korvei, and Saxo places it in a different reign than does his source; see Christiansen, 180n.70; Sawyer, "Conversion Histories," 96–97.

19. Saxo, *Gesta Danorum,* 10:11:6, p. 282; trans. Christiansen, 22.

20. Saxo gives a more positive picture of Olaf Haraldsson's Christianity: ibid., 10:16:2–3, pp. 288–29; trans. Christiansen, 30–31.

21. On Snorri's sources, see Theodore M. Andersson, "Kings' Sagas (*Konunga-sögur*)," in *Old Norse-Icelandic Literature: A Critical Guide,* ed. Carol J. Clover and John Lindow, Islandica 45 (Ithaca: Cornell University Press, 1985), 197–238.

22. Ólafs saga Tryggvasonar 27, in Snorri Sturluson, *Heimskringla,* ed. Bjarni

Aðalbjarnarson, Íslenzk Fornrit 26 (Reykjavík: Hið Íslenzka Fornrítafélag, 1941), 259–60; trans. Lee M. Hollander, *Heimskringla: History of the Kings of Norway* (Austin: University of Texas Press, 1967), 166–67.

23. Óláfs saga Tryggvasonar 33, p. 270; trans. Hollander, 173.

24. Óláfs saga Tryggvasonar 50, p. 299; trans. Hollander, 193.

25. In a scene common elsewhere in folklore, the hermit is able to determine that the tall, well-dressed retainer Olaf has sent in his stead is not truly the king. Peter Sawyer, "Ethelred II, Olaf Tryggvason, and the Conversion of Norway," *Scandinavian Studies* 59 (1987): 302.

26. Óláfs saga Tryggvasonar 31, p. 267; trans. Hollander, 170–71.

27. Óláfs saga Tryggvasonar 47, pp. 292–93; trans. Hollander, 189.

28. Óláfs saga Tryggvasonar 53, pp. 302–3; trans. Hollander, 195–96.

29. Óláfs saga Tryggvasonar 54, pp. 303–4; trans. Hollander, 196.

30. Óláfs saga Tryggvasonar 55, p. 305; trans. Hollander, 197.

31. Theodore M. Andersson, "The Conversion of Norway According to Oddr Snorrason and Snorri Sturluson," *Mediaeval Scandinavia* 10 (1977): 83–95.

32. Óláfs saga Tryggvasonar 57, 59, and 65–69, pp. 307–9, 314–18; trans. Hollander, 198–99, 205–8.

33. Óláfs saga Tryggvasonar 76, p. 323; trans. Hollander, 211. Olaf also tortured one Raud to death by forcing a snake down his throat: Óláfs saga Tryggvasonar 80, p. 327; trans. Hollander, 214.

34. Óláfs saga ins Helga 204, in *Heimskringla*, Íslenzk Fornrít 27, p. 354; trans. Hollander, 494.

35. Óláfs saga Tryggvasonar 61, p. 310; trans. Hollander 200–1. She later married Svein Forkbeard of Denmark, Olaf's enemy.

36. Óláfs saga Tryggvasonar 113, p. 372; trans. Hollander, 244.

37. Óláfs saga ins Helga 60, 64, 73, 176, pp. 77, 83, 101, 176; trans. Hollander, 292, 296, 309, 363.

38. E.g., Óláfs saga ins Helga 121, pp. 206–9; trans. Hollander, 387–89.

39. Óláfs saga ins Helga 112–13, pp. 184–90; trans. Hollander, 369–74. For discussion of this episode, see Theodore M. Andersson, "Lore and Literature in a Scandinavian Conversion Episode," in *Idee—Gestalt—Geschichte: Festschrift Klaus von See*, ed. Gerd Wolfgang Weber (Odense: Odense University Press, 1988), 261–84.

40. Óláfs saga Tryggvasonar 73, pp. 319–320; trans. Hollander, 209.

41. Óláfs saga Tryggvasonar 82, pp. 329–30; trans. Hollander 215–16.

42. Óláfs saga Tryggvasonar 84, pp. 332–33; trans. Hollander, 217–18.

43. See Jón Hnefill Aðalsteinsson, *Under the Cloak: The Acceptance of Christianity in Iceland, with Particular Reference to the Religious Attitudes Prevailing at the Time*, Acta Universitatis Upsaliensis, Studia Ethnologica Upsaliensia 4 (Stockholm: Almqvist & Wiksell, 1978), 61, on sources; see also *Kristni saga*, in *Biskupa Sögur*, ed. Hið Íslenzka Bókmentafélag (Copenhagen: S.L. Möller, 1856), 1:3–32, for a parallel.

44. *Brennu-Njáls saga* 100, ed. Einar Ól. Sveinsson, Íslenzk Fornrít 12

(Reykjavík: Hið Íslenzka Fornrítafélag, 1954), 255, trans. Magnus Magnusson and Hermann Pálsson (Harmondsworth: Penguin, 1960), 217.

45. *Brennu-Njáls saga* 100, p. 257; trans. Magnusson and Pálsson, 218.

46. *Brennu-Njáls saga* 102, p. 265; trans. Magnusson and Pálsson, 221.

47. *Brennu-Njáls saga* 103, pp. 267–69; trans. Magnusson and Pálsson, 223. See Ian Wood, "Christians and Pagans in Ninth-Century Scandinavia," in Sawyer, Sawyer, and Wood, *Christianization of Scandinavia*, 55, for earlier examples of how the efficacy of Christianity vs. paganism was judged.

48. *Brennu-Njáls saga* 105, pp. 271–72; trans. Magnusson and Pálsson, 225–26. See Aðalsteinsson, *Under the Cloak*, 103–22, for discussion of this incident, which he sees in terms of shamanism.

49. Paul Schach, "Antipagan Sentiment in the Sagas of Icelanders," *Gripla* 1 (1975): 109–11.

50. See discussion in Schach, "Antipagan Sentiment," 119–20.

51. Lönnroth, 24–27, would argue that they both included such a range that they might not have been all that different.

52 For bibliography on the sources for Scandinavian paganism see John Lindow, "Mythology and Mythography," in Clover and Lindow, *Old Norse-Icelandic Literature*, 21–67; see also Aðalsteinsson, *Under the Cloak*, 16–46, for a discussion of the evidence for pagan practice in Iceland.

53. Jón Viðar Sigurðsson, "Friendship in the Icelandic Commonwealth," in *From Sagas to Society: Comparative Approaches to Early Iceland,* ed. Gísli Pálsson (Enfield Lock, Middlesex: Hisarlik Press, 1992), 205–15.

54. *Laxdæla saga* 78, ed. Einar Ól. Sveinsson, Íslenzk Fornrít 5 (Reykjavík: Hið Íslenzka Fornrítafélag, 1934), 228.

55. Rimbert, *Vita Anskarii*, 20, ed. G. Waitz (Hannover: Hahn, 1884), 44–46.

56. As just one example, Bede's account of the conversion of Edwin of Northumbria, in which the Pope urged Queen Ethelburga to play a role: *Bede's Ecclesiastical History of the English People,* ed. and trans. Bertram Colgrave and R. A. B. Mynors (Oxford: Clarendon Press, 1969), II.9–II.14, pp. 162–88.

57. Jenny Jochens, "The Medieval Icelandic Heroine: Fact or Fiction?" *Viator* 17 (1986): 35–50, is the best discussion for the family sagas; Jenny Jochens, *Women in Old Norse Society* (Ithaca: Cornell University Press, 1995), expands the argument. For Saxo and Snorri see Birgit Strand [Sawyer], "Women in Gesta Danorum," in *Saxo Grammaticus: A Medieval Author Between Norse and Latin Culture,* ed. Karsten Friis-Jensen (Copenhagen: Museum Tusculanum Press, 1981), 135–67.

58. Birgit Sawyer, "Women and the Conversion of Scandinavia," in *Frauen in Spätantike und Frühmittelalter: Lebendsbedingungen—Lebensnormen— Lebensformen* (Sigmaringen: Jan Thorbecke Verlag, 1990), 265. Sawyer points out that although *Heimskringla* and the family sagas are less hostile to women, they still represent women's active roles as part of the pagan past.

59. Jochens, "Medieval Icelandic Heroine," 49–50.

7

Marriage and Conversion in Late Medieval Romance

Jennifer R. Goodman

Two of the favorite plotlines describing conversions to Christianity in later medieval romance center upon female characters. Both of these stories develop early in the history of medieval literature. In the first, a heroic Christian lady marries a pagan king and persuades him to accept her faith. This tale may spring from the historical account of the conversion of Clovis (ca. 466–511), the pagan king of the Franks, through the efforts of his Christian wife, the Burgundian princess Clothilde. The story attained new popularity in the fifteenth century, to some extent because of its interest for French royal propagandists. Perhaps for this reason, Clovis's conversion finds its way into a number of fifteenth-century prose romances.[1] Similar tales of long-suffering Christian queens struggling to convert their pagan or Moslem husbands attracted European authors and their early printers on into the sixteenth century. Margaret Schlauch's *Chaucer's Constance and Accused Queens* (1927) describes a substantial group of these romances.[2] Boiardo adopts a variant of this theme in *Orlando Innamorato:* there two long-lost princesses convert their parents and their kingdom. Evidently rediscovered, the charismatic heroine as an agent of conversion continued to charm innovative Renaissance poets as well as conservative printers and audiences across Europe.[3]

This plot demands to be set alongside a second motif, also widely represented in the fiction of the Middle Ages and Renaissance. In this complementary plotline, the female protagonist becomes the object of her lover's evangelism. Chivalric love acts in these stories as a force motivating the spread of Christianity. Saracen princesses and Amazon queens tend to populate this sort of tale from the twelfth century onward. In most cases these women prove the most active and forceful of the characters involved, contradicting their apparently passive role in the conversion story.[4]

Both of these kinds of stories attracted authors and audiences well beyond 1500. Some ingenious writers of the later fifteenth and early sixteenth centuries, like the Swiss Jean Bagnyon or the Italian poets Boiardo and Ariosto, managed to incorporate both varieties of conversion episode in their narratives. While both plotlines are well known to readers of medieval literature, few studies look at them together, as this one will do. Setting these two well-established patterns of feminine conduct against one another sheds light on their authors' theories of female psychology, marital relations, and divine providence operating in the domestic sphere. Romances containing powerful fantasies of female conversion and missionary action like these seem to have been read in a number of cases by mothers and daughters together.[5] Over a long period such romances helped to set patterns of conduct and to crystallize their readers' preconceptions of the psychology of religious conversion.

Before the effect of combining both stories in a single work can be assessed, each one should be discussed on its own. The simplest method would be to analyze them in chronological order. This plan may be frustrated by the fact that it is difficult to decide which tale appears earlier in the annals of European literature. The story of the Christian bride who persuades her non-Christian husband to be baptized was almost a thousand years old when it appeared in Bagnyon's *Histoire de Charlemagne*. It held great historical prestige for its medieval audiences, there and in other sources.[6] However, the romance of the Saracen princess in pursuit of the Christian knight also echoes ancient historical events and even older beliefs that associate marriage, religion, and sovereignty. On closer investigation it may prove the older story in terms of its underlying structure. Still, for the purposes of this study, it seems preferable to consider the Christian bride first.

The tale of the Christian princess who is given in marriage to a non-Christian king, and who succeeds in persuading her husband to accept baptism, achieved wide currency in medieval fiction. It also found its way into some of the most reputable history books of the era as an account of the advent of Christianity in France and England. This type of story attained special prominence in the fourteenth and fifteenth centuries: it is worth asking why. Jean Bagnyon would use it to begin his popular history of Charlemagne, a book that was to circulate in English, French, and Spanish and that plays a special role in the cultural history of Latin America.[7] The narrative may well have achieved its widest geographical spread in this form.

The pagan Frankish king Clovis's marriage in 493 to the Catholic Burgundian princess Clothilde is firmly established as a historical event. Twentieth-century historians differ in the amount of influence they assign to Clothilde as a factor in her husband's eventual conversion to the Catholic Christianity of Rome rather than to Arianism. Historians' treatment of this tale reveals their ideas about the relative weight that human relationships and cold political calculation ought to bear in decisions of this kind. It can also say much about a writer's views of women, or wives, as a force in government. H. A. L. Fisher's *History of Europe* of 1936, for instance, dilutes Clothilde's role:

> Whether the conversion of Clovis was due to the influence of his Catholic wife Clotilda, a Burgundian princess, or to his conviction that Christ had delivered the Alemans into his hands, or to a long-headed calculation of political chances, is of little moment compared with the fact that in 496 the leader of the Salian Franks, the most renowned of all the Germanic tribes, became a protagonist of the Catholic cause.[8]

The three possibilities are arranged in the sentence so as to emphasize the third, in all probability the one most attractive to Fisher as a hardheaded twentieth-century historian. This is also the one least supported by medieval accounts of the event. The first choice, that of the influence of Clothilde, is superseded by two more likely stories, and then all three are discarded as "of little moment." The grammatical sleight of hand merits recognition, as does the historical judgment behind it. Evidently twentieth-century students of history are not supposed to believe in these sorts of stories any more. Clovis's adoption of Catholic Christianity rather than Arianism to replace his original paganism is a momentous decision. It makes him the true founder of the French monarchy. Such a deed is not to be ascribed to a woman's influence, if at all possible. The level of resistance to Clothilde's story on the part of later historians might well prove a useful measure of their attitudes to women as a force in history. But this is another paper.

In many respects the tales of Clovis's marriage and conversion and that of Chaucer's Constance in the "Man of Law's Tale" are twins. One should stress, though, that Clothilde retains a confirmed historical status denied to Constance today. Both stories portray a reluctant Christian princess who is compelled by her male relatives to wed a non-Christian king. Indeed, Constance is compelled by force of circumstances to wed two of them. Bagnyon's Clothilde is a royal Burgundian lady who has fallen on hard times. Her uncle Agabondus has usurped the throne and eradicated the rest of her family. Clothilde has been spared on account of her beauty. Clovis hears of her through his messengers and sends an emissary to her to begin negotiations (*Charles the Grete*, 13). Clothilde's reception of the go-between, Clovis's trusted counselor disguised as a palmer, displays the princess's strength of character in action. Bagnyon's version of the story stresses her discernment in detecting that Clovis's messenger is no ordinary beggar and her prudence in refusing to commit herself to any firm engagement, though at the same time she intelligently retains the ring he sends her as a pledge of betrothal. In the event, her marriage will be a political arrangement between the two kings, Clovis and Agabondus. Unlike Chaucer's Roman princess Constance, dispatched to Syria in return for the promised Christianization of the country, Clothilde is married off without any commitment to conversion on the part of the Franks.

This summary begins to suggest some similarities of personality and situation linking the historical and the legendary princesses. Neither one enters into marriage with her non-Christian partner with any apparent enthusiasm, though both are elevated in rank by their marriages. Constance's elevation suffers a setback: the conversion of Syria is halted by her mother-in-law, the head of the conservative party, who engineers a *coup d'état,* executes her son and his supporters, and packs Constance off to sea on a rudderless boat. However, Constance does later marry a second pagan, King Alla of Northumberland, converting not Syria but England to Christianity. The point of this plotline is, in part, the inscrutability of divine providence in determining the religious destinies of nations.

In the *Histoire de Charlemagne,* Clothilde's married life begins with a bedroom scene in which she makes two requests of her husband, asking him to become a Christian and to recover her inheritance. Naturally, she chooses a strategic moment. "My right dere lord, I requyre the that it please the to graunte to me a lytel demaunde byfore or I entre in to thy bedde wyth the" (*Charles the Grete,* 15). Clovis responds that the second request seems much more feasible than the first. The scene parallels similar confrontations in lives of saints, though there the bride tends to announce maddeningly as well that she has taken a vow of perpetual chastity.[9] This cannot happen in the story of Clovis or of Constance, for obvious reasons. Both stories have strong dynastic implications. Clearly both virtuous ladies, whatever their level of personal piety, function as wives in every sense of the word.[10]

The comparative untidiness of Clothilde's story reflects its greater historical content. When Clothilde is married off to Clovis he is still a pagan. Her wedding-night plea for his conversion meets with no immediate success. It is not until several years and two children later that Clovis accepts Christianity. At that point, Clothilde's influence has been somewhat muted by the passage of time. The desire for victory over the Alemans may weigh more heavily with the canny—or desperate—Frankish king. Clothilde achieves her aim in the end but only after a turbulent phase of domestic friction.

Through all this Clothilde's offspring bear a definite religious significance, as instances of the Christian God's power and benevolence. Clothilde's faith, and her dynastic usefulness, are tested when the first child is baptized and then dies. Clovis blames Clothilde and Christianity for the event. "Wherof the kyng was euyl contente and sayd to the quene `Yf thou haddest gyuen hym and dedyed hym to my goddes he were now alyue'" (*Charles the Grete*, 16). Their second child, he suggests, might survive longer if allowed to remain a pagan. "`And now,' sayd he, `it shal none otherwyse be of this chylde but as it was of that other his broder, bycause ayenst myn entente thou doost thy wylle in baptysyng them'" (*Charles the Grete*, 17). Clothilde resists any such conclusion. This marital disagreement is presented as a test of faith for the Christian queen, who interprets the death of her firstborn otherwise: "The quene answerd `for this thyng I am noo thyng perturbled in my courage, but I rendre and gyue thankynges to god my creatour by cause he hath me so dygne and worthy that it hath plesed hym to take in to his royalme of heuen the fyrst fruyt of my wombe'" (*Charles the Grete*, 16–17). The loss does not shake her confidence in Christianity, nor her determination that her children shall be Christians, whatever her husband chooses to do.

In his presentation of this phase of Clothilde's career, Bagnyon elaborates on the queen's prayers. She prays for the survival of her second child: "thenne the quene for fere of the kyng prayed to god deuoutely for the helthe of hyr chylde" (*Charles the Grete*, 17). This one lives. Soon afterward, under the stress of battle and urged on by his wise counselor, Clovis decides in favor of his own baptism. Bagnyon's version of this story emphasizes Clothilde's involvement, even in her absence. Clovis's aide tells him he should accept the queen's god, and the king himself addresses his prayer to "Jhesu cryst on whom my wyf beleveth." She may be absent at the critical moment, but her persistent pleas have stamped her views on the men around her. Christianity for Clovis is his wife's religion: he mentions her name in his first prayer as if presenting a letter of introduction.

Bagnyon's description of Clovis's experience reflects—a thousand years later—elements of the Frankish marital customs discussed by Susan Wemple in *Women in Frankish Society*.[11] The episode of the ring rather confusedly preserves Clothilde's formal betrothal to Clovis, a formality that gave a woman some legal protection as she entered into marriage (Wemple, 37). Clothilde's request for a gift before the consummation of her marriage accords with the Germanic custom of the *morgengabe*—a gift from bridegroom to bride on the morning after the wedding. The usual gift would be material. Clothilde's second choice, the return of her just inheritance, strikes Clovis as the simpler of her two demands, as it is the more conventional (Wemple, 12). The story's later audiences might not obtain from Bagnyon much sense of the danger threatening Clothilde through the illness of her sons: Wemple observes that the Frankish wife who did not produce viable children could not expect to remain married for long. Merovingian wives were repudiated for barrenness or after the death of their offspring (Wemple, 59–61). This knowledge would add tension to the continuing dialogue between husband and wife. The point is also applicable to Chaucer's Constance.

Wemple begins her work by observing:

> Women played an important role in the creation of this new society although they seldom had access to the sources of public power. By marrying across ethnic lines and converting their husbands to Christianity, then bearing children and transmitting to them a mixed cultural heritage, they were instrumental in bringing about the demographic and cultural amalgamation of the people living in the Merovingian kingdom. (Wemple, 9)

This insight is pertinent to each of the stories of conversion under discussion here. The female characters who populate these stories are all engaged in the activities Wemple describes. These are romances of intermarriage, justifying and celebrating the courage of the woman who involves herself in such a partnership. In every case at issue in this paper, the narrative focuses with special attention on the personality and the experience of the woman as she weds a man of another religion and people. The woman's task as an agent of religious assimilation is clearly articulated through the tales of these heroines. The marriage across ethnic lines is depicted as historically momentous, a perilous adventure. For authors as different as Chaucer, Bagnyon, and Boiardo, this is how women change the course of history.

Chaucer's "Man of Law's Tale" takes a historical element similar to the story of the conversion of Clovis and combines it with incidents from folk sources to create a romance of the Christian bride afloat in a world of unbelief. When Chaucer adapted the story it was already current in Nicholas Trevet's chronicle as a narrative of the conversion of Northumbria to Christianity. As Chaucer presents the tale, it involves the Roman princess Constance, sent first to Syria to marry and convert the sultan, then, after his murder, carried in a rudderless boat to the coast of Northumberland, where she miraculously converts and marries King Alla (Ælle.) Falsely accused by her jealous mother-in-law of giving birth to a monster, she is sent off in the rudderless boat again, returning to Rome to be reunited in time with her scattered family.

This alternative history of the coming of Christianity to England needs to be set against the Venerable Bede's much better known story of Gregory the Great and the English slave boys. In that legend, the pope comes across a group of fair youths, *non Angli sed angeli,* whose blond beauty inspires Gregory to dispatch Augustine of Canterbury on his mission; while Augustine goes to Kent, the boys Gregory meets in the market are northerners, subjects of King Ælle of Deira.[12] That well-established tale contrasts with the story of Constance most strikingly in its masculinity. In Bede's tale, England receives Christianity through the good offices of an abbot-pope, a monk turned bishop, and a bevy of captive boys. The missionary enterprise is altogether male in inspiration and execution. Equally masculine are the later scenes in Northumbria where the king and his advisors debate their decision to accept this new faith.[13]

On the historical front, the Frankish wife of King Ethelbert of Kent, Bertha, would play a key role in 596, as her daughter Ethelberga would in Northumbria thirty years afterward. Without these queens and their families to insist that the Christian priests be received at court, it would have been much more difficult for the Roman missionaries to obtain a hearing in England. Bede's monastic account of the conversion of the English reaffirms the essential role intermarriage played in religious change during this period. It is true that in his presentation, as in J. M. Wallace-Hadrill's discussion of 1962, the princess is seen as the tool of male authorities.[14] Still, for the English as for the Frankish king, Jesus was the god "of whom my wife has spoken." Pope Boniface writes letters first to the king and then to his wife, urging her to exert herself to teach and encourage her husband to convert. Between the masculine tales of religious transmission, a woman's story much like that of Clothilde or Constance struggles to emerge. Once again, the story is of a secular woman, a wife.

The tale of Constance enhances the role of the wife. Any clerical assistants she may start out with fade into the background. The Christian bride becomes an emissary of God, sent by a devious route to fulfill a divine plan, supported by miracles throughout the hazards of her travels and marriages. The fictional events are bolstered by names of historical figures and actual places. Christianity is advanced in this story not by monks and popes but by a solitary wife and mother belabored by recurrent abuse. She is traduced—twice, sexually assaulted, accused of murder and of being a demon, and three times sentenced to die. Through all this, Chaucer's heroine remains maddeningly steadfast, accepting her subjugation meekly, her only protest a prayer. She is no eager missionary. In Constance's view of the universe, "women are born to thraldom and penance, / And to been under mannes governance" (ll. 286–87). It is made clear from the start that she leaves Rome with reluctance. The fact that she does feel sorry for herself makes Constance as human as she will ever be.

If Constance's story owes anything to Clothilde's, the tale seems to have been tidied up a bit as well as embellished with perils at sea and on land. Clothilde married her king first and attempted to convert him afterward, as did Bertha of Kent and Ethelberga of Northumbria. In the "Man of Law's Tale," both the Sultan of Syria and King Alla accept Christianity before marriage, agreeing to contracts more stringent than the conditional arrangement Bede describes between Ethelberga's family and King Edwin.[15] It would seem that later writers found the thought of intermarriage of an unconverted pagan and a Christian lady too repellent to depict without strong historical authority. Such a marriage would also be against the law in many medieval law codes: Clothilde indeed tells Clovis's messenger so: "it was not leeful to a paynym to haue to his wyf a crysten woman" (*Charles the Grete*, 14). The Kentish court tells Edwin on his first application for the hand of Ethelberga that "it was not permissible for a Christian maiden to be given in marriage to a heathen husband, lest the Christian Faith and Sacraments be profaned by her association with a king who was wholly ignorant of the worship of the true God" (Bede, *History*, 115). In the thirteenth-century *Siete Partidas* of Alfonso X the Wise, most sexual relationships between Moors and Christian women were punishable by death.[16]

In each of these stories the birth of a child turns into a crisis for the Christian queen, whether or not her husband has become a Christian. In both cases it is suggested that because of the mother's alien nature or customs, there must be something wrong with her child. Constance's mother-in-law pretends that the newborn child is deformed in an effort to persuade her son to repudiate Constance. When Alla refuses to do so, she forges a message of repudiation in his name. Clovis himself voices his suspicions that baptism is not a healthy practice. The threat of repudiation is never made explicit, but Clothilde's fear of her husband's displeasure is mentioned.

By doubling the tale of Constance's abortive attempt to convert Syria with its English parallel, her successful conversion of Northumberland, Chaucer's "Man of Law's Tale" stresses the mysterious nature of divine providence. Syria's loss is England's gain. This parallel also underlines the importance and the uncertainty of intermarriage as a mode of evangelization. In the Syrian case, the attempt to impose a new religion by royal mandate is foiled by hostility within the palace. In the case of England, a series of divine manifestations assures Constance's success. In both cases, the character who motivates all the action, the irresistible prize, is the Christian virgin, a figure perhaps to be identified with the Virgin Mary herself. The connection can be pushed at least so far: Constance is a maiden chosen by God for a great and mysterious purpose, who becomes the source of a people's salvation. The depiction of Constance with her infant, about to be pushed out to sea for the second time, unquestionably echoes portrayals of the Madonna in art and literature. The Christian bride in such stories might even have been read as a personification of Christianity, specifically of allegiance to Catholic orthodoxy. The Church is, after all, the Bride of Christ in any number of medieval allegorical texts and often in Christian interpretations of the love poetry of the *Song of Songs.*

Bagnyon's *Histoire de Charlemagne* of about 1470 offers a different form of doubling. Bagnyon follows the story of Clovis and Clothilde, the first historical event he describes at any length, with the complementary tale of Floripas, the Saracen princess, daughter of the Sultan of Babylon. He draws this second tale from the late thirteenth-century *chanson de geste* of *Fierabras,* one of the most widely disseminated medieval narratives of Charlemagne.[17]

At first sight the tale of Floripas seems not to complement but to clash against the tale of Clothilde. Notwithstanding the detailed studies of André de Mandach and others on possible historical models for the Saracen princess Floripas, she comes across to the modern reader as a most implausible being, the product of an energetic fictional imagination. When the reader first encounters her she is a glamorous beauty, dressed in fairy garments, enamored of Charlemagne's peer Guy of Burgundy, whom she has seen from afar but never met. She saves Charlemagne's captive peers from her father's dungeons by main force, murdering the jailor and her old governess in the process. Love motivates her actions. She proposes to accept baptism if she is given Guy of Burgundy as her husband. The peers agree — Guy of Burgundy with some qualms — and after a prolonged siege and rescue by Charlemagne, the romance ends with Floripas's baptism, marriage, and coronation, immediately preceded by the execution of her intransigent father, the Admiral Balan.

Like the stories of Clothilde and Constance, this is a romance of intermarriage, again resulting in the propagation of Christianity. The central figure — the Saracen princess — is altogether different in character, really the antithesis of the two Christian brides already discussed. For her twentieth-century critics Floripas may appear a repellent vehicle of anti-Islamic propaganda, a "Goneril virago," to borrow Dorothée Metlitzki's term for her.[18] Bagnyon finds Floripas's behavior so startling as to warrant authorial comment. Her murder of the jailor is indeed, in his view, the deed of a man (*euvre d'omme*), but it is a good deed, and a man would have been praised for it. Her determination to obtain her desire reflects the unprincipled volition common to the female sex. Her brother Fierabras, already a Christian, rebukes Floripas for her impatience as she waits her turn at the font while her father is resisting baptism, holding up her own christening and mar-

riage ceremonies. Here the princess about to be baptized herself offers neither tolerance nor sympathy for the Islamic loyalty of her parent. In fact,
she is presented as endorsing the extreme position—conversion or death—
that is later presented by Charlemagne to the remainder of the local populace.

Nicolàs de Piemonte's widely disseminated Castilian translation of about
1500 complicates the issue still further by revising Floripas's character to
suit its new Spanish audiences. The updated Saracen princess is craftier,
more self-conscious, and more prudent than her French model. She still
urges Charlemagne to kill her father, but she is allowed to defend her rea-
soning in answer to her brother. Balan should be killed because "even if he
allows himself to be baptized he will never be a good Christian."[19] In its
skepticism regarding the efficacy of forced baptism, this justification may
perhaps reflect the experience of the Spanish Inquisition among the unwilling converts of Spain.

Nicolàs de Piemonte's Floripas is also much more alert than the princess
in other versions of the same story to the double-edged nature of her own
decision. She addresses Charlemagne's twelve peers:

> "Noble and daring knights, since your fortune and my bliss have brought
> you to a time when you had need of my small and womanly strength; and
> since I purpose, forgetting my gods and the love of my father, of my
> family and my entire country, to save your lives, even at the risk of my
> own." [20]

In this passage, Floripas becomes a traitor-heroine of a complex kind, alert
to contrary analyses of her decision.

The effect of emphasizing these two contrasting ladies, Floripas and
Clothilde, as part of the same story deserves consideration. Taken together,
they celebrate intermarriage as a means toward religious assimilation. In
particular, their stories justify the woman's role in marrying outside her
own community of faith. Chaucer and Bagnyon create elaborate portraits
of women entering into such daring relationships. As Dorothée Metlitzki
noted in another connection, the Christian bride and the Saracen princess
are given opposing personalities. The Christian ladies are resigned, self-
effacing, and self-disciplined. The Saracens are aggressive, forward, pas-
sionate beings. Where the decorous Constance allows herself to become
the alluring object of the infidel prince's desire, Floripas asserts her own
unconventional choice of a mate. Clothilde and Constance are long-suffering souls, accepting the miseries imposed on them by an inscrutable God.
Floripas is prone to thump anyone who gets in her way. Where the Christian ladies remain models of wifely decorum, the Saracen can seem more

like a revenge fantasy, permitted to behave as outrageously as possible before baptism in fulfillment of the secret wishes of a fair number of young members of the audience who would love to push their governesses out of windows. Perhaps she gains this freedom because no one expects her to serve as an emblem of Christianity.

The Christian partner in these relationships is never allowed to express much enthusiasm for the marriage. Clothilde tells Clovis's messenger his king's request is unlawful, at the same time that she tucks his ring away in the royal treasury for safekeeping. Guy of Burgundy clings to the letter of the law as Floripas declares her love for him. Constance accepts both of her marriages in a spirit of resignation if not depression at the sad lot of woman. However seductively beautiful the Saracen princess may be, her Christian knight must never allow the balance of power to slip in her direction by admitting any attraction on his part. Other Frenchmen—the venerable Duke Naymes for one—do admire her; he cannot. Indeed, there are faint suggestions that a non-Christian ought to be physically repellent to a Christian in some subtle way: Floripas does not dare to kiss Guy on the lips, because she is still unbaptized. This curious inhibition remains unexplained; it may relate to popular beliefs about the physical impurity of the unbaptized.[21] Baptism will remove this taint, or so one understands. The saintly Christian maiden cannot be allowed to admit any pleasure even after marriage, but this inhibition might have trammeled her whomever she married.

To my knowledge the romances never depict any intermarriage in which the happy couple adopt the non-Christian partner's faith. The process is consistently portrayed as a one-way street.

These works continued to be published throughout the period when the Humanist historians of Europe were busy demolishing much of the legendary history of the Middle Ages and as busy creating a new one on classical models. Yet the much-translated chivalric literature of the day reemphasizes the role of the wife as a catalyst of religious change. Even as the Jesuits and Franciscans of Portugal, Spain, and France were marching out in all directions to preach Christianity to the heathen of the world, the early printers were advocating a different approach. Such works reflect a lingering recognition of the key role played by wives like Clothilde in the conversion of Europe to Christianity, in a sense celebrating the redemptive power of earthly love. Their continuing popularity among early printers indicates that the subject of conversion was still of acute concern to the West, under stress from the advancing Ottoman Empire, just as it was coming into contact with unimagined non-Christian peoples of Africa, the Americas, and Asia.

These varied romances perpetuate both history and fantasy. For a woman reader, the fantasy is of converting alien kingdoms; for a man, it is that of winning a glamorous alien princess and her lands. For readers of all sorts and conditions, these stories mingle sainthood, sovereignty, and secular delight. These tales of conversion stress the decisive importance of the secular woman—the maiden who becomes a wife—as a force in history. Through their complementary patterns of intermarriage, these authors reveal a little-explored aspect of European self-awareness and of religious ingenuity. In these secular fictions, conversion is not an enterprise of the clergy but of the marriageable female. Christianity is propagated through the will of a woman.

NOTES

The final draft of this paper was composed in Cambridge, England. I owe special thanks to Lady Jeffreys, Life Fellow of Girton College, for putting me up and for putting up with me at this time. As John Fisher said of Lady Margaret Beaufort, another lady eminent in the annals of that university, "She was also of singuler easynes to be spoken vnto, and full curtayse answere she wolde make to all that came vnto her." Fisher also remarked upon Lady Margaret's kindness to visitors: "Muche besynes there is in kepynge hospytalyte" ("The Months' Mind of Lady Margaret," *English Works*, Early English Text Society, e.s. 27, 1876; reprint, New York: Kraus, 1973, pp. 291, 296). I am glad of this chance to thank Lady Jeffreys for her hospitality and for her help and kindness. Thanks also to Jim Muldoon for much encouragement and many helpful references.

1. André Giacchetti, editorial introduction to *Ysaïe le Triste: roman arthurien du moyen âge tardif* (Rouen: Université de Rouen, 1989); cf. Jehan Bagnyon, *L'Histoire de Charlemagne (parfois dite Roman de Fierabras)*, ed. Hans-Erich Keller, Textes littéraires français (Geneva: Droz, 1992.) For the fifteenth-century English translation of Bagnyon, see William Caxton, trans., *The Lyf of the Noble and Crysten Prynce, Charles the Grete,* ed. Sidney J. Herrtage, Early English Text Society e.s. 36–37 (London: N. Teubner, 1881).

2. Margaret Schlauch, *Chaucer's Constance and Accused Queens* (New York: New York University Press, 1927.) On Constance, see Geoffrey Chaucer, "The Man of Law's Tale," in *The Riverside Chaucer,* ed. Larry D. Benson (Boston: Houghton Mifflin, 1987), 89–103. Chaucer's friend John Gower tells his own version of the Constance story in *Confessio Amantis* 2, ll. 587–1598. A date of about 1390 seems plausible for Chaucer's tale. The story comes from Nicholas Trevet's Anglo-Norman chronicle of circa 1334. Cf. *Riverside Chaucer,* 857. Perhaps not coincidentally, this chronicle was written for a female patron, Edward I's daughter Marie. Dorothée Metlitzki discusses the Constance story in *The Matter of Araby in Medieval England* (New Haven: Yale University Press, 1977), 154–56.

3. Matteo Maria Boiardo, *Orlando Innamorato,* trans. Charles Stanley Ross

(Berkeley: University of California Press, 1989); Fiordelisa converts her parents and the rest of the Armenians in II:32–35.

4. For detailed discussions of such figures, see Metlitzki, *The Matter of Araby*.

5. Cf. Jennifer R. Goodman, "'That Wommen holde in ful greet reverence': Mothers and Daughters Reading Chivalric Romances," In *Women, the Book, and the Worldly*, ed. Lesley Smith and Jane H. M. Taylor (Woodbridge: D. S. Brewer, 1995), 25–30.

6. Bagnyon takes this section of his romance from Vincent de Beauvais's thirteenth-century *Speculum Historiale*. The principal and rather erratic early source for Clovis's life and times is Gregory of Tours's *Historia Francorum*, book 2, a work of the second half of the sixth century. Brian Tierney characterizes Gregory's history as "a wild, barbaric tale of treachery, violence, and lust that seems more like a turgid historical novel than sober factual history" (Brian Tierney and Sidney Painter, *Western Europe in the Middle Ages, 300–1475* [New York: Knopf, 1970], 67).

7. See André de Mandach, *Naissance et développement de la chanson de geste en Europe, V. La geste de Fierabras: Le jeu du réel et de l'invraisemblable, avec des textes inédits*, Publications romanes et françaises 177 (Geneva: Droz, 1987), and Peter Burke, "Chivalry in the New World," in *Chivalry in the Renaissance*, ed. Sydney Anglo (Woodbridge: Boydell, 1990), 253–62.

8. H. A. L. Fisher, *A History of Europe* (London: Eyre and Spottiswoode, 1936; reprint, Frome and London: Collins, 1960), 121. In their medieval history text, cited in note six, Tierney and Painter omit any reference to Clothilde. They also regard Clovis's Christianity as questionable in the extreme, and deplore his personal character; in a notable understatement, they sum him up as "not really the model of a Christian gentleman" (49–50).

9. For an example, see the life of Saint Cecilia in Chaucer's "Second Nun's Tale," ll.120–75.

10. Cf. Chaucer, "Man of Law's Tale," ll.708–14.

11. Suzanne Fonay Wemple, *Women in Frankish Society: Marriage and the Cloister, 500 to 900* (Philadelphia: University of Pennsylvania Press, 1981.)

12. Bede, *Historia Ecclesiastica*, book II, chap. 1, toward the end of Bede's summation of Gregory's life; in English, *A History of the English Church and People*, trans. Leo Sherley-Price (1955; reprint, Harmondsworth: Penguin, 1972), 99–100.

13. Ibid., 126–28.

14. Ibid., 114–17. See J. M. Wallace-Hadrill, *The Barbarian West: The Early Middle Ages, A.D. 400–1000* (1952; rev. ed., New York: Harper & Row, 1962), 54: "As it happened, the pope was able to make use of a barbarian (and Catholic) princess, Theudelinda. . . . (He similarly made use of the Frankish princess Bertha, great-granddaughter of Clovis and wife of the Kentish Æthelberht.)" The account of Clovis on pp. 70–76 mentions Clovis's queen only as the person who involved Clovis in a family feud.

15. Bede, *History*, 115. Edwin agrees to allow his wife freedom of worship and

to become Christian himself "if, on examination, his advisers decided that [Christianity] appeared more holy and acceptable to God than their own [faith]."

16. For an English translation, see Emilie Amt, ed., *Women's Lives in Medieval Europe: A Sourcebook* (New York: Rutledge, 1993), 70.

17. A. Kroeber and G. Servois, eds., "Fierabras," in *Les Anciens Poètes de la France* (Paris: Vieweg, 1860). For discussion of Bagnyon's sources and their reception, see Jennifer R. Goodman, *Malory and Caxton's Prose Romances of 1485* (New York: Garland, 1987), 107–15. For more detailed discussions of Bagnyon's work and its fortune in medieval Europe, see de Mandach, *La chanson de geste*; Hans-Erich Keller, *Autour de Roland: Recherches sur la chanson de geste* (Paris: Champion, 1989).

18. Metlitzki, *The Matter of Araby,* 169–75, 184–87. For some medieval German approaches to the problem of the non-Christian woman, see Maria Dobozy, "Das Bild der Heidin in der deutschen Kreuzzugsdichtung," in *La Croisade: Realités et Fictions: Actes du Colloque d'Amiens, 18–22 mars 1987,* ed. Danielle Buschinger (Göppingen: Kiemmerle, 1989), 111–18. My thanks to Maria Dobozy for her helpful advice and for this reference.

19. Nicolàs de Piemonte, *Historia de Carlo Magno* (Seville, 1525), f. xxv (v). To my knowledge, there is as yet no modern critical edition of Nicolàs de Piemonte's *Historia de Carlo Magno.* For the Crombergers' editions of this volume, see Clive Griffin, *The Crombergers of Seville: The History of a Printing and Merchant Dynasty* (Oxford: Clarendon Press, 1988). I cite the 1525 Seville edition preserved at the Biblioteca Nacional in Madrid, which I have compared with the British Library copy of the 1544 Salamanca edition of Juan de Junta and with the undated edition of Padrino in the Biblioteca de Catalunya in Barcelona.

20. "Muy nobles y efforçados caualleros / pues que vuestra fortuna & mi dicha os ha traydo a tiempo que de mis pequeñas y mugheriles fuerças tuuiessedes necessidad: & por quanto tengo propuesto / oluidando mis dioses y el amor del padre: de los parientes & de toda la tierra / deslavuar vuestras vidas / aun que supiesse por ello perder la mia" (Nicolàs de Piemonte, *Historia de Carlo Magno,* f. xix r/v). The English translation is mine.

21. Compare the death of the Saracen knight Corsabryn in Malory's *Works,* ed. Eugène Vinaver (Oxford: Clarendon Press, 1973), II:666: "And therewithall cam a stynke of his body, whan the soule departed, that there myght nobody abide the savoure."

Conversion on the Eastern Frontiers of Christendom

8

Bargaining for Baptism
Lithuanian Negotiations for Conversion, 1250–1358

Rasa Mazeika

Fiercely pagan until 1387, the Baltic nation of Lithuania became in the later Middle Ages the last frontier for many who desired the perfection of chivalry attained by the warrior who fought for God. As effective war against Islam became ever more difficult,[1] medieval idealists and adventurers looked northward, to the crusade being waged by the military monastic order of the Teutonic Knights against Prussians and Lithuanians.[2] Originally founded to fight for the Holy Land, the Teutonic Order established itself in Prussia from 1230, and after 1237 also ruled Livonia (Latvia and parts of Estonia). Lithuania was thus under nearly constant attack on two fronts by these warrior monks and by knights and princes from nearly every European state, who came to join the papally approved Baltic crusade eager to win salvation while improving their swordplay.[3]

Yet Lithuania's pagan rulers maintained economic and diplomatic ties with all their Christian neighbors (including the Teutonic Order), and flirtations with Christianity were an important aspect of Lithuanian state diplomacy. Officially, Lithuania became Christianized only in 1387, after her ruler, Jogaila (Jagiello), accepted baptism to gain the kingdom of Poland and the hand of its heiress. This essay will deal not with that rather straightforward political transaction but with several examples of other pagan rulers' sophisticated use of conversion negotiations as a diplomatic tool and weapon.

Mindaugas: An Attempt at Conversion and Its Consequences

King Mindaugas (ca. 1240–63) is traditionally considered the founder of a unified Lithuanian state, although recent scholarship has modified this.[4] Lithuania's only anointed king, he was also the only ruler to convert before 1386.[5] Soon after Mindaugas had come to power, probably by murdering and exiling his relatives, one of the rival tribal princelings contesting his prominence formed an alliance with and accepted baptism from the Archbishop of Riga in Livonia. Mindaugas moved to neutralize any advantage derived by his rival.[6] He made peace with the Livonian branch of the Teutonic Order and accepted baptism under the sponsorship of its Grand Master, who undertook to obtain a royal crown for Mindaugas.

At peace with the Teutonic Order until 1261, his international position strengthened by his coronation in 1253, Mindaugas was now free to consolidate his power within Lithuania and to improve his kingdom's economy by encouraging trade with both Riga and the Order.[7] Yet he had paid a high price in grants of Lithuanian lands to the Teutonic Order. Probably supplementing authentic grants with forged donation charters, the Order would brandish these documents for centuries to buttress its claims to Lithuanian territory.[8] Mindaugas turned against the Order in 1261 and probably apostatized in an attempt to appease pagan opposition,[9] but this did not prevent his murder in 1263, caused partly by personal animosities and partly by an anti-Christian backlash that sought to expel all priests from Lithuania.[10] Decades of chaos followed. Mindaugas's successors might well conclude that an imprudent plunge into the waters of baptism could prove fatal.

Gediminas's Letters: A Pagan Ruler Offers Churches but not Conversion

Fraught with suffering for Western Europe, the fourteenth century was for Lithuania the period of her greatest power, based as much on clever diplomacy as on military resourcefulness, despite continuous bloody war with the Teutonic Order.[11] Gediminas, ruler of Lithuania ca. 1316–41, extended his control over large areas of present-day Russia and Ukraine.[12] A close alliance with the city and archbishop of Riga, who were in constant conflict with the Teutonic Order, fostered Lithuanian trade and gave the long-suffering townsmen military protection against the antics of the Teutonic Knights (whose favorite joke was that "the sword was Pope enough for them!").[13]

Thus allied with both eastern and western Christians, Gediminas provided for both in his country: he told envoys sent by papal legates in 1324 that he decreed, "Christians worship God according to their custom [morem],—the Russians according to their rite, the Poles according to their custom, And we worship God according to our rites, and we all have the one God" ("omnes habemus unum deum").[14] He built three Catholic churches, had Franciscan friars at his court as scribes and advisors, and had a "Metropolitan of Lithuania" for his Greek Orthodox Rus' subjects.[15]

When Gediminas's sons and daughters were sent to consolidate Lithuanian conquests or alliances through marriage to foreign ruling families, they usually adopted the religion of their Orthodox or Catholic spouses.[16] Such diplomacy was possible only because the Lithuanian ruler himself remained pagan—a worshipper of Indo-European nature gods who owed allegiance to no Christian church and thus could ally with both Catholic and Orthodox.[17]

Only once did the gods and goddesses of fire, earth, and oak seem in danger of abandonment. In 1322 and 1323, Gediminas wrote two letters to Pope John XXII, summarized in the Pope's reply, stating that he "lived in error unwillingly" and that he did he not attack Christians because he wished to destroy the Christian faith—rather he was defending himself against his enemies and was now ready "to receive the true faith" ("fidem recipere orthodoxam").[18]

Nevertheless, as S. C. Rowell points out, the papal summary also repeats Gediminas's request that the Pope send legates "to make peace and settle boundaries," and this was probably the Lithuanian ruler's main objective.[19] No specific mention was made of baptism or religious instruction.

While Gediminas had news by January of 1323 that the Pope would send some reply,[20] papal legates were sent to baptize Lithuania only in June 1324, after a long delay probably caused by papal politics.[21] Meanwhile, the Lithuanian ruler sent at least two more letters to the Pope and several letters to townsmen and monks in Saxony, claiming he was favorable to Christianity.[22]

In October 1323, a peace treaty was concluded between Gediminas, Riga, and the Livonian branch of the Teutonic Order with its secular vassals.[23] The link to negotiations for Lithuanian baptism is clear, since the Teutonic Knights of Livonia sent envoys to Gediminas beforehand with copies of his letters, asking if he would keep the promises they contained. The Lithuanian ruler answered rather evasively that he was awaiting the Pope's legate and "What I have in my heart, that God knows and I myself."[24]

Lack of a firm commitment on the question of baptism did not prevent the conclusion of the peace treaty, which does not mention Lithuanian conversion at all and is concerned with purely practical matters such as freedom of the roads and of trade. But the peace was only with the Livonian branch of the Teutonic Order—the main body, based in Prussia, would not adhere to the provisions of this treaty until it was ratified by the papal legates finally sent in 1324.[25]

These legates stopped in Riga, sent envoys to Gediminas, and immediately reconfirmed the peace treaty, warning the Teutonic Order not to violate it.[26] After hearing this welcome news from the legates' representatives, Gediminas (according to the envoys' report) "totally confirmed the tenor of the letters except baptism," disingenuously claiming that to be an obedient son in the lap of the Church and to receive the faith of Christ did not mean conversion (after all, remarked Gediminas, he called all older men "Father" as a mark of respect, so why not the Pope?). All misunderstandings were blamed on the hapless friar who had acted as scribe, and the Lithuanian ruler shouted, "If I ever had this in mind, may the Devil baptize me!"[27]

While the envoys evince in their report amazement and consternation at what they construe as Gediminas's change of mind (they clearly reject the contrived excuse of scribal error), it is interesting that neither the papal legates nor the Pope reacted by revoking the truce.[28] Despite the grumbling of the Teutonic Knights against a peace they considered forced upon them by the papacy,[29] and despite infractions by both sides, the truce probably stayed in effect for four years.[30] Gediminas unabashedly cited the papal confirmation of it in his complaints about truce infractions.[31]

Gediminas's letters have provoked much discussion among scholars: were they a diplomatic maneuver to secure a much-needed peace treaty or a real attempt to negotiate the baptism of the Lithuanians?[32] In the most recent monograph on Gediminas, S. C. Rowell suggests convincingly that the Lithuanian ruler adopted a "wait and see" attitude after initiating deliberately ambiguous proposals, and then decided that he had gained enough without baptism and that the Pope was not going to take sufficient action against the Teutonic Order to make Lithuanian conversion worthwhile.[33]

Whatever Gediminas's original intentions—and the sure reconstruction of states of mind, difficult enough for any historian, is impossible in Lithuanian history, where so many original sources have been lost—certain facts are clear. Baptism was dangerous: Gediminas was aware of the story of the first Lithuanian king, Mindaugas, who had accepted baptism but had been forced to apostatize and had eventually been murdered.[34] Conversion would not completely halt the attacks of the Teutonic Knights, who (as Gediminas pointed out) had not balked at attacking Catholic Riga yet would rob the Lithuanians of future opportunities to facilitate negotiations with Christians by flirting with the idea of baptism.[35]

Perhaps more light can be shed on Gediminas's attitude by closer study of letters he issued on May 26, 1323 addressed to the councilors of Lübeck and other North Baltic towns of the Hanseatic League and to the Franciscans and Dominicans of those towns. Most documents issued by Lithuanian rulers have been lost, but these letters were copied by a notary in Lübeck and have been preserved by the Teutonic Order in its archives. They offer a rare glimpse into a pagan's correspondence.

To Dominicans and Franciscans, the Lithuanian ruler writes that he has sent envoys to the Pope and has heard that the papal legates are coming soon. Baptism is not specifically mentioned, although a desire to convert is implied. There is no request for missionaries or religious instruction. The Dominicans are simply asked to spread the message that Gediminas invites soldiers, merchants, and artisans to his lands.[36] There is not even a specific invitation for Dominicans to come to Lithuania, although in the letter to the Hansa townsmen (see extract following), Gediminas promises to gather in Lithuania friars of both mendicant orders. The Franciscans are told that Gediminas has built two churches for them, one in Vilnius and one in Novgorodok. He asks that "for these this year four brothers knowing Polish, Semgallian and Prussian be ordained for us, of the sort who are now and were in the past" (in Lithuania?).[37] This is usually interpreted as a call for new missionaries[38] but may be only a request for renewal of already existing appointments.

Gediminas's letter to the Hansa towns is even more practical and bears looking at in more detail:[39]

[Gediminas greets the councilors, merchants, and artisans of Lubeck, Rostock, Stralsund, Greifswald, Stettin (Szczecin), and Gotland]:

" . . . For a long time now, you have crossed our borders without any inspection in order to visit Novgorod and Pskov. We have permitted all for the sake of future benefits. . . .

Our forefathers sent you their envoys and letters, opened their land to you, not one of your people came. . . . If they [our forefathers] promised one thing, God willing we will do doubly as much, the more so because we have sent letters to our father, the most holy lord Pope, for union with the Church of God and are awaiting with indescribable impatience the coming of his legates. . . .

Once you have taken counsel about it among yourselves, and sent to us on behalf of all of you high-ranking true envoys . . . we will ordain such a mutual peace, as Christians have never known.

We will assemble bishops, priests, religious of the Dominican and Franciscan orders, whose lives are praiseworthy and upright: we do not want those to come, who make their monasteries a refuge for bandits [refers to Cistercians selling an abbey to the Teutonic Order]. . . .

Moreover, we grant as our royal gift now in the present charter, that our land is free from duties or tolls, exactions or extra charges . . . to all merchants, knights, vassals (to whom I will grant income, to each according to his status), to craftsmen of all sorts, namely to smiths, cobblers, carpenters, stonecutters, saltmakers, bakers, silversmiths, crossbowmen, fishermen, and others of whatever condition in life, let them come with their children, wives, and livestock. . . .

To farmers wishing to enter and stay in our kingdom, we grant and concede that they may cultivate freely for ten years without taxes, and meanwhile let them be exempt from all royal work duties. . . .

Let the civil law of Riga be used by all the people. . . .

So that we might render you more sure and secure, we have had erected two churches for the Franciscans, one in our royal city called Vilnius and the other in Novgorodok, and a third for the Dominicans, so that everyone may worship God according to his rite. . . ."

[Gediminas then notes that he has appended his seal to show] "that this our grant of gifts should remain unchangeable. Know this, that we have sent the same seal to our lord and Holy Father. . . . We repudiate those who contradict this seal as malicious destroyers of the Faith, heretics and liars."

[The letter ends with assurances that Gediminas will keep his word, instructions on the safest route to Lithuania, and a request that recipients copy the text and send it on to another town.]

Clearly, material rather than spiritual concerns dominate here. Mention of a desire for "union with the Church" and of the imminent arrival of papal legates establishes Gediminas's friendliness toward Christianity and Christians. Overtures to the Pope are linked to invitations to immigrants: Hansa merchants have been traveling through Lithuania for years, but previous attempts to get them to settle have failed. Gediminas will do more than his predecessors because he has sent letters to the Pope. The stress is on material inducements to soldiers, merchants, artisans, and farmers. Churches built in Lithuania are mentioned only as one of the comforts of home, as it were, provided so that every Christian might feel more "secure" and "worship God according to his rite." This is the logical place for Gediminas to point out that he plans to join that rite, but no such assurance is given. Even the invitation to bishops and priests is limited to those who do not displease Gediminas.

Privileges and tax incentives are promised in Lithuania to professionals and skilled labor: merchants, fighting men, craftsmen, farmers—and priests, so long as they stick to their job and do not create problems for Gediminas! The Pope has a "job" as well: his prestige is supposed to safeguard Gediminas's seal and make heretics out of the Teutonic Knights who had broken this seal on previous letters.[40]

At least some of the Lithuanian requests were in fact granted. Lübeck and Stralsund discussed the letters in council.[41] All three letters were copied in Lübeck, probably as a prelude to being sent farther, and one copy, now lost, was put in the town archives.[42] The Franciscans, at least, were ready to accept Gediminas' invitation, petitioning in 1323–24 for papal permission to build houses in Estonia and Prussia to serve as bases and halfway houses for missionaries traveling to Lithuania.[43] The Pope for various political reasons chose to ignore the lack of real conversion and threw his support behind Gediminas's peace treaty.[44] Lithuanians had at least briefly won Catholic support without conversion and its attendant dangers. Flirtation with baptism would prove a useful technique again and again in the coming decades.

Algirdas: Baptism Negotiations as Tool and Weapon

During the reign of Algirdas [Olgerd] (1345–77), several unsuccessful attempts were made to negotiate the conversion of Lithuania.[45] Here we will review only one set of negotiations, which seemed to offer the most hope of success and which bear some resemblance to the negotiations of 1323, when Algirdas was already a grown man and quite capable of profiting from example.

In April of 1358, perhaps at the urging of Pope Innocent VI, whose attention had just been directed to the problem of Lithuanian conversion by King Casimir the Great of Poland,[46] Emperor Charles IV wrote "to the Lithuanian princes" inviting them to accept baptism and sending as his envoy Henry von Plauen.[47] The sequence of events, often confused by modern scholars, is quite clear from many sources.[48]

Lithuanians replied quickly and favorably: in July of the same year, according to the chronicle of Henry of Rebdorf, "the pagan king of Lithuania sent his brother to the lord Emperor Charles, who was then in Nuremberg, stating that he and his land wished to receive the Christian faith ("recipere fidem christianam").[49]

If Rebdorf is actually quoting the words of the Lithuanian ruler (and we have no way of knowing this), it may be significant that the same phrase ("recipere fidem") is used to signify conversion as Gediminas used in his letters to Pope John XXII.[50] Of course, this is a common enough expression to be coincidental, but it may also reflect a use of Gediminas's letters to the Pope as models by his son Algirdas.

Rebdorf's information that Lithuanians came to the emperor's court is confirmed by a second imperial letter to Lithuania of July 21, 1358.[51] It states that Emperor Charles IV had sent Heinrich von Plauen to the Lithuanian prince and his brothers and they had "given hope that they would accept the Christian faith," sending their own envoys to accompany von Plauen back to the emperor's court. Henry von Plauen is identified by Herman of Wartberg, a chronicler of the Teutonic Order, as a defector from that Order,[52] and one document does mention a brother "Heinrich von Plawen" in Prussia eight years earlier.[53] Wartberg blames "Plawe" for giving the emperor the idea of negotiating with the Lithuanians for a baptism which would put the Teutonic Knights out of business, but this may simply be a way of deflecting blame from Charles IV, with whom the Teutonic Order could not quarrel openly.[54]

Many sources agree that Charles IV then appointed high-ranking envoys to Lithuania.[55] According to the emperor's letter in July, they carried an invitation for the ruler of Lithuania to send one of his brothers to Bohemia, where the emperor would await him.[56] We know that in November of 1358 Charles IV indeed went to Wroclaw [Breslau], by then part of Bohemia, and stayed there until February of 1359, possibly accompanied by King Casimir of Poland.[57] The chronicler Rebdorf says he was awaiting "the pagan king of Lithuania," who had promised to be baptized in that city at Christmas.[58]

Led by the Archbishop of Prague, as befitted a religious mission, the imperial envoys arrived in Prussia by November 19.[59] Grumbling about the expense and trouble, Teutonic Knights escorted them to the Lithuanians.[60]

Suddenly, the Lithuanians changed their tune, just as Gediminas had done. Chronicle accounts of this episode differ but present a coherent picture: to the emperor's envoys and perhaps in a letter, the Lithuanian ruler, Algirdas, at the end of 1358 set conditions for conversion which do not seem to have been mentioned before. The Teutonic Order should give up to the Lithuanians Baltic lands it had conquered and castles it had built — the most detailed account by Wartberg delineates an area reaching from Konigsberg to Riga, including half of Prussia and Livonia. According to Wartberg, the Lithuanians even demanded that the Teutonic Knights move to the Russian steppes to protect Christendom against the Mongols, without gaining any jurisdiction over the Rus peoples because "All of Rus ought to belong to the Lithuanians."[61]

Negotiations ended abruptly. The Teutonic Order was a valuable imperial ally in the Italian wars,[62] and the emperor could not allow its military and financial base to be destroyed.

Oddly enough, the fantastic Lithuanian demands of 1358, made by a prince with decades of experience in negotiating with other rulers and with the Teutonic Order and possessing a reputation for unusual craftiness,[63] have been accepted at face value by many historians.[64] Algirdas is portrayed as ready to receive baptism if only the necessary conditions were met, and naive enough to believe that the Teutonic Order would simply pack its bags and quietly vacate its lands.

Yet like his father Gediminas in 1323, Algirdas had already benefited from the months when baptism negotiations were being arranged. In the summer of 1358, King Casimir of Poland traveled to the Polish-Lithuanian border, accompanied by many important officials. As H. Paszkiewicz pointed out, he quite possibly was conducting secret negotiations with the Lithuanians.[65] In early August of 1358—that is, shortly after the appearance of Lithuanian envoys at the imperial court in July—Lithuanian princes signed a border treaty with Ziemowit III of Mazovia, vassal of the king of Poland.[66] This agreement left the Poles free to attempt recovery of conquered Mazovian lands from the Teutonic Order without fear of infringing on Lithuanian claims and having to fight on two fronts.[67] Like the peace made by Gediminas in 1323, this treaty may have continued in force even after the Lithuanian refusal to accept baptism.[68]

In 1359 Algirdas's daughter married Casimir's grandson, a union of two close relatives (the groom's grandmother was also the bride's aunt) for which papal dispensation was petitioned and granted as an encouragement to Lithuanian conversion.[69] Although Poland had been at war with the Lithuanians since 1340 over areas of present-day Ukraine, after this marriage Casimir mounted no major offensive on this front until 1366.[70]

The Prussian branch of the Teutonic Order, which at the beginning of 1358 had joined in a devastating invasion of Samogitia, does not seem to have made war on the Lithuanians from the beginning of baptism negotiations in the spring of 1358 until 1360.[71] Perhaps the truce that the emperor's envoys were supposed to arrange between the Teutonic Knights of Prussia and the Lithuanians was in fact secretly signed and kept for two years.

Algirdas would have found peace with Poland and Prussia especially useful in 1358–59, since Mongol power was weakening in Russia after the death of Khan Janibeg in 1357. Lithuania seized this opportunity to expand eastward greatly.[72]

Whatever they had intended, in 1358, as in 1323, the Lithuanians had achieved the respite they needed from constant attack simply by undertaking negotiations for baptism, without having to undergo the risks actual acceptance of Christianity would bring. On the other hand, the Polish king and the Teutonic Order, both recently reprimanded by the Pope for secret treaties with the "infidel" Lithuanians in 1355–56, won the opportunity to make legitimate truces and agreements with the pagans when they were ostensibly considering baptism.[73]

Most probably, the Lithuanians deliberately prolonged baptism negotiations in 1358 while other agreements, advantageous to all parties, were being made. Then negotiations were broken off by the expedient of new demands which were deliberately meant to be insulting, or at least were interpreted that way by the Teutonic Knights, who later called the whole episode an insulting jest.[74] Like Gediminas's letters to German cities and friars, in which he could advertise the advantages of Lithuania and complain about its blockade by the Teutonic Order, the negotiations of 1358 were a sort of advertisement—in this case of optimal Lithuanian land claims. Since negotiations had broken down over these, useful propaganda was provided for Lithuanian complaints that the Teutonic Knights valued their lands more than the prospect of converting pagans. Once again, the question of conversion provides a convenient cover for varied diplomatic maneuvers by Christians and pagans alike.

Gediminas had declared to envoys sent to him in 1323 who asked about his intentions concerning baptism: "I permit any man to live in my land according to his customs and his Faith."[75] This view of the Christian faith as an ethnic custom does not seem to have shocked the medieval Christians with whom the Lithuanians dealt. Vague hints of conversion were sometimes an admission ticket to serious negotiations for peace, but it was not considered necessary, even by the papacy, for the pagans actually to accept Christianity before concluding mutually advantageous agreements with Christians. For Gediminas and Algirdas, retention of paganism provided a useful diplomatic tool and weapon, without exposing them to the danger of sharing the baptized Mindaugas's fate. Little wonder that the two most powerful rulers in Lithuania's history were unwilling to abandon the paganism that allowed them to use promises of conversion as a means of preserving their power and independence.

Abbreviations for Sources Used

CEV   *Codex epistolaris Vitoldi*, ed. A. Prochaska, *Monumenta media aevi historica* VI (Cracow: Academia Literarum Cracoviensis, 1882).

GL   *Gedimino Laiskai* [Letters of Gediminas], ed. V. Pasuta and I. Stal (Vilnius: Mintis, 1966).

LUB   *Liv-, Esth-und Curländisches Urkundenbuch*, Abteilung I, vols. 1–6 (Reval and Riga, 1853–73; reprint, Aalen: Scientia, 1967–74).

MGH   *Monumenta Germaniae Historica, Scriptores Rerum Germanicarum.* 32 vols. (Hanover-Leipzig, 1826–1934), n.s. 12 vols. (Berlin and Weimar, 1922–).

MPV   *Monumenta Poloniae Vaticana,* 3 vols. (Cracow, 1913–14), vol. 3, J. Ptasnik, *Analecta Vaticana* (Cracow: Academia Literarum Cracoviensis, 1914).

Napiersky   K. E. Napiersky, ed., *Rusko-Livonskie Akty/ Russisch-Livländische Urkunden* (St. Petersburg: Buchdrukerei der Kaiserlichen Akademie der Wissenschaften, 1868).

PSRL   *Polnoe Sobranie Russkikh Letopisei* (St. Petersburg and Moscow: Arkheograficheskaia Kommmissiia & Akademia Nauka, 1843–1965).

Raczynski   E. Raczynski, ed., *Codex Diplomaticus Lithuaniae* (Wroclaw: Sumptibus Sigismundi Schletter, 1845).

SRP   *Scriptores Rerum Prussicarum,* vols. 1–3 (Leipzig, 1863, 1866; reprint, Frankfurt am Main: Minerva, 1965).

VMPL   A. Theiner, ed., *Vetera Monumenta Poloniae et Lithuaniae,* vol. 1 (Rome: Typis Vaticanis, 1860; reprint, Osnabrück: Otto Zeller, 1969).

Notes

1. K. M. Setton, R. L. Wolff, and H. W. Hazard, *History of the Crusades* (Madison: University of Wisconsin Press, 1975), 3:3–26.

2. Recent works in English on this crusade: E. Christiansen, *The Northern Crusades* (London and Minneapolis: Macmillan and University of Minnesota Press, 1980); N. Housley, *The Later Crusades* (Oxford: Oxford University Press, 1992), 322–75; Jonathan Riley-Smith, *The Crusades, A Short History* (London: Athlone, 1987), 161–65, 212–15; Setton, Wolff, and Hazard, *History of the Crusades,* 545–85; M. Giedroyc, "The Arrival of Christianity in Lithuania," *Oxford Slavonic Papers* n.s. 18 (1985): 1–30.

3. W. Paravicini, *Die Preussenreisen des europäischen Adels,* 2 vols. (Sigmaringen: Jan Thorbecke, 1989–95); V. Matuzova, "Anglai Prusijoje," *Lietuvos Istorijos Metrastis* (1989): 5–15.

4. E. Gudavicius, "Del Lietuvos valstybes kurimosi centro ir laiko," *Lietuvos TSR Mokslu Akademijos Darbai* Serija A (1983): 61–70; M. Giedroyc, "The Rulers of Thirteenth Century Lithuania," *Oxford Slavonic Papers* n.s. 17 (1984): 5–9.

5. Vaisvilkas (Voishelk) (r. 1264–67) was Eastern Orthodox but had converted long before he inherited the throne.

6. Z. Ivinskis, "Mindaugas und seine Krone," and M. Hellmann, "Der Deutsche Orden und die Königskrönung des Mindaugas," both in *Zeitschrift für Ostforschung* 3 (1954): 360–96.

7. *LUB,* vol. 1, cols. 312–13, no. 243.

8. Grants: *LUB,* vol. 1, cols. 333, 371, 382, 394, 436, 442, 449, 462, nos. 252, 286–87, 294, 308, 342, 347, 354, 363. Order still citing these in 1409: *CEV,* p. 996. On authenticity, K. Maleczynski, "W sprawie autentycznosci dokumentow Mendoga," *Ateneum Wilenskie* 11 (1936): 1–56; Gudavicius, *Kryziaus karai Pabaltijyje ir Lietuva XIII amziuje* (Vilnius, 1989), 122, 133.

9. Controversy over apostasy is summed up in H. Paszkiewicz, *Jagiellonowie a Moskwa* (Warsaw: Fundusz Kultury Narodowej, 1933), 92–100, and J. Jakstas, "Lietuvos krikstas," *Aidai* no. 1 (1987): 4–6.

10. Personal feuds: S. C. Rowell, "Between Lithuania and Rus': Dovmont-Timofey of Pskov," *Oxford Slavonic Papers* n.s. 25 (1992): 4. One of Mindaugas's murderers urges him to apostatize and kill Christians: *Die Livlandische Reimchronik,* ed. L. Meyer (Paderborn, 1876; reprint, Hildesheim: Georg Olms, 1963), lines 6347–6460. Cf. chronicle of Hermann von Wartberg, *SRP,* 2:42: Mandaugas expels Christians.

11. S. C. Rowell, "Pagans, Peace and the Pope, 1322–1324: Lithuania in the Centre of European Diplomacy," *Archivum Historiae Pontificiae* 28 (1990): 63–98; A. Nikzentaitis, "Lietuvos . . . uzsienio politikos veiksmu programa," *Lituanistica* 3 (1990): 31–40.

12. H. Jablonowski, *Westrussland zwischen Wilna und Moskau* (Leiden: E. J. Brill, 1955; reprint, 1961), 11–13; S. C. Rowell, *Lithuania Ascending: A Pagan Empire within East-Central Europe, 1295–1345* (Cambridge: Cambridge University Press, 1994), 82–117.

13. Riga and Gediminas: *LUB,* vol. 6, col. 466, no. 3068; cols. 472–77, no. 3072; *GL,* nos. 7, 15. On sword as Pope, see W. Urban, "The Sense of Humor among the Teutonic Knights," *Illinois Quarterly* 42 (1979): 45. On trade, R. Mazeika, "Of Cabbages and Knights: Trade and Trade Treaties with the Infidel on the Northern Frontier, 1200–1390," *Journal of Medieval History* 20 (1994): 63–76.

14. *LUB,* vol. 6, col. 479; *GL,* p. 129. Yet Gediminas allowed other religions only if they did not insult him or his pagan gods. He executed two missionaries who enraged a marketplace crowd in Vilnius by urging abandonment of "false and superstitious gods": *Analecta Franciscana* (Quaracchi: Collegium S. Bonaventura, 1897), 3:535–36; R. Mazeika and S. C. Rowell, "Zelatores maxima: Pope John XXII, Archbishop Frederick of Riga and the Baltic Mission, 1305–1340," *Archivum Historiae Pontificiae* 31 (1993): 59–60.

15. Churches and Franciscans: *LUB,* vol. 6, cols. 468, 480, nos. 3069, 3073, vol. 2, col. 146; *GL,* pp. 31, 45, 53–55. Metr. of Lith.: J. Meyendorff, *Byzantium and the Rise of Russia* (Cambridge: Cambridge University Press, 1981), 95; Rowell, *Lithuania Ascending,* 155–56.

16. S. C. Rowell, "Pious Princesses or the Daughters of Belial: Pagan Lithuanian Dynastic Diplomacy," *Medieval Prosopography* 15, 1 (1994): 3–79.

17. On Lithuanian religion: M. Gimbutas, "The Pre-Christian Religion of Lithuania," in *La Cristianizzazione della Lituania* (Vatican City: Libreria Editrice Vaticana, 1989), 13–26; W. Mannhardt, *Letto-Preussische Götterlehre* (Riga: Lettische Literarische Gesellschaft, 1936).

18. Gediminas reports writing to Pope John XXII in a letter to Lübeck and other towns dated January 25, 1323: *LUB,* vol. 6, col. 467, no. 3069, and *GL,* no. 3, p. 29. Papal reply: *VMPL,* p. 193.

19. Rowell, *Lithuania Ascending*, 197; papal letter, *VMPL*, p. 193, no. 293.

20. ". . . patri nostro sanctissimo sub catholice fidei receptione direxisse, cuius responsum novimus." *GL*, no. 3, p. 29; *LUB*, vol. 6, col. 467, no. 3069.

21. R. Mazeika, "The Context of Pope John XXII's Letters to Gediminas," in *Gedimino laiku Lietuva ir jos kaimynai* (Klaipeda Universiteto Vakaru Lietuvos ir Prusijos Istorijos Centras, in press); Mazeika and Rowell, "Zelatores," 59–60.

22. *LUB*, vol. 6, col. 467, no. 3069, vol. 2, cols. 139–46; Raczynski, 27–32; *GL*, nos. 2–5, 6, 10. The *GL* publication is easily available but has many errors: P. Rabikauskas, "Commentary on the 'Letters of Gediminas,'" *Lituanus* 15, 4 (1969): 47–54 (includes English translations of some letters). New critical edition: S. C. Rowell, *Chartularium Lithuaniae* (Vilnius, in press).

23. *GL*, pp. 65–75, no. 8. *LUB*, vol. 2, col. 150, no. 693.

24. *LUB*, vol. 6, no. 3070, col. 469. My thanks to Janet Ritch of the University of Toronto for her help with medieval German translation. Cf. ibid., nos. 3071, 3072.

25. As Rowell points out: *Lithuania Ascending*, 214–15.

26. *LUB*, vol. 2, col. 184, no. 708; Rowell, *Chartularium*.

27. Report of the envoys of the papal legates: *LUB*, vol. 6, col. 479, no. 3073; *GL*, no. 14, p. 127; Rowell, *Chartularium*, no. 51.

28. Envoys' reaction: *GL*, 135–45. Gediminas writes as if peace still in effect: *LUB*, vol. 6, col. 484.

29. Teutonic Order chroniclers Peter Dusburg (*SRP*, 1:191) and Herman of Wartberg (*SRP*, 2:61–62).

30. Paszkiewicz, *Jagiellonowie*, 279–80; Rowell, "Pagans, Peace and the Pope," 92. Infractions: *GL*, nos. 16, 17; Dusburg, *SRP*, 190, 192.

31. *GL*, p. 167; *LUB*, vol. 6, col. 484.

32. J. Jakstas, "Vokieciu Ordinas ir Lietuva Vytenio ir Gedimino metu," *Senove* 2 (1936): 5–45; K. Forstreuter, *Deutschland und Litauen im Mittelalter* (Cologne: Bohlau Verlag, 1962), 43–60; H. Spliet, *Die Briefe Gedimins and Ein Quellenkritische Ubersicht zu den Gediminbriefen* (Sinsheim: G. Beckersche Buchdruck, 1953, 1959); Paszkiewicz, *Jagiellonowie*, 266–68; S. C. Rowell, "The Letters of Gediminas: 'Gemachte Lüge'?" *Jahrbücher für Geschichte Osteuropas* 41 (1993); A. Nikzentaitis, "Del Gedimino laisku autentiskumo," *Lietuvos TSR Mokslu Akademijos Darbai* Serija A 101 (1987): 92–99 and (1988): 66–76.

33. Rowell, *Lithuania Ascending*, 211, 224.

34. Gediminas mentions Mindaugas: *GL*, p. 23; *LUB*, vol. 2, col. 140.

35. *GL*, p. 129; *LUB*, vol. 6, col. 479: attacks on Riga mentioned by Gediminas.

36. My thanks to S. C. Rowell for providing me with a copy of his new critical edition of this document from *Chartularium Lithuaniae*, now in press. Cf. Raczynski, 27–32; *LUB*, vol. 2, nos. 691, 688, 689, 690; *GL*, nos. 4–6.

37. Raczynski, p. 30; *GL*, p. 55.

38. Nikzentaitis, "Del Gedimino laisku," 95; Rowell, *Lithuania Ascending*, 207.

39. Raczynski, 28–30; *GL*, no. 4; corrected by Rowell, critical edition.

40. Cf. letters to Dominicans and Franciscans: *GL*, pp. 49, 57; *LUB*, vol. 2, cols. 142, 144; Raczynski, 28, 31.

41. Raczynski, 27, 30; *LUB*, vol. 2, cols. 146, 147; cf. Rowell, *Chartularium*.

42. Lübeck's copy was lost or destroyed during World War II: Rowell, "Gemachte Lüge," excursus D.

43. Ptasnik, *MPV*, vol. 3, no. 177, p. 235.

44. See note 21.

45. Mazeika, "The Relations of Grand Prince Algirdas with Eastern and Western Christians," in *Cristianizzazione* (as in note 17), 63–84; M. Giedroyc, "The Arrival of Christianity in Lithuania," *Oxford Slavonic Papers* n.s. 22 (1989): 37–52; A. Nikzentaitis, "Die friedliche Periode . . . und das Problem der Christianisierung Litauens," *Jahrbücher für Geschichte Osteuropas* nf 41 (1993): 1–22.

46. Ptasnik, *MPV*, vol. 3, no. 375, p. 357.

47. Critical edition: H. Grundmann, "Das Schreiben Kaiser Karls IV. an die Heidnischen Litauer-Fursten 1358," *Folia Diplomatica* 1 (1971): 89–103. Cf. K. Conrad, ed., *Preussisches Urkundenbuch [PrUB]*, vol. 5, bk. 2 (Marburg, 1973), no. 642, p. 361.

48. Sources viewed as contradictory and unclear: K. Conrad, "Litauen, der Deutsche Orden und Karl IV," *Zeitschrift für Ostforschung* 21 (1972): 24–26; A. Nikzentaitis, "Lietuvos diplomatijos veikla," *Lituanistica* (1991): 3–11.

49. *MGH, Scriptores*, vol. 1, *Die Chronik Heinrichs Taube von Selbach* (Berlin, 1922), pp. 112–13.

50. *GL*, pp. 27, 95; *VMPL*, no. 293, p. 193.

51. J. Karwasinska, "Zlote Bulle Karola IV w sprawie chrztu Litwy," *Cultus et Cognitio: Studia z dziejow sredniowiecznej kultury* (Warsaw: Polska Akademija Nauk, 1976), 233–49.

52. *SRP*, 2:79.

53. B. Jähnig, "Der Deutsche Orden und Karl IV," *Blätter für deutsche Landesgeschichte* 114 (1978): 135; *PrUB*, vol. 4, no. 553, p. 504.

54. *SRP*, 2:79. Evidence is lacking for Conrad's theory that von Plauen was divulging secret baptism negotiations between the Lithuanians and the Teutonic Order (Conrad, "Litauen," 34). "Plawe . . . divulgavit" may mean only "Plauen spread the rumor."

55. Chronicles of Rebdorf, and Wartberg, also the July letter of Charles IV (notes 49, 51, 52 above); *PrUB*, vol. 5, bk. 2, nos. 690, 691.

56. Karwasinska, "Zlote Bulle," 242.

57. Conrad, "Litauen," 24; J. F. Böhmer and A. Huber, *Regesta Imperii*, vol. 8, *Die Regesten des Kaiserreichs unter Kaiser* (Innsbruck: Wagnerischen Universitäts Buchhandlung, 1877), nos. 2865–2913.

58. *MGH, Scriptores*, 1:113.

59. *PrUB*, vol. 5, bk. 2, no. 691.

60. Wartberg, *SRP*, 2:79–80.

61. Ibid.; cf. Rebdorf, *MGH, Scriptores*, 1:113; Henry of Diessenhoven, *SRP*, 3:420.

62. *PrUB*, vol. 5, bk. 1, nos. 292, 339, 386–87.

63. R. Mazeika, "The Role of Pagan Lithuania in Roman Catholic and Greek Orthodox Religious Diplomacy" (Ph.D. dissertation, Fordham University, 1987), 36–78, 110–66. Russian chronicles, even those hostile to Algirdas, report that he had "great intellect and self-restraint" (*PSRL*, 18:118; 15, col. 117; 5:236.

64. V. Gidziunas, "The Introduction of Christianity to Lithuania," *Lituanus* 13 (1957): 12; A. Kucinskas, *Kestutis-Lietuviu tautos gynejas* (Marijampole, 1938; reprint, Vilnius: Mokslas, 1988), 137; Z. Kaczmarczyk, *Kazimierz Wielki* (Warsaw: Wyd. S. Arcta, 1948), 171–72; Nikzentaitis, "Die friedliche Periode," 5–8, 21–22.

65. H. Paszkiewicz, *Polityka ruska Kazimierza Wielkiego* (Warsaw: Instytut Popierania Nauki Warszawa, 1925), 199–200.

66. T. Lubomirski, ed., *Kodeks dyplomatyczny ksiestwa mazowieckiego* (Warsaw: Druk Gazety Polskiej, 1863), no. 80, pp. 72–74.

67. G. Rhode, *Die Ostgrenze Polens* (Cologne and Graz: Bohlau Verlag, 1955), 1:217, argues that neither Mazovia nor Lithuania in 1358 held all the lands named in the treaty—some were in territories of the Order. Thus the treaty was an agreement on which lands Poles and Lithuanians would try to conquer.

68. Algirdas's relatives helping to defend Polish fortress: *Codex Diplomaticus Prussicus*, vol. 3, ed. J. Voigt (Königsberg, 1848), no. 87, noted by Rhode, *Ostgrenze*, 217.

69. *MPV*, vol. 3, p. 371.

70. Kucinskas, *Kestutis*, 110; Rhode, *Ostgrenze*, 199.

71. Herman of Wartberg, *SRP*, 2:79–80; Wigand of Marburg, *SRP*, 2:524.

72. R. Batura, *Lietuva tautu kovoje pries Aukso Orda* (Vilnius: Mintis, 1975), 232–34; Jablonowski, *Westrussland*, 13–15.

73. Papal reprimands: *VMPL*, nos. 769, 776, pp. 577, 581.

74. *CEV*, p. 997.

75. *LUB*, vol. 6, col. 469.

9

✠

Conversion vs. Baptism?
European Missionaries in Asia in the Thirteenth and Fourteenth Centuries

James D. Ryan

European missionaries entered the fields of the Lord in the thirteenth and fourteenth centuries in unprecedented numbers, to convert all mankind, thereby to usher in the final days and God's reign on earth. They were active on every flank of Europe, even in Asia, where the faith was carried *ad Tartaros* (to the Tartars). That effort was different from prior and contemporary medieval missions. Most evangelization had taken place on the borders of emerging European civilization, in circumstances which encouraged acculturation between contiguous communities, to bring peoples living adjacent to, or in the midst of, established Christian communities into the fellowship of faith.[1] Evangelists to eastern Asia, however, advanced into a non-Christian world, as in Apostolic times, when the first missionaries took up the gospel challenge: "Go, therefore, and make all nations your disciples: baptize them in the name of the Father and of the Son and of the Holy Spirit" (Matt. 28:19).

The problems they encountered in Asia ought to have made missionaries reevaluate the meaning of conversion and how it should be fostered. Not surprisingly, reports from the missions and instructions sent to Asia do provide insights into what missionaries (and the larger society that sent them) thought they were about. Unfortunately, the few surviving sources convey only the outline of this mission. Lacunae in the record notwithstanding, the mission ad Tartaros well illustrates the diverse and sometimes contradictory facets of the medieval movement to convert all mankind. Like their counterparts closer to Europe, missionaries in Mongol lands usually relied on preaching and personal example to win converts. But because they were embarked on high adventure and incredibly difficult travels, they improvised boldly in the exotic environment Mongol patronage provided. The records suggest that, as missionaries were making converts in Asia, they and the church that sent them were inventing the foreign mission, laying foundations for future evangelization.

A recurring theme in missionary reports from Asia is the evangelists' success in conferring baptism, sometimes in questionable circumstances. Perhaps to justify their heroic efforts, missionaries report thousands of baptisms, but give scant evidence that recipients experienced meaningful conversion. Inner conversion should have been a prime concern, even for those working in Tartar lands. Canon lawyers and university doctors had discussed the respective roles of God and man in the processes of redemption for more than a century, refining conceptualizations of free will and grace. Commentaries and *Summae* mandated catechesis before the administration of baptism, insisting that no one be christened unless there was a reasonable expectation that they would thereafter lead a Christian life. Speculation about what ought to be done with neophytes seems to have had little impact in the mission field, however, where converts were being baptized. Reports from eastern missions, in particular, leave the clear impression that pagans desiring the sacrament were speedily brought to the font. If baptism was performed casually in Asia, with scant instruction and little expectation that recipients would undergo a lasting change of life, this would have been contrary to accepted European practice. This concern provides a central focus for the following review of missionaries' actions and intentions in Asia in the thirteenth and fourteenth centuries.

The Beginning of the Mission to the Mongols

A papal-sponsored mission to the Tartars began in 1245, after they stormed into eastern Europe, when Innocent IV (1243–54) dispatched diplomatic probes to the Mongol khans.[2] The Franciscan friar John of Plano Carpini, one of these emissaries, was in Mongolia at the coronation of Great Khan Güyük (1246–48). He later wrote a *History of the Mongols,* reporting on their lands and customs and how their hordes might be resisted.[3] Dominican-led embassies, launched at the same time, made contact with lower-ranking Mongol leaders in territories adjacent to the Middle East.[4] These early envoys carried letters urging the khans to convert, but their chief aim was to open political dialogue and assess the Mongol threat. A religious mission began almost immediately, however, because a Mongol prince, Buri, had carried German Christians into Central Asia as captives in the 1240s. Their plight moved William of Rubruck and others to undertake missions in which political concerns played little or no part.[5] Rubruck is unique among such early missionaries because he left us a highly personal report, his *Itinerarium* (translated by P. Jackson as *The Mission of Friar William of Rubruck*), detailing his route, observations, and activities as he traveled in Asia from late spring 1253 until early 1255.[6]

In the report Rubruck makes clear that preaching salvation and comforting Christian captives were his prime desires. He denied political purpose as he set out for the east. "I stated publicly in a sermon at St. Sophia . . . that I was not [King Louis IX's] envoy . . ., but that I was going among these unbelievers in accordance with [the Franciscan] Rule" (MR 66–67). On his way he inquired concerning "Buri's German slaves," making "numerous enquiries about them at [several Mongol] courts" (MR 144). Although he later referred to them as his "chief reason for going" into Asia, circumstances prevented him from ever reaching them (MR 226). Some historians have pictured Rubruck a royal envoy because the *Itinerarium* was a report to King Louis IX, but he was not. When he arrived in southern Russia in search of Sartaq, a son of Batu Khan reputed to have received baptism, Rubruck "took good care at no point to say that I was [the French king's] envoy" (MR 97).[7] He later reiterated his missionary purpose to Khan Möngke (1251–59): "We are not fighting men, and it is our desire that the world should be ruled over by those who would govern it most justly, in accordance with the will of God. It is our task to teach men how to live in accord with God's will, and for that purpose we came into these parts" (MR 238). Even as he was ordered to return west he insisted that the khan's letter, which he was asked to carry to Louis IX, clearly state his station: "Originally they referred to us [in the letter] as . . . envoys, whereupon I told them 'Do not call us envoys.' . . . I told them to strike out the word 'envoys' and to call us monks or priests" (MR 250).

At this juncture circumstances militated against the development of a religious mission in Asia. Plano Carpini and Rubruck noted the good order which the Mongols maintained, their general religious tolerance, and the influence of Christian sects, especially Nestorianism, among them, but neither saw Asia as ripe for proselytization. Rubruck twice remarked on the alien nature of that milieu: "When we first came among these barbarians, . . . I felt . . . that I was entering another world" (MR 70–71, 97). He also found the Tartars inhospitable: "in no locality . . . were we given enough for our needs . . . [and] it was seldom that we found anything there for sale" (MR 252). Even more crucial was Mongol unwillingness, at this period, to endorse missionary efforts. After agreeing to carry his letter west, Rubruck asked Khan Möngke himself for permission to serve the religious needs of German slaves: "'they need a priest . . ., and I should be happy to settle with them. . . . [W]ith your consent I should return.' At this he was silent for a long time" (MR 238–39). Denied license to preach, Rubruck was forced to leave for home in July 1254. Returning through Armenia in February 1255, he encountered "five Preaching brothers . . . carrying letters of the Lord Pope to . . . Mangu [i.e., Möngke] Chan . . ., requesting they be allowed to stay in [Tartar] territory and preach the word of God . . . . When I told them, however, what I had seen and how I was being sent back, they altered course" (MR 271–72).[8] No doubt he also informed them of his lack of missionary success: "We baptized [in Mongol lands] a total of six souls" (MR 253). Rubruck flatly discouraged future missions: "It [is] inadvisable for any friar to make any further journeys to the Tartars, as I myself did or as the Preaching Friars are doing"(MR 278).

William of Rubruck's six baptisms in the Orient, and the circumstances under which they were administered, beg further examination. Given his uncertain standing during the years he spent in the Mongol empire, six baptisms is not an especially small number. Scrupulous adherence to normal procedures vis-à-vis the conferral of baptism should not have yielded many christenings. Even if teaching or example had moved infidels to convert, he was in no position to teach or guide them in their new faith, because he could not remain in contact with them. Without extensive instruction before conferral of the sacrament, and lacking an institutional framework to ensure new converts opportunities to strengthen their faith later, the ready—as it were, nonchalant—administration of baptism would have violated established doctrine and custom of the western church.

Teachings Concerning the Conferral of Baptism

Although theologians and canon lawyers still differed over the validity of orders conferred by heretics or schismatics, there was little debate concerning baptism. Gratian's *Decretum* of 1140 clearly enshrined the teaching of Augustine: that baptism is always conferred if properly administered and that the disposition of the recipient determines whether grace is bestowed.[9] The Roman church rejected the position taken by eastern churches, that baptism by defective ministers was invalid and had to be repeated.[10] Thomas Aquinas, restating opinions concerning baptism that prevailed through the thirteenth century, put the matter clearly in his *Summa Theologica*: Baptism was valid whenever the matter and form of the sacrament were correct. "Even an unbeliever can confer a true sacrament, provided that the other essentials be there."[11] Nevertheless, he emphasized the recipient's disposition, making it illicit to administer the sacrament under duress. "On the part of the one baptized, it is necessary to have the will or intention of receiving the sacrament. . . . If an adult lack the intention . . . he must be rebaptized," but using the conditional form.[12] For the same reason there was a duty to catechize before conferring the sacrament. "Because Baptism is the sacrament of faith . . . in order that a man receive the faith he must be instructed therein. . . . Therefore . . . catechism should precede Baptism."[13] Baptism was rarely withheld from anyone requesting it, and it was common for catechumens to undergo instruction in the faith after the event, but as a general rule adults were catechized before christening.[14] Under such guidelines, Rubruck should have been slow to confer the sacrament unless there was a reasonable expectation that the newly converted could pursue a Christian life. Thus it would be no surprise if all those baptized were Christian captives' children in the east, and none pagans. In fact, the only three he specifically mentions were "sons of a poor German" who had been carried to Karacorum (MR 246).

Surprisingly, Rubruck was not reluctant to christen potential converts, even without extensive preparation, as one anecdote in his *Itinerarium* makes clear. A Muslim visited the friars shortly after they entered the Tartar realm. "While he was talking to us we began to expound the Faith. And on hearing of God's favour shown to the human race . . ., and how cleansing from sin lay in baptism, he said he wanted to be baptized. But *when we were getting ready to baptize him* he suddenly mounted his horse [to] . . . go home and consult his wife."[15] Thus a chance encounter, cursory discussion of the Christian faith, and an expression of interest in becoming Christian almost occasioned a baptism that very instant, without preparatory catechization and with little reason to expect that the new "convert" would be able to follow a Christian life or receive fuller indoctrination.

The story of the potential Muslim convert raises disturbing questions about procedures followed by the friars, but it also illustrates the paucity of our data concerning circumstances under which converts might have been baptized. William tells this story to illustrate the importance of *comos*, fermented mare's milk, which remains a major source of nutrition on the Mongolian steppe.[16] Although an essential food, for eastern Christians it was unclean and forbidden. "Russians, Greek and Alan Christians who live among [the Tartars] and who wish strictly to observe . . . do not drink *comos*, and [if they do], their clergy reconcil[e] them as if they had abjured the Christian faith" (MR 101). William enjoyed *comos* and rejected their prohibition. "On [first] swallowing it I broke out in a sweat all over from alarm and surprise, . . . but . . . I found it very palatable, as indeed it is" (MR 99). Counseling Alans, "Christians of the Greek rite who . . . have Greek priests but . . . are not schismatic," who asked "whether they could be saved, since they were obliged to drink *comos*," Rubruck "set them right as best [he] could, instructing them and strengthening them in the faith" (MR 102–3). It is in this context that Rubruck tells of the reluctant Muslim. After consulting his wife, the Muslim reported that "he did not dare . . . receive baptism, since this meant he would not drink *comos* . . ., and he could not survive in the wilderness without this drink. [William] was wholly unable to disabuse him of this idea. . . . How far they are alienated from the Faith by such a notion," William lamented (MR 104). William's discourse on *comos* prompted him to include circumstances surrounding this potential missionary baptism, detail which few documents from the era provide. Although Rubruck's *Itinerarium* is a lengthy narrative, baptisms are mentioned only on this occasion and as regards the christening of the three German children. Given Rubruck's many attempts to explain his beliefs in the east, the incident with the Muslim suggests that he was ready, at virtually any occasion, to bring those expressing the least desire for baptism to the sacramental font. William was surely aware that baptism should not be administered lightly, and his apparent willingness to christen any infidel with an interest in becoming Christian prefigures the activities of later evangelists, all of whom seem to have counted their successes in terms of the numbers that they baptized.

Mission Expansion into Eastern Asia

After Qubilai (1260–94) succeeded his brother Möngke as Great Khan, Mongol attitudes about the acceptance of western missionaries changed. According to Marco Polo, his father and uncle brought a request from Qubilai, about 1270, that the pope "send him a hundred men of learning, thoroughly acquainted with the principles of the Christian religion . . . and qualified to prove to the learned of his dominions . . . that the faith possessed by Christians is superior to, and founded upon more evident truth than any other."[17] Although this request came to nothing,[18] the court of the Ilkhans, established in Persia about 1261 by Qubilai's brother, Hülegü, made repeated contact in search of Christian cooperation against the Mamluks and gave western missionaries license to preach in Persia. Mongol toleration also allowed the mission to spread north of the Black Sea; a license to preach (a *yarligh* of privileges) was issued to Franciscan missionaries in the Khanate of the Golden Horde (Kipchak) at least as early as the reign of Möngke Temür (1267–80).[19] Thus encouraged, Franciscan and Dominican friars, preeminent in mission work in that era, had established convents on the western threshold of the silk routes, north of the Black Sea, in Persia, and in Mesopotamia, well before the close of the thirteenth century.[20]

Expansion of the mission into east Asia awaited the election of Jerome of Ascoli, Nicholas IV (1288–92), the first pope from the Franciscan order.[21] His interest in mission activity was stimulated in 1287, before his reign began, by a Turkic Nestorian monk, Bar Saüma, an ambassador for both Ilkhan Arghun (1284–91) and the Nestorian Catholicus Mar Yabhalaha III.[22] Because the monk arrived during a papal interregnum, several cardinals, among them Jerome of Ascoli, interviewed him. When they showed surprise that the Ilkhan would send a monk, he replied: "You must know that many of our fathers have gone to the land of the Mongols, the Turks, and the Chinese, and have taught them. Today many of the Mongols are Christians; there are princes and queens who have been baptized and confess Christ."[23] Moreover, Saüma reported Arghun's promise, to be baptized in Jerusalem, after its liberation from the Mamluks.[24] Following a trip to the courts of France and England, Saüma returned during Lent (1288), after Nicholas IV's election, and was invited to full participation in the liturgy. On Palm Sunday the pope "gave the communion first to Rabban Saüma after he had confessed his sins."[25] The ecumenical openness shown to Saüma is consistent with the missionary outreach that characterized Nicholas IV's brief reign.[26]

The Mission to China

Nicholas IV launched the mission to China in 1289, when he sent John of Montecorvino to Cathay. The pope's letter to Great Khan Qubilai explains the circumstances. "Shortly after . . . our promotion we received . . . messengers . . . [who] earnestly begged . . . that we should send some Latin monks to your court."[27] John and his companions were in fact to be the wise men from the west whom Qubilai had repeatedly requested. John of Montecorvino became the first Archbishop of Khanbaliq (modern Beijing), and his letters (translated by C. Dawson in *Mission to Asia,* hereafter MA) are a major source of information on Mongol China; after the Asian mission collapsed he was virtually forgotten, to be rediscovered only in the seventeenth century.[28] The twenty-seven letters John carried when he left Italy with a large party of friars show that he intended to follow the silk route, across Central Asia.[29] War between Mongol princes in Chaghatai Khanate blocked that way, however, detaining him in Persia until 1291, when he set out with only one companion, Nicholas of Pistoia, on the long sea passage via India, where that friar died. It was 1294 before Montecorvino reached "Cathay . . . the kingdom of the Emperor of the Tartars, who is called the Great Chan. Indeed I summoned the Emperor himself to receive the Catholic faith . . . with the letters of the Lord Pope, but he was too far gone in idolatry. Nevertheless he behaves generously to Christians" (MA 224–25). In fact, it was not Qubilai whom John summoned to conversion but his successor, Temür Öljeitü (1294–1307), who granted the western holy man the same public largess received by other religious in residence at his court.

John's letters reflect the self-effacing modesty of a Franciscan friar, but he reported mission successes almost always in terms of numbers of those baptized. His first letter from China, in 1305, reported both hostility from the numerous Nestorian clergy already established in China (who "call themselves Christians, but behave in a very unchristian manner") and mission success; a church had been constructed in Khanbaliq and six thousand people had been christened. But "for the . . . slanders [of the Nestorians, he wrote] I might have baptized 30,000 more, for I am constantly baptizing" (MA 224–25). Shortly after his arrival he had converted an important Tartar vassal from Nestorianism to Latin Christianity, "[King George] of the family of Prester John."[30] George was an Öngüt prince, whose people, Turkic converts to Nestorian Christianity, enjoyed great influence in the Mongol world because of their leaders' intermarriage with the descendants of Chingiz Khan. George (K'uo-li-chi-ssu in the *Yüan shih*) was, for example, first married to Qubilai's sister, and after her death to his daughter.[31] Montecorvino reports in his second letter that George "brought a great part of his people to the true Catholic faith, and built a fine church, . . . call[ing] it 'the Roman church' [in his capital, Tenduk] . . . twenty day's journey" from Beijing (MA 225–26). When George died, however, his Nestorian brothers reversed his policies, and that sect again predominated in Tenduk. Montecorvino clearly believed an opportunity for mass conversion had been lost and urged that reinforcements be sent; "if a few fellow workers would come, I hope in God that all could be restored" (MA 226). Recent scholarship makes John's expectations appear overly sanguine. Chinese sources show George also a devotee of Chinese culture and Confucian values, so his commitment to Christianity may have been quite superficial.[32] Although he felt isolated in China, John noted in 1306 that he had a secure position in the khan's court "and right of access to it as legate of the Lord Pope" (MA 231). He built two churches in Beijing and established a nucleus of Latin worship in them by purchasing "forty boys . . . sons of . . . pagans, [whom he] baptized . . . and taught Latin. [T]hey keep choir and say office as in a convent whether I am there or not" (MA 231). John's second letter claims he had already "baptized several thousand" in Cathay, and during that winter he was christening at the rate of one hundred souls a month.[33]

The resumption of diplomatic traffic between Khanbaliq and khanates to its west allowed John's letters to be sent and made reinforcing the mission possible. Thus his 1305 letter "beg[ged] for some brethren to come, if they are . . . anxious to offer themselves as an example," and "ask[ed] the brethren who . . . receive this letter . . . to bring its contents to the notice of the Lord Pope" (MA 226–27. Thomas of Tolentino was carrying word of

John's mission successes to the papal court at Avignon before the second letter from China was written. Tolentino, who had left Italy with Montecorvino in 1289 but remained in Armenia, "rehearsed in a wonderful speech before the lord Pope and the Cardinals and Prelates these wonderful works of our God so well begun . . . by Brother John, . . . asking the lord Pope . . . to take care that [they] be increased and perfected."[34] In response, Clement V instructed the Franciscans to select seven friars to be consecrated bishop and sent into China, to carry a pallium to Montecorvino and anoint him archbishop of a newly created see of Khanbaliq, with authority to organize a hierarchy for the entire Tartar empire.[35]

In fact, Clement V ordained suffragan bishops to assist Montecorvino on at least two occasions, and no fewer than four of these made it to China. Three of the batch ordained in 1307–8 survived, reaching John in 1313. From letters sent home by two of these, Brothers Peregrine and Andrew of Perugia, we know that they consecrated Montecorvino and that he established a suffragan see at Zaitun, in Fukien province near modern Quanzhou.[36] Renewed fighting in Chaghatai Khanate had forced them to retrace John's footsteps through India, where three of their number perished. Three more were consecrated bishops in 1310–11 to reinforce the China mission, at a time when the route across Central Asia seems again to have been clear.[37] We can trace their progress into Kipchak Khanate,[38] and several sources name one of them, Peter of Florence, successor bishop to the see of Zaitun.[39] Letters from China all report good progress in proselytization and mention baptisms, with much of this work among those already Christian. Peregrine's 1318 letter testifies that Montecorvino had "converted [the Nestorian King George] completely . . . and the king himself in one day converted several thousand of his people. And had he lived, we should indeed have subdued his whole people and kingdom to Christ" (MA 232). He credits Friar John with having broken the "power of the Nestorians, who [had] prevented . . . Christians of whatever nation or class . . . [from] erect[ing] an oratory, however small . . ., or a cross" (MA 232). John had "erected a number of churches," and given opportunity to other "Christian peoples who hate the schismatic Nestorians" (MA 232). These included both the Armenians and Alans. The former were "building for themselves a remarkable church and intend to give it to [Montecorvino]. Wherefore he is constantly with them and has left the Latin Church to the other brethren" (MA 232). The Alans, a community of thirty thousand mercenaries from the southern Russian steppes, he calls "good Christians, . . . and these men with their families come to Brother John; and he preaches to them and encourages them" (MA 232–33). Because all the letters mention western merchants in China, clearly they also constituted a congregation for the missionaries. Western merchants and mercenaries in Mongol China must have been a significant community.[40] A chance archeological find, the 1342 headstone for an Italian merchant's young daughter, Catherine Vilioni, carved with vignettes from the life of St. Catherine of Alexandria in Chinese style but inscribed in Old Gothic lettering, gave proof that some merchants even reared families in the Orient.[41]

In addition to serving religious needs of fellow Christians, friars preached to and baptized Mongols, Chinese, and other Asians. With the khan's support, they could preach freely and even expounded their faith in the Muslim quarter; Peregrine reported:

> Among the infidel we can preach freely and in the mosque of the Saracens we have preached often that they might be converted, and to idolators likewise . . . by means of two interpreters. Many come together and wonder greatly and enquire diligently about these things. . . . [W]e have good hope, seeing the crowds eager to hear and running to where we preach. Truly we believe that if only we possessed their languages, God would show . . . wonders. [T]he harvest is great [but] the laborers are few and they have no sickle . . . [f]or we brethren are . . . unskilled in . . . languages. (MA 233)

Franciscans laboring in China were typical of their order. Few had mastery of languages (Montecorvino seems an exception to the rule), but their indifference to language is understandable on two counts. By the fourteenth century, perhaps because of the presence of western merchants, serviceable interpreters seem to have been relatively easy to find. In addition, Asian mission fields offered so many different peoples and tongues that preparatory linguistic training was a practical impossibility. As Andrew of Perugia remarked in his letter from Zaitun: "In this vast empire there are verily men of every nation under heaven and of every sect; and each and all are allowed to live according to their own sect. For this is their . . . error, that every man is saved in his own sect" (MA 237). This did not daunt the friars, who believed that good example and preaching, even if in a language unintelligible to the auditors, would promote conversion among infidels.[42]

Their preaching did have results, as Andrew's letter attests. "We can preach freely and securely, but of the Jews and Saracens none is converted. Of the idolators, exceeding many are baptized: but when they are baptized they do not strictly adhere to Christian ways" (MA 237). Clearly baptism was being freely conferred in China on pagans who did not adopt a Christian life. These christenings appear to be different from the thousands reported by Montecorvino in the first decade of the fourteenth century, which well may have come from within communities of Christians resident in the east, such as the Alans, some of whom Rubruck had encountered a half-century earlier.[43] Christianized as Greek Orthodox about the beginning of the thirteenth century, only a few years before their first contact with the Mongols, the Alans had submitted to Möngke in 1235, becoming auxiliary troops and armorers. After Qubilai's conquest of Sung China, they became bodyguards of the Yüan court.[44] Cut off from the Orthodox Church and its clergy, and apparently unwilling to be rebaptized as Nestorians, the Alans became a congregation for Montecorvino in China. The numerous baptisms claimed by Montecorvino could have been performed for the Alan community, but not the "exceedingly many" idolaters whom Andrew of Perugia baptized and whom he characterized in the passage already quoted as not adhering "strictly to Christian ways." If those were converts from the many who ran to where the friars preached, baptism was being conferred casually in a pagan wilderness, with little hope that recipients would lead a Christian life.

Andrew of Perugia's report of numerous, if lukewarm, converts seems to refer to ethnic Chinese. Conversions among the Chinese have often been called into question, doubted on the grounds that Christianity held no attraction for this group.[45] This a priori judgment is based on an evaluation of Chinese society and the sophistication of its religious expressions, but it may not be valid for the Yüan period, as the history of Taoism in that era demonstrates. The amalgam of beliefs and practices subsumed under the heading of Taoism were not always encouraged in China, where Confucianism generally assumed the role of official creed. Nevertheless, Taoism did enjoy official patronage from time to time, and under the Yüan dynasty, a period of intellectual and religious ferment, several new Taoist sects appeared. Among these was *Ch'üan-chen*, the "integral perfection" sect, which promoted religious syncretism, reflecting the notion (generally popular in China) that its three religions (Buddhism, Confucianism, and Taoism) share an essential unity. This sect produced the *Li-chiao shih-wa lun*, "Fifteen Essays on Religion," a sort of breviary condensing the teachings of those three faiths into fifteen succinct points.[46]

The Mongol period in China occasioned increased interest in religion and syncretism, as the appearance of such Taoist sects indicates. In this environment conversions to Christianity, superficial or otherwise, might have been relatively commonplace. An important study of the "sinicization" of other Asians in China, which documents the apparent frequency and ease of "conversion" between religions under the Mongols, bears this out.[47] It gives numerous examples of converts to Confucianism, Chinese Buddhism, and/or Taoism from within Moslem, Christian, Buddhist, and

Manichaean families, including many who seem to have converted several times. These conversions would not have been the type described by Monte-corvino, when he purchased and baptized forty boys to provide his newly founded mission with worshippers and a choir. They would have been the indifferent converts responding to preaching, such as those Andrew of Perugia bewailed, who could have been drawn from the many Chinese who embraced amorphous syncretism. Because one element of their belief, the Way (Tao), encouraged openness to all religious mysteries, it was easier for the friars to attract potential Chinese converts to their sermons and in-struction. Ironically, underlying concepts of Tao also made western con-version—unreserved acceptance of dogmatic belief—more difficult. Giving oneself completely to any faith is antithetical to Tao, which holds that you must always be ready to go beyond the understanding you have currently achieved. No explanation of the nature of the universe or of man's place in it could be wholeheartedly embraced without losing one's way (*tao*) in the search for truth.[48] Thus Taoism, because it prevented those under its influ-ence from any meaningful conversion to Christianity, made it virtually im-possible for friars to capture its adherents in a European-style commitment to the Christian faith.

In any case, the mission in China continued and expanded throughout the first half of the fourteenth century. The Franciscan establishment there had grown by the time Odoric of Pordenone visited China (1325–28). Making his way to the east via India, Odoric spent three years in Cathay before returning across Asia to Italy, were he dictated his *Relatio*, a travel narrative, shortly before his death in 1331.[49] In it he mentions many anony-mous friars at work in China, with mission stations in several cities, and attests to the success of their efforts. Odoric casually mentions, for ex-ample, convents both at Hangchow (staffed by at least four friars, who had converted a local high official), and at "Iamzai," or Yangchow (where there were also three Nestorian churches).[50] When he describes the extent of the court at Khanbaliq, Odoric summons authority for his assertions: "I . . . [made] diligent enquiry from Christians, Saracens, and all kinds of idolaters, and *likewise from our converts to the faith, of whom there be some who are great barons at that court,* and have to do with the king's person only."[51]

From the tone and content of Odoric's *Relatio*, he hardly seems a mis-sionary. It is replete with charming vignettes and details concerning travel in Asia, but it provides so few facts concerning the mission effort that Odoric almost seems disinterested in proselytizing, and he claims no conversions.[52] Among his rare mentions of mission baptisms is the report near the end of his *Relatio* of wonders performed by friars in "greater Tartary," perhaps

Chaghatai Khanate. For missionaries there it was "a mere nothing to expel devils from the possessed . . . [of whom] there be many in those parts both men and women." Because of this power, the local population "bind and bring [the possessed] to our friars . . . [who] bid the demons depart. . . . Those who have been delivered . . . straightway cause themselves to be baptized."[53] After baptism the nomads let the friars consign their felt idols to a bonfire, and although devils shrieked in displeasure, the friars commanded their departure. "In this way our friars baptize great numbers in that country," Odoric reported.[54] It seems here that thaumaturgy, not proselyzation, is the stimulus for baptisms performed "straightway."

Odoric was far from being disinterested in the mission, despite the slight mention of it made in his recollections. His hagiographic *vita,* written by those who had known him, asserts that he went out to win souls, and he was seeking papal permission to collect a party of fifty missionary recruits for China when he died.[55] Such an expedition would have been most welcome in China, where replacements for the friars in residence were eagerly sought. Peregrine had written in 1318 that "we . . . Friars cannot live long, and no others have come," and Andrew wrote in 1326 that "I alone remain [of the suffragan bishops]" (MA 234, 237). These lamentations notwithstanding, it is clear that missionaries were still being sent east. One example is Friar Nicholas, whom John XXII dispatched in 1334, with a retinue of twenty Franciscan priests and six lay brothers, to succeed Montecorvino as archbishop.[56] The pope described Nicholas as learned and virtuous in his letter of accreditation to the khan, but the records, including the papal registers, are so defective that little else is known concerning him. Fragments of information about the mission that do survive draw glaring attention to the deficiencies. We have no trace, for example, of letters accrediting James of Florence, who became bishop of Zaitun and was later martyred in 1362.[57] We do know, however, that he received a subsidy for departing *ad partes Cataye* on February 14, 1333.[58] Because we lack other reports from China, only Odoric of Pordenone and John of Marignolli (who was in China from 1342 to 1345) inform us concerning the extent of the Franciscan mission there.

Friar John of Marignolli, who was sent into Asia by Benedict XII in 1339, is the last western witness to the mission in China. An urbane and erudite Florentine, he produced a narrative that is an invaluable, but unusual, source. After his 1353 return, he was rewarded with a bishopric and employed by Emperor Charles IV in Bohemia to compile a chronicle for that kingdom. Because Marignolli lacked enthusiasm for his task, to relieve boredom he interspersed recollections of his thirteen-year trip in its chapters. There they lay undetected until the late 1700s, and they were not

edited as a coherent travel account until 1820.⁵⁹ The genesis of the expedition Marignolli helped lead was the arrival at Avignon, in 1338, of ambas-
sadors from the Alans and Khan Toghon Temür, requesting an archbishop
for Khanbaliq to replace Montecorvino, who died in 1328 or 1329. The
Alans' letter, full of praise for Montecorvino, begged a "good, capable and
wise legate who may care for our souls; . . . we stand ill without a head,
without instructor, and without comforter."⁶⁰ Obviously, Archbishop Nicholas (Montecorvino's designated replacement) had not arrived in China, leaving the see of Khanbaliq without an incumbent and the office of legate to
the khan unfilled. This vacancy, according to the Alans, caused "the Christians in these parts . . . great shame." For his part, the khan hoped "to
open a way for the frequent sending of envoys" between the pope and
himself, and "ask[ed] the Pope . . . to send his blessing," as well as "horses
and other wonderful things." In response Benedict XII dispatched Marignolli
and his companions, a large entourage which led a Frankish war horse
across Asia as a present to delight the Yüan emperor.⁶¹

John's long stay in China began with a procession into the royal court at
Khanbaliq. "Ceremonially dressed, with a most beautiful cross which went
before me with candles and incense, singing *I believe in one God,* we entered into the presence of the Kaan. . . . I gave a full benediction which he
received with humility."⁶² During almost three years there, he and his party
of thirty-two were treated very liberally—"[the khan] spent more than the
value of 4000 marks for us"; John does not mention missionary activities
there, only "many glorious disputations against the Jews and other sects."⁶³
After leaving Beijing he journeyed "with magnificent provisions . . . and
about 200 horses" to Zaitun, whence he embarked for India.⁶⁴ Zaitun he
describes as "a wondrous seaport and a city of incredible size, where our
Friars Minor have three very fine churches . . . . They have also some fine
bells of the best quality, two of which were made to my order, and set up
with all due form in the very middle of the Saracen community."⁶⁵ The
friars delighted in tweaking Muslims, who abhorred bells, by placing campaniles in proximity to Islamic quarters. Marignolli mentions neither preaching to pagans nor serving the religious needs of the Alan community, although some of his party may have been left in China to help staff Franciscan
churches and minister to the Alans.

An Example of Catechization in the Eastern Missions

Marignolli's fragmentary and episodic testimony is crucial in documenting
the range of postures concerning catechization and baptism in Asia. Clearly,
if an eastern ruler had expressed a desire for baptism, any of the missionar-

ies would happily have made the best of such a conversion, and worked to promote Christianization later. A similar willingness to accept the instant conversion of individual nonbelievers is demonstrated in Rubruck's report and inferred in the letter of Bishop Peregrine. No source, except Marignolli, explicitly shows a missionary-preacher who, having moved an auditor to seek baptism, withheld the sacrament pending catechization. An incident during his stay in Quilon, India, where at least one catechumen received lengthy instruction before baptism, makes it clear that catechistics were not completely ignored in the east. Quilon, an important port in southwest India, was home both to a large indigenous Christian community, the St. Thomas Christians, and to western missionaries; some fifteen years before Marignolli's arrival, Pope John XXII had erected a Latin bishopric there.[66] During John's year-long stay a Brahman ascetic requested baptism, declaring Marignolli a divine messenger he had been told by an idol to seek out. In this complicated tale the Brahman was reunited with his long lost son, who had been purchased by a Genoese merchant from pirates. Now baptized, the boy (Marignolli's interpreter) and the old man recognized each other in John's presence. Whether or not the story can be taken at face value, it provides details usually lacking; Marignolli agreed to baptize the man but only after extensive catechization. "After three months instruction I baptized him . . . Michael, and blessed him, and sent him away, whilst he promised to preach to others the faith that he had acquired."[67] This instance contrasts with Rubruck's conduct in the thirteenth century and earlier fourteenth-century examples in China; here there was no rush to confer the sacrament without proselytization.

Marignolli appended another vignette to his recollections, a kind of post-script, which contrasts with the picture from Quilon. In 1342 Marignolli tarried, before entering China, at "Kamul" (modern Hami), an oasis east of the Tien Shan, where caravan routes north and south of those mountains converge. Marignolli recounted his visit there while discussing tithing. "As long as the church is provided for . . . [perhaps] the tithe should [not] be imposed. . . . As a case occurred from my own experience at Kamul, when many Tartars and peoples of other nations, on their first conversion, refused to be baptized unless we would swear [that we would later] extract no temporalities from them; nay, on the contrary, that we should provide for their poor of our own means. This we did and a multitude of both sexes in that city did then most gladly receive baptism."[68] It is highly doubtful that there was a mission in Kamul; nevertheless the inhabitants, "Tartars and peoples of other nations," were solicited to receive baptism by Marignolli and his party as they passed through the city. This seems another lapse in orthodoxy, but a phrase Marignolli uses may be significant: they refused baptism "on their *first* conversion" unless reassured that no exactions would be made of them. Although Marignolli does not elaborate, this implies a distinction between the first impulse to convert, on which baptism would be bestowed, and a subsequent, fuller turning toward Christianity expected after catechization.

Conclusion

As it turned out, subsequent instruction by missionaries active in Asia proved impossible. Plague struck before another major expedition could be organized in Europe, and the climate of toleration in Asia soon ended. Before Marignolli returned to Europe "the way by land [through Chaghatai] was closed on account of war," hence his journey via India.[69] Chaghatai Khanate finally disintegrated shortly thereafter, its western regions becoming Transoxania, ruled by a Turkish, Muslim, nobility intolerant of Christianity.[70] The mission effort in China was effectively over, as well. Anti-Mongol revolutionaries overwhelmed Zaitun in 1362, and James of Florence, its last Latin bishop, was put to death in Chaghatai Khanate that year, probably while in flight from his see.[71] After the Yüan dynasty was crushed in 1368, vestiges of all it had fostered, including Christianity, were suppressed.[72]

Fourteenth-century sources, however fragmentary, disclose a substantial mission effort which, before midcentury, had created a network of convents and churches in central and eastern Asia. In conformity with long-established practice, missionaries there urged the khans to receive baptism in the Roman Church. At the same time, through interpreters, they preached personal salvation to the masses. Reports from these missionaries, which seldom make mention of catechization, give the impression that preaching yielded converts, and that baptism was administered upon request. This behavior was consistent with the political naiveté of the missionaries, who shortsightedly accepted identification with the Yüan regime in China and were perceived as foreigners in Mongol employ. Because they did not appreciate the abject dependence of the entire eastern mission on Mongol toleration, their mission was doomed when the Yüan dynasty collapsed. Their abiding faith, that God would show great things through them, came to nothing as the window of mission opportunity slowly closed.

This judgment should be tempered, however, by evidence in their reports of attention to long-range missionary goals. While they hoped for the conversion of one or more khans, they also worked to create a foundation of belief within the societies in which they worked. Because no single people—not the Alans, the Öngüts at Tenduk, nor the Mongols themselves—

would have provided a solid base for Christianity in Asia, the missionaries preached to and baptized the general populace wherever allowed. Thereby they sought to create a vital Christian community in the east, and success in that task could be validated only by enumerating those introduced to salvation through baptism. If faulted for being too ready to baptize, missionaries could have defended their actions; without baptism the gates of heaven remain closed to sinful man, and each person baptized was another soul saved for paradise.

The emphasis on preaching and conferring baptism, however, was complemented by practices showing that missionaries sought evidence of inner conversion through patient instruction. Although it is abundantly clear that the sacrament was often freely conferred on those who sought it, missionaries sometimes insisted on a period of instruction before baptizing, and certainly expected those baptized to continue in the practice of their new faith. John of Marignolli's comments, in particular, argue that fourteenth-century missionaries to Asia tempered the urge to count christenings by adhering to the duty to catechize. Sometimes this was done before baptism, as in the case of the old Brahman, but probably more frequently in preaching and teaching after the "first conversion" Marignolli mentions in his anecdote concerning Kamul. In so comporting themselves, the missionaries to Asia conformed to European ideals and practice by moderating their wild enthusiasm with a mature grasp of theological principles. Thus their concept of conversion went beyond simple faith, that God might move through them, to adherence to realistic practices, including catechization, which might have provided a foundation for lasting communities of their faith in the east, had political realities not intervened to nullify their efforts.

NOTES

Research in Vatican and French archives was partially supported by grants from the City University of New York PSC-CUNY Research Award Program.

1. For an overview of medieval mission activity see Kenneth Scott Latourette, *A History of the Expansion of Christianity*, vol. 2, *The Thousand Years of Uncertainty* (New York: Harper, 1938).

2. For Western diplomatic and missionary contact with the Mongols, see J. Richard, *La papauté et les missions d'Orient au moyen age (XIIIe–XVe siècles)* (Rome: Ecole française de Rome, 1977); I. de Rachewiltz, *Papal Envoys to the Great Khans* (Stanford: Stanford University Press, 1971); and G. Soranzo, *Il Papato, L'Europa Christiana e i Tartari* (Milan: Università cattolica del Sacro Cuore, 1930). Good surveys are also provided by J. Bentley, *Old World Encounters: Cross-Cultural Contacts and Exchanges in Pre-Modern Times* (New York and Oxford: Oxford University Press, 1993), 155–64, and J. R. S. Phillips, *The Medieval Expan-*

sion of Europe (Oxford: Oxford University Press, 1988), 57–140. Collections of primary sources concerning these encounters include A. Van den Wyngaert, ed., *Sinica Franciscana*, vol. I, *Itinera et relationes fratrum Minorum saeculi XIII et XIV* (Quaracchi: College of St. Bonaventure, 1929), hereafter cited as *Sinica Fran.*; G. Golubovich, ed., *Biblioteca Bio-Bibliografica della Terra Santa e Dell'Oriente Francescano,* vols. 1–5 (Quaracchi: College of St. Bonaventure, 1906–29), hereafter *BTS*; C. Dawson, ed., *Mission to Asia* (originally *The Mongol Mission* [1955], reissued Toronto: University of Toronto Press, 1980); and H. Yule and H. Cordier, eds., *Cathay and the Way Thither,* 2d ed., 4 vols. (London: Hakluyt Society, 1913–16), hereafter Yule, *Cathay*. D. Morgan, *The Mongols* (London: Blackwell, 1986) outlines Mongol history and provides an excellent bibliographical study. The style he adopts in transliterating Mongol names, which vary widely in still standard reference works, is followed herein whenever possible.

3. *Sinica Fran.*, 27–130, translated in Dawson, *Mission to Asia,* 3–72.

4. These were Ascelin of Cremona and Andrew of Longjumeau; see *The Mission of Friar William of Rubruck,* trans. P. Jackson, with introduction and notes by P. Jackson and D. Morgan (London: Hakluyt Society, 1990), ser. II, no. 173 (hereafter cited as *MR*), 30–32, and the works cited therein.

5. The papacy had dispatched Dominicans as early as July 23, 1252, perhaps to minister to captives encountered earlier by Andrew of Longjumeau. See *Acta Innocentii PP. IV*, ed. E. Berger, 4 vols. (Paris: P. Thorin, 1884–1911), no. 7753, 3:457.

6. *Sinica Fran.*, 164–332. The latest critical translation is Jackson's *Mission of Rubruck.*

7. See also introduction, *MR*, 44.

8. *MR*, 271–72. Concerning this mission, see Paul Pelliot, "Les Mongols et la papauté," *Revue de l'Orient Chrétien* 22 (1922–23): 3–30; 24 (1924): 225–335; 28 (1932): 3–84; 24: 216–20.

9. *Dictum Gratiani post* c. 97, C. I, q. 1, in *Decretum Gratiani, emendatum etc.*, 3 vols. (Taurinae, 1638), endorsed the teaching in Augustine's *De Baptismo Contra Donatistis,* lib. V, c. 20, in *Corpus Scriptorum Ecclesiasticorum Latinorum,* 5:51 (Vindobonae, 1866), 79. See A. A. Reed, "The Juridical Effects of Baptism—Canon 80" (Ph.D. diss., Catholic University of America, 1956), 3–4, 10–12.

10. L. Salet, *Les Reordinations* (Paris: J. Gabalda, 1907), 11, contrasts opinions on baptism.

11. *Summa Theologica,* III, q. 64, a. 9 (complete English edition in 5 vols., trans. by the Fathers of the English Dominican Province; rev. ed., 1920: Christian Classics Reprint, 1981).

12. Ibid., III, q. 68, a. 7.

13. Ibid., III, q. 71, a. 1.

14. B. Kedar, *Crusade and Mission* (Princeton: Princeton University Press, 1984), 151–53, gives examples from contemporary accounts of infidel baptisms.

15. *MR*, 104, emphasis added. This was on Pentecost, June 8, 1253.

16. A modern American described *comos* (*qumiz* in Turkish) as having "the flavor of buttermilk mixed with champagne." W. O. Douglas, "Journey to Outer Mongolia," *National Geographic* 121, 3 (March 1962): 325.

17. *The Travels of Marco Polo,* ed. M. Komroff (revised from Marsden's translation; New York: Boni & Liveright, 1926), 8. For the historicity of Polo's book see L. Olschki, *Marco Polo's Asia: An Introduction to his "Description of the World" Called "Il Milione,"* trans. J. A. Scott (Berkeley and Los Angeles: University of California Press, 1960).

18. Two Dominicans departed with the Polos but lost heart and turned back (*Travels of Marco Polo,* 12–13).

19. Richard, *La papauté,* 187.

20. R. Grousset, *The Empire of the Steppes* (1939), trans. N. Walford (New Brunswick: Rutgers University Press, 1970), 353–71; de Rachewiltz, *Papal Envoys,* 150–54. See also K. M. Setton, *The Papacy and the Levant (1204–1571)* (Philadelphia: American Philosophical Society, 1976), 1:115–17, 120.

21. A. Franchi, *Nicholas Papa IV (Girolamo d' Ascoli)* (Ascoli Piceno: Grafiche d'Auria, 1990), is a long overdue biography of this important pope.

22. A detailed account of Saüma's trip is preserved in *History of Mar Yabhalaha* (a biography of the Catholicus). The most recent critical edition is F. Altheim and R. Stiehl, "Rabban Sauma Reise nach dem Westen, 1287–88," *Geschichte der Hunnen,* Bd. III (Berlin: de Gruyter, 1961), 190–217. Others that remain useful are W. Budge, *The Monks of Qubilai Khan* (London: Religious Tract Society, 1928); J. A. Montgomery, *History of Yaballaha Before 1550* (New York: Columbia University Press, 1927); and A. C. Moule, *Christians in China Before the Year 1500* (New York: Society for the Promoting of Christian Knowledge, 1926), 94–127.

23. Moule, *Christians in China,* 107.

24. Ibid., 114.

25. Ibid., 111.

26. See J. D. Ryan, "Nicholas IV and the Evolution of the Eastern Missionary Effort," *Archivum Pontificiae Historiae* 19 (1981): 79–95.

27. This letter is abridged in Moule, *Christians in China,* 168–69.

28. Luke Wadding found Montecorvino's letters (in a manuscript now in the Bibliothèque Nationale) and published them in 1636 in vol. 3 of *Annales Minorum,* 2d ed. (16 vols., Rome, 1731–36), hereafter cited as *Ann. Min.* Critical editions include *Sinica Fran.* 340–55 and *BTS,* 1:86–95. They are translated in *MR* (Dawson, *Mission to Asia),* 222–31; Moule, *Christians in China,* 166–81; and Yule, *Cathay,* 3:45–70, who also includes John's letter from India, discovered later.

29. *Registres de Nicholas IV,* ed. E. Langlois (Paris: A. Fontemoing, 1905), nos. 2218–44.

30. George, or Kerguz, was head man of the Öngüt Turks (*MR,* xxxii. Polo (*Travels of Marco Polo,* 102–3) also mentions "George, the present King [of Tenduk] . . . fourth in descent from Prester John." Tenduk was in China's northwest, in the loop of the Huang He (Yellow) River.

31. C. Yüan, *Western and Central Asians in China under the Mongols: Their Transformation into Chinese* (Los Angeles: Monumenta Serica at the University of California, 1966), 54. The *Yüan shih* is the official Chinese history of the Yüan dynasty, compiled after its fall.

32. Yüan, *Asians under the Mongols*, 53–57. See also Bentley, *Old World Encounters*, 161.

33. Dawson, *Mission to Asia*, 229, 230–31. Dated "1306 in the month of February, on Quinquagesima Sunday" (February 13), it states, "Since the Feast of All Saints [November 1] . . . more than four hundred people" were baptized.

34. Moule, *Christians in China*, 182.

35. For these events see Moule, *Christians in China*, 182–89. Clement V, by creating a hierarchy for Mongol Asia, initiated a new mission strategy. See Richard, *La papauté*, 123–24, 144 ff.

36. Peregrine's letter of 1318 and Andrew of Perugia's of 1326 (*Sinica Fran.* 356 ff. and *BTS*, 1:96 ff.) are translated by Dawson, *Mission to Asia*, 232–37.

37. *Regestrum Clementis Papae V*, edited by the Benedictines in 8 vols. (Rome: Typographia Vaticana, 1885–92), 6, nn. 7480, 7481 (both December 20, 1310), and 7482 (February 19, 1311). See also *Ann. Min.* 6:184.

38. There one of them, Jerome of Catalonia, stopped to found a bishopric at Kaffa; see Richard, *La papauté*, 157–58. G. Fedalto finds the title episcopus Caffensis as early as 1317; see *La chiesa latina in Oriente* (Verona: Mazziana, 1973), 1:441–42.

39. Peter's presence in China is attested to, inter alia, in "The Book of the Estate of the Great Caan," probably written ca. 1330 by John of Cora, Archbishop of Soltanieh, translated in Yule, *Cathay*, 3:89–103; see also 100.

40. See L. Petech, "Les merchands italiens dans l'empire mongol," *Journal Asiatique* 250 (1962): 553–58.

41. The stone was discovered in 1951. Rubbings from it are reproduced in F. A. Rouleau, S.J., "The Yangchow Latin Tombstone as a Landmark of Medieval Christianity in China," *Harvard Journal of Asiatic Studies* 17 (1954): 346–68.

42. For complementary explanations of this phenomenon, see E. R. Daniel, *Franciscan Concept of Mission in the High Middle Ages* (Lexington: University Press of Kentucky, 1975), and R. I. Burns, "Christian-Islamic Confrontation in the West: The Thirteenth Century Dream of Conversion," *American Historical Review* 76 (1971): 1386–1434.

43. Rubruck also celebrated mass for Alans at Karacorum (Easter, 1254), who had not "set eyes on the sacrament . . . [since] Nestorians would not admit them into their church . . . unless they were re-baptized" (*MR*, 213).

44. F. W. Iklé, "The Conversion of the Alani by the Franciscan Missionaries in China in the Fourteenth Century," *Papers in Honor of Professor Woodbridge Bingham*, ed. James B. Parsons (San Francisco: Chinese Materials Center, 1976), 31–32. The Mongols first fought their way through the northern Caucasus in 1223, eventually subjugating the Alans.

45. Iklé summarizes this view: "To the Chinese, as is well known, Christianity made no appeal, since it furnished neither a more highly developed system of religion . . ., nor did it represent a superior civilization. Political power [another reason for conversion] . . . was totally lacking" ("Conversion of the Alani," 30).

46. F. Baldrian, "Taoism," trans. C. Le Blanc, in *The Encyclopedia of Reli-*

gion,, M. Eliade, editor in chief (New York and London: Macmillan, 1987), 14:288–306. All three sects—the others were *T'ai-i,* "supreme unity," and *Chen-ta-tao,* "authentic great way"—disappeared after the fall of the Yüan (see 296–97); see also I. Robinet, *Histoire du taoîsme des origines au XIV siècle* (Paris: Editions du Cerf, 1991), 210–11.

47. Yüan, *Asians under the Mongols,* 18–120.

48. I am indebted to Prof. Charles Le Blanc, University of Montreal, for this insight. For a fuller discussion of Taoism, see Robinet, *Histoire du taoîsme,* and H. Maspero, *Taoism and Chinese Religion,* trans. F. A. Kierman, Jr. (Amherst: University of Massachusetts Press, 1981).

49. For Odoric's *Relatio,* see *Sinica Fran.* 411–95, and the annotated translation in Yule, *Cathay,* 2:97–277.

50. Yule, *Cathay,* 2:200, 209–10.

51. Ibid., 225–26. The emphasis is mine.

52. The *Relatio* claims no baptisms, but Odoric's *vita* (composed less than forty years after his death) does: "In [Odoric's] sixteen years . . . [across the sea] he baptized twenty thousand infidels and subdued them to the catholic faith." A. C. Moule, "A Life of Odoric of Pordenone," *T'oung Pao* 20 (1920): 279.

53. Yule, *Cathay,* 2:260–61. The setting is "magna Tartaria" (*Sinica Fran.* 490–91), but no specific location is given.

54. Yule, *Cathay,* 2:262. The felt idols, described by both Plano Carpini (*History of the Mongols,* in Dawson, *Mission to Asia,* 9) and Rubruck (*MR,* 75–77, 156), played an important role in Mongol religious practice.

55. Moule, "A Life of Odoric," 289, and Yule, *Cathay,* 2:275–77.

56. Nicholas was designated archbishop on September 8, 1333, and carried letters recommending him to the Great Khan, the king of Korea, various Tartar khans, the King of Armenia and the Tartar people. *Ann. Min.* 7:138–44.

57. James was killed by Moslems in Chaghatai, perhaps en route home after being expelled from China. *BTS,* 5:92 and Moule, *Christians in China,* 197.

58. See Richard, *La papauté,* 152n.107.

59. For Marignolli's life and his reports see Yule, "Recollections of Travel in the East," *Cathay,* 3:209–69; and Moule, *Christians in China,* 254 ff.

60. For these letters, dated July 11, 1336, see Moule, *Christians in China,* 252–54.

61. Chinese sources record this gift; see H. Franke, "Das 'himmilische Pferd' des Johann von Marignolla," *Archiv für Kulturgeschichte* 50 (1968): 33–40.

62. Moule, *Christians in China,* 257.

63. Ibid., 258.

64. Ibid., 252.

65. Marignolli's "Recollections," in Yule, *Cathay,* 3:229–230. The friars also had a *fondaco* there, an inn with a warehouse used by merchants as a depository.

66. For missionary contact with India and the St. Thomas community see J. D. Ryan, "European Travelers Before Columbus—the Fourteenth Century's Discov-

ery of India," *Catholic Historical Review* 79 (October 1993): 648–70, and works cited therein.

67. Marignolli's "Recollections," in Yule, *Cathay*, 3:258.

68. Ibid., 265–66.

69. Marignolli's Chronicle, in Moule, *Christians in China*, 259.

70. Mongol hegemony in Chaghatai collapsed after Khan Kazan (1339–46) was killed doing battle against the Turkish nobility in Transoxania. L. Kwanten, *Imperial Nomads: A History of Central Asia, 500–1500* (Philadelphia: University of Pennsylvania Press, 1979), 249–50; J. A. Boyle, "Caghatay Khanate," *The Encyclopaedia of Islam*, new ed.(Leiden: E. J. Brill, 1965), 2:4.

71. See above, note 57.

72. Richard (*La papauté*, 154–55) points out that the new Ming dynasty was not systematically xenophobic and did receive later archbishops of Khanbaliq.

Jews, Muslims, and Christians as Converts

From Jew to Christian?

Conversion and Immutability in Medieval Europe

Jonathan M. Elukin

Origins of the idea of race—as a scientifically defined biological category—are usually traced to European societies of the nineteenth and twentieth centuries. In this milieu, conversion to Christianity for modern European Jews never effaced completely their Jewish identity. Some scholars have tried to push back the historical origins of such racial ideology into premodern times. Yosef Yerushalmi, for example, has argued that the purity of blood laws of Spain show that in the fifteenth century people were already thinking in racial terms.[1] Such attempts have not been welcomed by historians of the Middle Ages. Generally, the Middle Ages have been promoted as the last time when, despite all the horrible persecutions inflicted upon Jews by Christians, Jews were still able to convert and thus find a refuge in which they could leave behind their Jewish identities.[2]

The experience of medieval Jews who converted to Christianity was more ambiguous than this idealized picture would suggest. Throughout the Middle Ages, Jews who converted to Christianity found it difficult to convince Christians that they had abandoned their Jewish identities. Perhaps it would be more accurate to say that Christians continued to insist that Jewish converts had retained some element of Jewishness. Was the source of this attitude an incipient racial ideology? In other words—did Christians of the Middle Ages see Jewishness as a physical characteristic that conversion could not eradicate?

Simply to answer in the affirmative would distort the reality of medieval society and transpose modern conceptions of race back into an equally complicated medieval ideology. Instead of imposing modern categories of thought on medieval people, we should explore the particular medieval sentiments that promoted a deep suspicion of Jewish conversions to Christianity. Before looking for explanations—some of which are necessarily tentative—we need to set out the parameters of our study.

The most conservative generalization will have to suffice: by the thirteenth century, a converted Jew faced Christians who were deeply suspicious of his new Christian identity. It is difficult, of course, to decide whether the increasing evidence of problematic Jewish conversions from the twelfth and thirteenth centuries shows an intensification of ambivalence toward Jewish converts during the course of the Middle Ages or is simply the result of the more abundant literary evidence available in the High Middle Ages. Antagonism to Jews certainly increased dramatically after the twelfth century.[3] This does not necessarily explain the ambivalence to Jewish converts. On the other hand, suspicion of converts may have increased as a by-product of this more generalized antagonism to Judaism.

We have to use the evidence we have without discounting its shortcomings. To that end, let us first ask about the Jews who converted to Christianity. Can we recover anything of their historical experience? To do so, we will necessarily range rather broadly across evidence from Late Antiquity through the thirteenth century.

Let us begin with a text from the New Testament. In Acts 6:1 we read that "during those days, when the disciples were increasing in number, the Hellenists complained against the Hebrews because their widows were being neglected in the daily distribution of food." Here we have evidence that the Gentile Christians of the early Church, although not yet dominant, discriminated between converts from Judaism and those from among the Gentiles, strongly suggesting that a person's former identity was not lost upon baptism. The language of the thirteenth-century collection of saints' lives, the *Golden Legend,* was more explicit: "As the number of the disciples increased, the Christians of Gentile origins began to murmur against those converted from Judaism, because the widows among the former were being neglected in the daily ministry."[4] The medieval readers of the *Golden Legend* also learned that converts from Judaism could still be identified by their Jewish origins and be expected to act malevolently.

The Jewish identity of other converts never completely disappeared, at least as that identity was perceived by historians who recorded these idiosyncratic conversions. The early fifth-century Greek historian Socrates records in his *Ecclesiastical History* the account of one converted Jew whom he described in terms of his Jewishness even after he converted: "Marcian had promoted to the rank of presbyter a converted Jew named Sabbatius, who nevertheless continued to retain many of his Jewish prejudices; and moreover he was very ambitious of being made a bishop."[5]

Such ambivalence survived into the early medieval west. Sidonius, a fifth-century Gallo-Roman nobleman, seemed to have quite amicable relations with several Jews. In one letter, he wrote to a friend, "I commend to you Promotus, the bearer of my letter, who is already known to you, but has recently, through your prayers, been made a member of our tribe. A Jew by race, he has now chosen to be accounted an Israelite by faith rather than by blood."[6] Sidonius acknowledges Promotus' new identity as a Christian—a (true) Israelite by faith. This new identity supersedes the one derived from Promotus' lineage as a Jew and, more importantly, as a non-Roman. Nevertheless, Sidonius' identification of Promotus as a former Jew leaves open the question of the perceived completeness of his conversion.

Later in the Middle Ages, it would make sense to a medieval reader that a residual Jewishness could influence the actions of a convert. Indeed, it even made sense that someone with Jewish parentage would be involved in host desecration. In a thirteenth-century account, we find the story of an individual who received the host and then—against Church decrees—removed it from his mouth to find that it had miraculously turned into a tiny infant. The author identified the perpetrator as the son of a convert.[7]

The famous thirteenth-century autobiography of Herman-Judah gives us another opportunity to see the perceived difficulties of converting a Jew into a Christian. The authenticity of the text has recently been questioned and has provoked a spirited debate among historians.[8] I cannot mediate that dispute here. Indeed, I am not sure whether one side has definitively made the case for authenticity or forgery. In any event, the text still reflects what Christians in the Middle Ages believed was the course of a convert's transformation.

From "Herman's" point of view, his conversion was being constantly undermined by demonic attacks and obstacles. It was the interference of the diabolical "Enemy," according to the text, that led Herman to believe he needed to be immersed only once rather than the threefold immersion that was normative in the Church:

> I stepped into the waves of the life-giving font. Immersed in it once, toward the east, I believed that that one immersion sufficed for the renewal of the ancient state. But the clerics standing around the baptistry shouted that I ought to be immersed more times. Having already just left the font, I could not hear their voices distinctly, nor, since water was running down the hairs of my head, could I see clearly the gestures that they were making to me. Therefore, wiping the water from my face with my hands, I heard what they wanted, but, stiff with the bitter cold of the font, I at first did not willingly yield to their wish; but, bent by the gentle

admonition of my baptizer, I did what had to be done for salvation. And so, considering that I had satisfied the divine mysteries by the second dipping, I began to want to get out of the font. I was almost frozen rigid by its extreme cold. But again the clergy clamored with loud shouts that to complete the sacrament I had humbly to submit to be immersed to the south in the saving waves. Overcome therefore by diabolical fraud, I suspected that they were making a laughingstock of me.

We need to imagine how a Christian audience would have read this anecdote of Herman's conversion. Herman's mistaken understanding of baptism would have confirmed for a Christian audience that Jews were untrustworthy neophytes. That is, if left to themselves, the Jews would get Christianity wrong, in both its rituals and its content. In order to prove the validity of his conversion, Herman has to explain away his perceived ignorance and the ever present potential that he could be accused of an insincere conversion. The entire autobiography can be seen as testimony to the need to establish a new identity in a world that is loath to accommodate such transformations and to excuse mistakes that might seem to undermine that new identity. The writing of the autobiography, and the account of Herman's later successes in the Church (his fluency in Latin, for example), were ways to construct a new identity and to fight off perceived doubts about the indeterminacy of conversion from Judaism.[9]

The ambivalence of Christians toward new converts from Judaism can also be seen in the bureaucratic language used to describe them. Here we have evidence about how verifiably real people negotiated the transition from Judaism to Christianity. Documents from medieval governments and the institutions of the Church identified Jewish converts in ways that preserved the memory of their conversion. That is, they appear in the surviving documents identified as *conversus* or *quondam judeus*. For example, Roger the Convert and John the Convert became favorites of Henry III of England, yet they still carried their past identities with them.[10] Perhaps in some cases the appellation was meant to honor the commitment of the convert. I think it is more likely that concealed behind this seemingly neutral terminology, however, was distrust that could grow easily into open antagonism.

One seemingly successful English convert who came under intense suspicion because of his perceived Jewishness was the former Jew Henry of Winchester, knighted by Henry III after being baptized. Edward I remembered Henry of Winchester's transformation: "The lord king Henry, our father, of happy memory, freed Henry of Winchester, knight, from Judaic error and converted him to the unity of the holy faith, immersing this same

Henry in holy baptism and causing him to be called by his own name, Henry, and then, out of affection which our father had for this man Henry, caused him to be decorated with the belt of knighthood."[11] This newly made favorite of the king worked as the king's notary in the Jewish Exchequer, the court entrusted with cases involving Jews, but he continued to be involved with at least one other Jew in the buying and selling of Jewish bonds. He also seems to have been implicated in the coin-clipping scandal of 1278–79 but obtained a pardon for his involvement—perhaps by betraying his Jewish accomplice to the royal judges.

Ironically, Winchester was assigned to act as a judge in the coin-clipping trials under Edward but his perceived Jewishness offended Bishop Thomas Cantilupe. In the fourteenth-century dossier of the canonization of Thomas, Ralph de Hengham, later chief justice of the Court of Common Pleas, recounts how Thomas was scandalized by the convert's challenge to established norms of Christian authority. It was unacceptable that "a certain knight who was a Jew and called Henry of Winchester, the Convert, should have *testimonium et recordum* over Christians who clipped or forged the king's money—that is to say, that he should have authority and power such that at his command and testimony, or by his written record, other men could lose life and limb. Thomas, who was a member of the council, objected and said to the king that it was not proper that this convert and Jew should have such power over Christians." Indeed, according to the dossier, "[Thomas objected] because he judged it unworthy and not pleasing to God for the faithful of Christ and those born to Christian parents to be subject to a man recently converted from Judaism to Christ and for their lives and limbs to be in the power of such a man, whose conversion and fairness he perhaps held suspect, on account of Jewish perfidy and the ancient hatred of the Jewish people for Christians."

Edward was persuaded by Thomas's arguments and withdrew the appointment of Henry. In this case at least, baptism had not effaced the visible Jewish identity of a convert. Such discomfort, Robert Stacey believes, was common in England by the thirteenth century: "Integration had its limits, even for a man who had been knighted by the king himself. By the middle of the thirteenth century in England, there was clearly an irreducible element to Jewish identity in the eyes of many Christians, which no amount of baptismal water could entirely eradicate, at least, from a layman. Through baptism, converts from Judaism became Christians, but this did not mean that they had entirely ceased to be Jews in the eyes of their brothers and sisters in Christ."

Despite their rhetoric of welcoming Jews into the fellowship of Christian truth, it seems that many Christians during the Middle Ages were often reluctant to help support individual converts. This reluctance can only be effectively explained by suspicions about the new convert's identity. The papal archives preserve many instances of the Pope insisting, cajoling, or ordering local authorities to provide for the support of deracinated Jews.[12] To continue with evidence from England, many years after the founding of the *domus conversorum,* the halfway house for converts, the royal government was still farming out converts to various religious houses because it could not or would not support the converts itself.[13] Converts were not always well received by the institutions of the Church. Many were forced to wander from monastery to monastery before they were finally accepted. One particularly articulate convert, whose letters of appeal reached the king, compared herself to Hagar and Mary Magdalene.[14]

Local bishops also had to coerce church officials to support indigent converts. We have one letter from Anselm of Canterbury to the prior and archdeacon of Canterbury in which the reluctance of clerics to help converts forced Anselm to insist upon the obligations of Christian charity. After a certain Robert had decided to flee Judaism for Christianity, Anselm beseeched all Christians to help this Jew, who on account of Christ had left his parents. Anselm declared that it was disgraceful for Christians and particularly members of the clergy to abandon the convert.[15] We do not know if Anselm's entreaties were successful. Such hesitancy about accepting converts was thus widespread, and we can be confident that the reluctance derived from Christian ambivalence about the true identity of converts from Judaism.[16]

The local churchmen who had to implement the programs of the papacy no doubt had to weigh the accommodation of these new Christians against limited finances. However, the recourse of the popes to language about the importance of accepting the converts whose conversion was somehow in danger suggests that it was less a question of money than of what the converts represented. These conversions were not secure. Judaism always lurked as a seductive refuge unless Christians accepted them. To various popes, converts were examples of the victory of the Gospel. To local churchmen who would have to be responsible for the support and welcome of the converts among their congregations, it was much harder to overcome a lingering discomfort and reluctance.

One of the most fully developed cases of this kind to survive in the archives concerns Milo, a Jewish convert, who sought a prebend from the bishop of Tournai in the early 1170s. Pope Alexander III had ordered the bishop and chapter to accept Milo. The convert was forced to seek another papal injunction when the chapter apparently pretended that it had never received the first papal letter. The Pope already suspected the true reason behind the unwillingness to admit Milo was his former Jewish identity. Alexander had to remind the bishop that Christ himself was a Jew—whence salvation came—and one should rejoice over Milo's conversion.[17]

Alexander's strong words were obviously not enough for the willful bishop and chapter. Another letter followed quickly, warning the chapter to accept Milo and to desist from harassing him because he had once been a Jew. The Pope had heard that many of the clerics looked down upon Milo, asserting that it was indecent to offer a prebend to such an uncivilized and ignoble man and one born in the Jewish *gens:* "There are many of you, as we have heard, who are scorning a little the reception of the aforesaid 'M,' and some of you are asserting that it is indecent that a man both shameful and ignoble and born from the Jewish race be received into canonical orders and to obtain a prebend in your church." Alexander reminded the clerics of the origin of the Jewish people, which was not ignoble at all. Rather the Old Testament records their descent from the most noble patriarchs: "they have proceeded by physical descent from those most noble patriarchs, namely Abraham, Isaac and Jacob." Thus, Alexander concluded, Milo should be received by the chapter and not molested. It is interesting that the letter does not urge the chapter to ignore his Jewish ancestry. Rather, the Pope tries to show that his Jewishness was not a disability.[18]

The language of the letter forces us to consider the motivations of the clerics of Tournai. They may have had a particular grudge against Milo and were trying to make his candidacy unappealing by exploiting his origins. This may have been a cynical ploy on their part, but they must have believed it would have some meaning and effect on their audience in the papal curia or the local clergy. It seems more likely, given what we know of Christian concerns about Jewish conversion, that their anxieties were genuine. They must have been strongly motivated to risk the displeasure of the papacy, particularly in a case where the Pope felt such a strong personal connection to the convert. The dignity of the chapter was at stake, and as we know, as the elites of feudal Europe stabilized from the eleventh century, the conditions of birth became of paramount importance in both lay and religious circles.[19]

Doubts about the sincerity of conversions by Jews brought Innocent III to rely on an account of miraculous conversion in order to support one convert. In a letter from the papal archives dated June 8, 1213 and issued from Rome, Innocent III ordered Peter of Corbeil, archbishop of Sens, to provide the Jewish convert "N," formerly Isaac, and his family with the necessities of life. Innocent made the converts more attractive by confirming that they had witnessed a miracle of the Eucharist, which prompted them to convert. A Christian woman, by the name of Christiana, lived with the Jews. She apparently was being seduced away from the Catholic faith, and on the feast of the Resurrection, she hid the host in her mouth and brought it to Isaac. ("Ecce Salvator meus, ut asserunt Christiani.") Isaac hid the host in a chest full of money. When he later opened it, the chest was full of hosts ("sed hostiis plenam vidit"). Persuaded by the miracle, the Jews decided to accept the Christian faith ("deliberaverunt ad fidem accedere Christianam").[20]

The Pope was recounting the story for the Jews' potential patron in order to establish their pedigree. We will see how important miraculous conversions were in convincing Christians of the sincerity of Jewish converts. If the Pope thought in this case that his churchmen were anxious about the nature of the Jews' religious rebirth, and that he could confirm it by telling the story of the miraculous host, it makes sense that the other cases of reluctant support for the Jews were influenced in some way by uncertainty over the sincerity and reality of their conversion. Unfortunately for the papal authorities in those other cases, there was no convenient miracle story to buttress the conversions.

Jewish actions may have also contributed to the Christian belief in the inefficacy of conversion. Groups of converted Jews banded together informally and often demonstrated a particular group identity. For example, the papal registers record that a group of converted Jews in 1235 in Paris petitioned the Pope to be exempted from attending court outside Paris provided that they appear before the bishop of Paris.[21] They could obviously identify each other and were identified by the church bureaucracy as recent converts. By associating with former coreligionists, these converts may have been acknowledging the difficulties of integrating fully into Christian society. In addition, they were certainly encouraging Christians to suspect that the ties of family and religion had not been broken by baptism.[22]

At the same time, attempts by Jews to bring converts back to Judaism might have raised doubts in the minds of Christians about the fixity of baptism. Christians in England would have heard of the famous story of Juliana of London, who converted to Christianity in 1274 and then was kidnapped by nine Jews who tried to smuggle her out of the country.[23] Caesarius of Heisterbach recounts in his thirteenth-century collection of *exempla* the story of one Jewish woman whose mother promised her that "'I can easily undo your baptism . . . I would draw you,' said the Jewess, 'three times through the opening of the latrine, and thus the virtue of your baptism would be left behind.'"[24] Even the Duke of Louvain was perfectly willing to restore a converted Jewess to her father and had to be warned: "Sir, if you commit this crime against God and His church, never can your soul be saved."[25] If Christians were aware of rabbinic thought on the inefficacy of baptism, this might have contributed as well to a suspicion that Jewish identity remained immutable.[26] In Christian eyes, the connections between converts and Jews remained; it was a bond that could easily undermine the conversion.

How can we explain this predisposition among Christians, firmly established in the evidence by the thirteenth century, to look at Jewish converts as still retaining something of their Jewishness? There are several possible explanations, and the relative hierarchy of these answers is uncertain.

The perceived nature of conversion itself led Christians from Late Antiquity onward to doubt that Jewish identity could be transformed in the waters of the baptismal font. It is a central paradox of Christian religious history that even as baptism was held out as the way to salvation for all people, it was understood as an ongoing process and not as a sudden shift that fundamentally and completely transformed the life of the convert.[27] Christians needed to believe in the possibility of total conversion because their personal religious experiences forced them to confront the imperfect process of conversion. Robin Lane Fox has described, at least for the early centuries of Christianity, the long process of initiation for the catechumen as representative of Christian understanding of conversion: "It is certainly not a process dominated, or largely explained, by sudden miracles . . . The years of instruction and preparation became, in their turn, one of the faith's particular appeals. People felt that they were exploring a deep mystery, step by step. They were advancing with a group of fellow explorers along a route which required a high moral effort."[28]

Conversion was thus a journey that continued throughout a life of contemplation, study, and prayer. It was a journey, however, marked by uncertainty. No one could be assured of the gift of God's grace, the only sure guarantee of salvation. The pressing need to ensure that vulnerable infants were prepared for heaven led to infant baptism, a ritual which suggested that faith could be granted substantively to a passive recipient. However, baptism never was completely divorced from a conscious acceptance of faith. When Christians extended baptism to infants by the fifth century, it was on the condition that godparents would speak the *professio* on the infants' behalf. Eventually, some began to consider that it was the Church, and not uninstructed godparents, who made the *professio* for the child. In either case, there was some active will that created an effective baptism. It was not simply a passive act.[29] The sincerity of the candidate for baptism thus remained a factor in the perceived success of the transformation. The community could often see its own uncertain experience of *transitus,* it has been argued, even in children about to be baptized.[30]

Even if the human will could be neutralized, Christians did not think that the human person was so malleable. Baptism was unlikely to transform an individual's religious personality if it could not even neutralize sexuality. The early Church father Tertullian, for example, was not certain that baptism could efface the deep and dangerous sexuality of women. He was concerned that their sexuality, as Peter Brown argues, was "sunk deep into the human body" and "Christian baptism did nothing to change this fact."[31] Baptism, as Brown has written, did free people from slavery to their bodies. It "weakened a little the grip of the demonic powers that ruled the pagan world outside its walls." However, after the ceremony, one did not find "oneself shot free, if even for one highly stylized moment, of the huge gravitational pull of human nature."[32]

Christianity was thus a religious culture built upon the idea of incremental and imperfect conversion. By its very nature, then, conversion promoted suspicion of converts. Karl Morrison has recently argued that "insofar as converts aroused suspicion, the entire community of believers was shot through with universal and mutual suspicion . . . [and] the suspicion of crypto-belief in former ways was endemic in a society of converts."[33] Imagining the quandary of medieval Christians when faced with newly converted Jews, Morrison writes that medieval Christians would have asked themselves "how could those [Jews] whose minds had not been impregnated with divine love be won from their depraved and animal understanding to true belief."[34] The question became: when was a conversion a true conversion?

In this society of converts, then, an outward sign might guarantee the legitimacy of the conversion.[35] Accounts of forced conversions were also recast in the light of a pseudomiracle. Gregory of Tours recounted the events surrounding the conversion of the Jews of Clermont in the sixth century to make it seem as if the bishop had in some way persuaded the Jews to have a fundamental change of heart. Gregory described the city as torn apart by a religious feud that began at Easter when a Jewish convert was attacked by another Jew. The following Ascension, the Christian mob destroyed the synagogue. Then, according to Gregory's version, Bishop Avitus sent envoys to the Jews saying, "I do not incite you by force to believe in the Son of God, but I preach and convey the salt of wisdom to your hearts . . . Therefore, if you wish to believe as I do, be one flock under me. But otherwise, leave this place." The Jews were "moved by conflicting emotions and hesitated, but on the third day [after Ascension]—as I believe, overcome by the bishop—they agreed and sent a reply to him, saying, 'We believe that Jesus is the Son of the living God promised us by the prophets, and therefore we beseech that we might be washed by baptism, lest we persist in this fault.' The bishop rejoiced at the message. After celebrating the nocturns of holy Pentecost, he left for the baptistery outside the walls, and there the whole multitude, prostrate before him, asked for baptism."[36]

By suppressing the fact that a Christian mob had driven the Jews into a house and besieged them there—a fact we know from the parallel poem account of Venantius Fortunatus—Gregory removes the immediate threat of violence to the Jews. Even in his version, the destruction of the synagogue—which might be considered intimidation enough—is displaced by the sudden and quasimiraculous change of heart of the Jews, a model of conversion that Gregory applied to other pagan groups like Clovis's Franks.[37] The immediate baptism of the Jews and the flight of those Jews who chose not to convert underscores the completeness of the conversions. The validity of the conversion under Avitus, at least in the eyes of Gregory, is further set off by his derogatory account of the forced conversions orchestrated by King Chilperic.[38]

In other cases the conversion of a particular Jew was confirmed by a divine sign. At the forced baptism of a Jewish child who had been seized in Rouen during the First Crusade, and who later became a monk at the monastery of Fly, Guibert of Nogent was told that "after the holy words had been said and the sacrament performed, when they came to the part where a candle is lighted and the melted wax is dropped on the water, a drop of it was seen to fall separately all by itself, taking the shape of a tiny cross on the water so exactly in its minute substance that no human hand could have made a similar one so small."[39] Guibert was still a little suspicious of the sign, even though it was verified by the boy's patron and "by the priest, both solemnly protesting by God that the tale was true." Guibert admits that he would have "treated the incident less seriously had I not seen without any doubt the remarkable progress of the boy." In the context of the boy's religious career, the meaning of the tiny wax cross was clear: "Therefore the cross at his baptism seems to have been formed not by chance but by Providence, as a sign of the future religious faith of a man of Jewish origin, which in our days is unusual."[40] For Guibert, the sign confirms the convert's religious transformation, which might still have been regarded with suspicion by his readers.

Even better were the conversions associated with miraculous events surrounding the Eucharist. In the archetypical host desecration story, a Jew of Paris at Easter of 1290 obtained a host and then attacked it with knives and cast it into boiling water. The host turned into an image of the crucified Christ in the cauldron. The Jew was executed but his family—convinced by the apparition—converted to Christianity, and his daughter entered a convent.[41] These miracles, significantly, could also be repeated, making conversion seem an ever-present possibility.

In addition to the nature of conversion itself, the sociology of the Middle Ages made it more difficult for Jews to "convert" fully. The Jews were the one immediately and constantly present non-normative group that lived—except for periodic expulsion—within Christian society.[42] At the same time, Jews always converted *into* an established Christian society. Other ethnic groups that converted did so as embryonic national groups or looked on as passive witnesses to a royal acceptance of Christianity, as in the case of Clovis's conversion. In either case, a coherent local society of converts was created, which could thrive in the new religion despite carping by Church authorities as to the efficacy of the conversion. The Jews, on the other hand, had no ethnic or national refuge in which to convert.

Even the relatively tolerant and multiethnic society of the early Middle Ages may have worked against creating a model of full Jewish conversion. Scholars have offered many different interpretations to explain the relatively tolerant attitudes of Christians in the early Middle Ages as compared to the aggressively anti-Judaic attitudes current after the eleventh century. The multiethnic character of the early Middle Ages, with different barbarian tribes moving into the Roman orbit, has recently been emphasized as a factor in giving the Jews room to thrive.[43] However, this environment of multiple ethnicities may in fact have sensitized Christians to the continuing reality of ethnic groups. Thus, it may have been harder for Jews in this environment to escape their so-called ethnic origins.

We also know that Christians were accustomed to thinking in terms of descent. We find that Augustine promoted a deep sense of the continuity of the Jews: "In fact, even after losing their temple, their sacrifice, their priesthood, and their kingdom, they hold on to their name and race in a few ancient rites . . . Like Cain, who in envy and pride killed his just brother, they have been marked with a sign so that no one may kill them."[44] This attitude penetrated royal legislation deep into the Middle Ages. According to the thirteenth-century Spanish law code, the *Siete Partidas,* the Jews were protected so "that they might live forever as in captivity and serve as a reminder to mankind that they are descended from those who crucified Our Lord Jesus Christ."[45] At the same time, national distinctions across European society often became reified into permanent differences that to modern readers reflect a biologically inflected racial prejudice.[46]

Indeed, male Jews had to overcome the problematic mark of circumcision. Conversion could not efface this sign which remained imprinted on their bodies. Christian suspicion of conversion often focused on the ineradicable nature of circumcision. Indeed, in one case in 1230, Christians expressed their opinion of the efficacy of one Jew's conversion by circumcising his child.[47] The possibility of Christians converting to Judaism and undergoing circumcision particularly enraged Christian authorities. Gerald of Wales in the twelfth century denounced the circumcision of two monks who thus became the "most vile enemies of Christ."[48] Punishment for this self-mutilation, when it could be enforced, was swift and brutal. A deacon in the thirteenth century who, Maitland tells us, turned Jew out of love for a Jewess, was immediately burned.[49] The mark may have been thus so disfiguring that it made converted Jews seem only half Christian.

Conversely, once Christians were circumcised, they still could be identified as former Christians. At least this is what Bernard Gui, the famous inquisitor of the thirteenth century, asserted in his *Manual for the Inquisitor.* When Jews circumcise Christian children, according to Gui, they cut the foreskin of the penis only halfway around the organ. For Jewish children, they circumcise by cutting the skin all the way round. Why would Gui be interested in preserving this information—accurate or not—about Jewish circumcision? What did he believe that this difference in circumcising techniques demonstrated about Jews and Christians? Such a vision of a Jewish standard that discriminated between "real" Jews and Christian converts was comforting to Gui, for it meant that one could still make a distinction between true Jews and the unfortunate Christian apostates who had been attracted to the *perfidia judeorum.*[50]

The rhetoric surrounding the famous controversy in the papal schism of 1130 between Anacletus II and Innocent II suggests that some Christians held ambivalent views of the descendants of Jewish converts, particularly when the descendants had access to real power. In the propaganda war during the schism, Anacletus' Jewish lineage (his great-grandfather had been Jewish) became a central issue. Bernard of Clairvaux spoke for many when he protested that Anacletus' pretensions to the papal throne were an outrage: "It is clear that it is an injury to Christ for [one] of Jewish lineage/race to occupy the seat of Peter."[51] Bernard could not have made up this language out of whole cloth. Because he was engaged in a crucial public debate, he had to believe that his propaganda and what it said about Jewish identity had a reasonable chance of making sense to his audience. The question remains: what drove Christians like Bernard to reify Jewishness into a physical attribute transmitted by descent and impervious to the effects of baptism?

This sensitivity to the physical distinctiveness of the Jews permeated many aspects of medieval Christian culture. Art provided an idiom in which physical distinctiveness, defined as grotesque disfigurement, became a living style of discourse to describe Jews as well as other marginal figures.[52] At least some medieval physicians sought to describe Jews as marked by unique physical disabilities.[53] Thus, while Robert Bartlett is right to emphasize that medieval ethnicity is largely a cultural construct of language, geography, and law, he underestimates the persistent emphasis on lineage, descent, and physical appearance that informed much of the medieval attempt to define ethnic identity.[54]

Can we then describe Christian suspicions about converted Jews as deriving from a sense of their *racial* distinctiveness? We should be wary of importing modern language into a medieval reality. There was a matrix of ideas in the Christian culture of the Middle Ages that presented different aspects of Judaism as immutable. For example, Christians thought that Jewish history had not changed since the time of Jesus. The language of the Jews, Hebrew, also was considered anachronistic. Indeed, Christians thought that the Jews themselves—represented by the Pharisees—had remained unchanged since the first century.[55]

Christian culture by the twelfth century thus created a way of thinking about the immutability of Jews that drew its strength largely from religious ideas rather than from conceptions of the biological distinctiveness of Jews. This perception of immutability, when combined with the emphasis on lineage and the embryonic ideas of the physical distinctiveness of the Jews through which lineage was expressed, made it easier for Christians to imagine that Jews were incapable of being assimilated into Christian society. The Christian culture of conversion, as I have tried to show, provided fertile ground for these impulses. A sensitivity to ethnic identity certainly existed in the Middle Ages, but it was not the biologically defined racism of modern Europe. It is difficult to sum up such a complicated spectrum of ideas, but at least one medieval writer has provided us with a convenient commentary. Joachim of Fiore, the twelfth-century mystic, captured the medieval sentiment about the fixed nature of the Jews when he wrote in a quietly derogatory way: "Noluerunt . . . ipsi Judaei mutari cum tempore"—those Jews did not wish to change with the times.[56]

NOTES

This paper is a much revised version of two chapters from my dissertation. I am grateful to James Muldoon for the invitation to contribute to this volume and for his acute substantive and editorial comments.

1. Yosef H. Yerushalmi, *Assimilation and Racial Anti-Semitism: The Iberian and the German Models* (New York: Leo Baeck Institute, 1982). See also Jerome Friedman, "Jewish Conversion, the Spanish Pure Blood Laws, and Reformation: A Revisionist View of Racial and Religious Antisemitism," *Sixteenth Century Jour-*

nal 18 (1987): 3–31. I have not seen B. Netanyahu's *The Origins of the Inquisition in Fifteenth Century Spain* (New York: Random House, 1995). For general comments on Jewish conversion to Christianity, see Jeremy Cohen, "The Mentality of the Medieval Jewish Apostate: Peter Alfonsi, Herman of Cologne, and Pablo Christiani," in *Jewish Apostasy in the Modern World*, ed. Todd M. Endelman and Jeffrey Gurock (New York: Holmes & Meier, 1987), 20–47, and William C. Jordan, "À travers le regard des enfants," *Provence historique* 37 (1987): 531–43.

2. Robert Bartlett, *The Making of Europe* (Princeton: Princeton University Press, 1993), 197. Peter Browe, "Die kirchenrechtliche Stellung der getauften Juden und ihrer Nachkommen," *Archiv für katholisches Kirchenrecht* 121 (1941): 3–22, 165–91, believes that Jewish converts in the Middle Ages were fully integrated into Christian life. The same conclusion about the efficacy of baptism can be found in Garth Fowden, *Empire to Commonwealth: Consequences of Monotheism in Late Antiquity* (Princeton: Princeton University Press, 1993), 68: "Once reborn in the waters of Christian baptism one was in the fullest sense a member of the Church community, but not so in the synagogue." Here Fowden seems more interested in proving the seemingly "racist" leanings in Jewish thought about converts. For a more balanced treatment of the Jewish material, see Gary G. Porton, *The Stranger within Your Gates: Converts and Conversion in Rabbinic Literature* (Chicago: University of Chicago Press, 1994).

3. In a forthcoming article, "The Pharisee and the Interior Jew," that will appear in a volume of essays from the University of Notre Dame conference "In the Shadow of the Millenium: Jews and Christians in 12th-Century Europe," I argue for the importance of the twelfth century's "discovery of the self" as a crucial factor in increased suspicion of Jewish converts.

4. Jacobus de Voragine, *The Golden Legend: Readings on the Saints,* trans. William Granger Ryan, 2 vols. (Princeton: Princeton University Press, 1993), 1:45 (chap. 8, St. Stephen).

5. Socrates, *The Ecclesiastical History of Socrates Scholasticus: A Select Library of Nicene and Post-Nicene Fathers of the Christian Church,* ed. A. C. Zenos (New York: Christian Literature Company, 1890), 2:129 (book V, chap. 21). See also Socrates' account of one upwardly mobile convert from Judaism who tried baptism in several heretical churches before coming to Paul, bishop of the Novatians. When the Jew entered the baptismal font, God apparently made the water disappear on account of his previous baptisms (book VII, chap. 17). In Vincent of Beauvais' retelling of the episode in his thirteenth-century encyclopedia, the *Speculum Historiale*, the emphasis is now placed on the Jewishness of the man seeking baptism. The fleeing water showed the "virtutem dei et iudei perfidiam." *Speculum Quadruplex sive Speculum Maius. Speculum Historiale*, 4 vols. (Douai, 1624; reprint, Graz, Austria, 1965), 4:733–34.

6. Sidonius, *Poems and Letters*, trans. W. B. Anderson, 2 vols. (Cambridge: Harvard University Press, 1965), 2:483.

7. Miri Rubin, "Desecration of the Host: The Birth of an Accusation," *Christianity and Judaism*, ed. Diana Wood (Oxford: Blackwell, 1992), 171.

8. *Hermanus quondam Iudaeus, Opusculum de conversione sua.* See Karl F. Morrison's recent translation in *Conversion and Text: The Cases of Augustine of Hippo, Herman-Judah, and Constantine Tsatsos* (Charlottesville: University Press of Virginia, 1992). On the authenticity of the work, see the recent articles by Avrom Saltman, "Herman's *Opusculum de conversione sua:* Truth or Fiction?" *Revue des études juives* 147 (1988): 31–56, and the response by Aviad Kleinberg, "Hermanus Judaeus's *Opusculum:* In Defense of Its Authenticity," *Revue des études juives* 151 (1992): 337–53. See also Anna Sapir Abulafia, "The Ideology of Reform and the Jews," *Jewish History* 7 (1993): 43–63, and Arnaldo Momigliano, "A Medieval Jewish Autobiography," in his *On Pagans, Jews, and Christians* (Middletown, Conn.: Wesleyan University Press, 1987), 222–31.

9. See Morrison, *Text,* 98–108 (chaps. 11–19). Sander L. Gilman, *Jewish Self-Hatred* (Baltimore and London: Johns Hopkins University Press, 1986), 31: "He [Herman] must reify the abyss demanded by the Church between the Christian and the Jew. Such a demand places Herman, or any other convert, in an untenable position. For the dichotomy between Christian and Jew does not provide for a true identification with the persona of the former. There remains always the stigma of being the convert. (Indeed, this seems to be one of the demons that Herman is exorcising in his letter.) In order that the 'seeing' Jew may be an even better Christian than his coreligionist, the convert must turn this stigma into a sign of higher status."

10. On the English cases, see Robert C. Stacey, "The Conversion of Jews to Christianity in Thirteenth-Century England," *Speculum* 67 (1992): 276.

11. The following discussion and quotations are drawn from Stacey, "Conversion," 276–77.

12. See, for example, Shlomo Simonsohn, *The Apostolic See and the Jews: Documents,* 492–1404, Studies and Texts 94 (Toronto: Pontifical Institute of Medieval Studies, 1988). See Documents, no. 196, Lyons, July 15, 1250, 203–4, and no. 197, Lyons, November 13, 1250, 204–5.

13. F. Donald Logan, "Thirteen London Jews and Conversion to Christianity: Problems of Apostasy in the 1280s," *Bulletin of the Institute of Historical Research* 45 (1972): 214–29.

14. Joan Greatrex, "Monastic Charity for Jewish Converts: The Requisition of Corrodies by Henry III," in Wood, *Christianity and Judaism,* 133–45.

15. Anselm, *Epistola* 117, *Patrologia Latina,* ed. J. P. Migne, vol. 159, col. 154.

16. Simonsohn, *Documents,* no. 222, 1265–1268, 227. Sometime between the years 1265 and 1268, Pope "X" (Clement IV?) sent a command to William de Gres (or Renaud de Nanteuil), bishop of Beauvais, to provide for two converts, one Guillermus de Sancto Evultio and Maria, his sister. The Pope was concerned that once having converted, they would return to the blindness of Judaism unless provisions were made for them. Simonsohn, *Documents,* no. 50, Benevento, March 7, 1169, 52, concerning one Peter, "olim Judaeus, nunc autem Christianus."

17. Simonsohn, *Documents,* no. 52, 1173–1174, 54.

18. Ibid.

19. Marc Bloch, *Feudal Society*, trans. L. A. Manyon, 2 vols. (Chicago: University of Chicago Press, 1961), 2:325.

20. Simonsohn, *Documents*, no. 93, Rome, June 8, 1213, 98.

21. Ibid., no. 207, Rome, December 9, 1255, 212.

22. See the articles by Logan, note 13, and Stacey, note 10, above.

23. Barrie Dobson, "Jewish Women in Medieval England," in Wood, *Christianity and Judaism*, 167.

24. Caesarius of Heisterbach, *The Dialogue on Miracles*, trans. and ed. H. Von E. Scott and C. C. Swinton Bland, 2 vols. (New York: Harcourt, Brace and Company, 1929), 1:110 (book II, chap. 26).

25. Ibid., 107 (book II, chap. 25). Guibert of Nogent also suggested to his readers that conversion could be reversed. About the boy converted at Rouen, he wrote that since his patron "feared that he might be recovered by his family and returned to his earlier condition, he entered him in the monastery of Fly." For an English translation, see *Self and Society in Medieval France,* ed. and trans. John F. Benton (New York: Harper & Row, 1970), 136 (book II, chap. 5).

26. On rabbinic precepts about the perceived inefficacy of apostasy, see Jacob Katz, "Although He Sinned, He Is an Israelite," *Tarbiz* 27 (1958): 203–17 (Hebrew).

27. Karl Morrison, *Understanding Conversion* (Charlottesville: University Press of Virginia, 1992), 75–77.

28. Robin Lane Fox, *Pagans and Christians* (New York: Knopf, 1987), 314.

29. John Van Engen, "Faith as a Concept of Order in Medieval Christendom," *Belief in History: Innovative Approaches to European and American Religion*, ed. Thomas Krelman (Notre Dame and London: University of Notre Dame Press, 1991), 19–67.

30. On the flexible symbolism of infant baptism, see Peter Cramer, *Baptism and Change in the Early Middle Ages, c. 200–c. 1150* (Cambridge: Cambridge University Press, 1993), 116.

31. Peter Brown, *The Body and Society: Men, Women, and Sexual Renunciation in Early Christianity* (New York: Columbia University Press, 1988), 81–82.

32. Ibid., 81. For a discussion of the perceived limited power of baptism to transform Jews in the Visigothic society of early medieval Spain, see P. D. King, *Law and Society in the Visigothic Kingdom* (Cambridge: Cambridge University Press, 1972), 136.

33. Morrison, *Conversion*, 73. Here would be an interesting point to pursue in a comparative study with Islam. Was there the same persistent suspicion of converts or fellow believers in Islamic culture?

34. Morrison, *Conversion*, 45.

35. Gregory of Tours, *History of the Franks*, book V, chap. 11; see the translation in Walter Goffart, "The Conversions of Avitus of Clermont," in his *Rome's Fall and After* (London: Hambledon Press, 1989), 309–10.

36. Gregory of Tours, *History*, book V, chap. 11 (Goffart, "Conversions," 309–10).

37. For different treatments of the Clermont drama, see Brian Brennan, "The Conversion of the Jews of Clermont in A.D. 576," *Journal of Theological Studies* 36 (1985): 321–37; and Michel Rouche, "Les baptèmes forcés des juifs en Gaule Mérovingienne dans l'Empire d'Orient," *De l'antijudaïsme antique à l'anti-sémitisme contemporain*, ed. V. Nikiprowetzky (Lille: Presses Universitaires de Lille, 1979), 105–25.

38. See Goffart, "Conversions" 302–4.

39. Benton, *Self and Society*, 135–36 (book II, chap. 5).

40. Ibid.

41. Rubin, "Desecration of the Host," 169–70.

42. Gavin Langmuir has also argued that Christians were wont to be particularly suspicious of Jews since Jews articulated criticisms of Christianity that Christians themselves suppressed. See Langmuir, "Doubt in Christendom" and "Peter the Venerable: Defense Against Doubts," in his *Toward a Definition of Antisemitism* (Berkeley and Los Angeles: University of California Press, 1990), 100–135, 197–209.

43. Mark Cohen, *Under Crescent and Cross: The Jews in the Middle Ages* (Princeton: Princeton University Press, 1994), 119.

44. Augustine, Sermon 201, *The Fathers of the Church*, vol. 38, *The Writings of Saint Augustine* (New York: Cima Publishing Company, 1947). Augustine's idea that all men were present in Adam when the first man sinned speaks to this overriding sense of the continuing presence of past generations. See Elaine Pagels, *Adam, Eve and the Serpent* (New York: Vintage, 1988), 108–9, citing Augustine, *City of God*, book XIII, chaps. 3, 14. Successive generations of Jews were linked together in the eyes of Christians who sought to indict them for the Crucifixion. See Jeremy Cohen, "The Jews as Killers of Christ in the Latin Tradition from Augustine to the Friars," *Traditio* 39 (1983): 1–27, and Kenneth Stowe, *Alienated Minority* (Cambridge: Harvard University Press, 1993), 16.

45. Dwayne E. Carpenter, *Alfonso X and the Jews: An Edition of and Commentary on Siete partidas 7.24 "De los judíos"* (Berkeley: University of California Press, 1986), 28.

46. Paul Meyvaert, "'Rainaldus est malus scriptor Francigenus'—Voicing National Antipathy in the Middle Ages," *Speculum* 66 (1991): 743–64, and Richard C. Hoffman, "Outsiders by Birth and Blood: Racist Ideologies and Realities Around the Periphery of Medieval Culture," *Studies in Medieval and Renaissance History* 6 (1983): 14–27.

47. W. Rye, "The Alleged Abduction and Circumcision of a Boy at Norwich in 1230," *The Norfolk Antiquarian Miscellany* 1 (1877): 319, cited in Sophia Menache, "Faith, Myth, and Politics—The Stereotype of the Jews and their Expulsion from England and France," *Jewish Quarterly Review* 75 (1984–85): 354n.14.

48. Gerald of Wales, *Speculum Ecclesiae. Giraldi Cambrensis opera*, ed. J. S. Brewer (London: Longman & Co., 1873), 4, 139 [Rolls Series, no. 21]. On general Christian abhorrence of circumcision, see John Gilchrist, "The Perception of

the Jews in the Canon Law in the Period of the First Two Crusades," *Jewish History* 3 (1988): 9–24, and the references in Walter Pakter, *Medieval Canon Law and the Jews* (Ebelsbach: Verlag Rolf Gremer, 1988).

49. Frederic W. Maitland, "The Deacon and the Jewess: Or Apostasy at Common Law," in his *Collected Papers*, 2 vols. (Cambridge: Cambridge University Press, 1898), 1:385–406.

50. Bernard Gui, *Manuel de l'inquisiteur,* ed. and trans. G. Mollat, 2 vols. (Paris: Champion, 1927), 2:13 (book V, chap.3).

51. Bernard of Clairvaux, Epistle 139, cited in Mary Stroll, *The Jewish Pope: Ideology and Politics in the Papal Schism of 1130* (Leiden: E. J. Brill, 1987), 156–68. See the discussion of Anacletus II in Herbert Bloch, *Monte Cassino in the Middle Ages*, 3 vols. (Cambridge: Harvard University Press, 1986), 2:946–69. Aryeh Grabois, "From Theological to Racial Antisemitism: The Controversy of the Jewish Pope in the Twelfth Century," *Zion* 47 (1982): 1–17 (Hebrew), overstates the influence of the forced conversions of Jews during the First Crusade and their later return to Judaism as an explanation for the racial language present in the discourse about Anacletus.

52. For evidence of the perceived disfigurement of medieval Jews after the twelfth century, see Ruth Mellinkoff, *Outcasts: Signs of Otherness in Northern European Art of the Late Middle Ages*, 2 vols. (Berkeley: University of California Press, 1993).

53. On medical approaches to the persistent physical distinctiveness of Jews, see Gilbert Dahan, *Les Intellectuels Chrétiens et les Juifs au Moyen Age* (Paris: Editions du Cerf, 1990), 528–29, and Peter Biller's excellent article "Views of Jews from Paris around 1300: Christian or 'Scientific,'" in Wood, *Christianity and Judaism*, 187–207.

54. Bartlett clearly recognizes that racial feelings grew in intensity by the later Middle Ages. See *Making of Europe*, 236–42. But even earlier, the imposition of some legal and linguistic barriers seems more an expression of an already deeply felt antagonism based on ethnicity rather than an attempt to construct ethnicity, particularly since the cultural barriers were imposed by conquering peoples on already subject groups.

55. See the discussions in my dissertation, "The Eternal Jew in Medieval Europe: Christian Perceptions of Jewish Anachronism and Racial Identity" (Princeton University, 1993).

56. Amos Funkenstein, *Perceptions of Jewish History* (Berkeley: University of California Press, 1993), 177, citing Joachim's *Tractatus super quattuor Evangeliarum.*

Multidirectional Conversion in the Frankish Levant

Benjamin Z. Kedar

Albert of Aachen, a chronicler of the First Crusade, recounts that during the siege of Jerusalem in the summer of 1099, the crusaders took a Muslim nobleman prisoner. Baldwin of Bourcq, later to become the second Frankish king of Jerusalem, and other crusading leaders conversed with the prisoner, trying to convert him to Christianity. When he refused to profess the Christian faith, he was brought before the Tower of David, the Muslim-held citadel of Jerusalem, and Baldwin's esquire decapitated him in view of all, to terrify the citadel's defenders.[1]

This account of crusader leaders attempting to convert a Muslim prisoner to Christianity during the siege of Jerusalem has not received the attention it deserves, possibly because it appears in the work of a chronicler who did not join the expedition, or because it deviates from the conventional image of the First Crusade. Yet the episode's credibility is enhanced by a parallel account contained in a letter written only one year after the crusader conquest of Jerusalem. This letter, sent to Egypt by the leaders of the Karaite Jewish community of Ascalon, tells how the crusaders urged a captive Jerusalemite Jew of a respected family to convert and become a Christian priest. The prisoner refused—just like the noble Muslim in the story told by Albert of Aachen.[2] In the summer of 1099, then, there were in Jerusalem some crusaders eager to convert unbelievers.

Not infrequently, unbelievers did convert, as we learn from various pieces of evidence on conversion to Christianity in the Frankish Kingdom of Jerusalem. Most of the evidence pertains to converts from Islam. The phenomenon is not surprising: an all-Mediterranean perspective reveals that wherever Christians brought a Muslim population under their rule, some of the conquered converted to the religion of the conquerors. This was true of the Byzantine reconquest of Crete and Asia Minor in the tenth century as well as of the subsequent Latin reconquests. As early as 972, when the Christians routed the Muslims of Fraxinetum on the Provençal coast, some of the defeated Muslims converted to Christianity. In Spain and in Sicily too, the Christian conquest resulted in partial Muslim conversion, and the same holds true for the Frankish Levant.[3] What does merit surprise is that the quite extensive evidence on Muslim conversion in the Frankish Kingdom of Jerusalem has been until now largely ignored. I should like to survey the principal testimonies and attempt to characterize the phenomenon.

Latin chronicles tell of Muslims who converted and entered the service of Godfrey de Bouillon and Baldwin I, the first two rulers of the kingdom. Godfrey had a Muslim ally who rode by his side in the battle of Ascalon in August 1100 and was persuaded by Godfrey to convert. (Albert of Aachen, telling of this event, adds that he is uncertain whether the baptism took place before or after the battle, thus increasing the story's credibility).[4] In November 1100, Baldwin I set out for the Dead Sea in the company of "local inhabitants who were previously Saracens [i.e., Muslims], but have recently become Christians."[5] Baldwin I also baptized a Muslim, christened him with his own name, and included him in his entourage—until, during the siege of Sidon in 1110, this convert allied himself with the Muslims of the besieged town and was caught and hanged.[6] We hear of another Muslim convert who gained Baldwin I's confidence and in 1112 averted a Muslim attempt to infiltrate the city of Jerusalem.[7] These cases of conversion are not reported as anomalies, and the Muslim converts are mentioned only because of the role they played in the events described. Therefore we may assume that there were more such converts whose existence remains undocumented as they did not take part in events the chroniclers saw fit to recount.

Some baptized Muslims participated in warfare alongside the Franks; thus, it has been persuasively argued that the first nucleus of the Turcopoles—that is, the light cavalry—was formed of Muslim converts of Turkish origin.[8] The Muslims viewed such converts as traitors, of course: after the Muslim victory at Chastellet in 1179, Saladin ordered the execution of all Christian warriors who had formerly been Muslims.[9] Conversion to Christianity appears to have occurred also among Muslim peasants. In a still unpublished treatise on shaykhs, or elders, active in villages of the Nablus region in Frankish and Ayyubid times, Diya al-Din al-Maqdisi mentions a formerly pious Muslim "who entered a church and became a Christian"; the event is not presented as exceptional.[10]

There are several references to the conversion of Muslim slaves. Frankish law, like that of Catalonia, set down that a converted slave should be set free.[11] The results were twofold: first, slaves would convert in order "to be freed from servitude" (por estre delivres dou servage).[12] Second, Frankish lords would prevent the conversion of their slaves so as to avoid the obligation of releasing them. Jacques of Vitry, bishop of Acre in the years 1216–28, sternly reproved the lords on this account.[13] Similarly, Pope Gregory IX denounced the Frankish lords who forbade their Muslim slaves to attend sermons given by missionaries and to be baptized. Gregory did more than denounce: in two letters of 1237–38 he ordered the lords to allow their slaves to accept baptism, abolishing simultaneously the *consuetudo terrae* that promised the manumission of a baptized slave.[14] But even this compromise between Faith and Mammon failed to surmount the lords' resistance, and fifteen years later a papal legate had to threaten them with excommunication if they refused their slaves Christian instruction. The legate, Odo of Châteauroux, harbored no illusions as to the lords' reaction. He expected their resistance to continue and therefore decreed that his statute, promulgated in Jaffa in 1253, was to be read out twice a year in all churches throughout the Frankish East.[15] And as late as 1298 an ecclesiastical council in Nicosia had to threaten to excommunicate any lord refusing to allow his slaves to be baptized.[16]

There can be no doubt that Muslim slaves and other Muslims of low social standing did convert to Christianity. In 1264 Pope Urban IV wrote to the patriarch of Jerusalem that the poor Muslims who were coming to Acre to be converted should be provided sustenance during the days in which they were to receive Christian instruction.[17] In the same year, a burgess of Acre, an Oriental Christian by the name of Saliba, drew up his will. This is the sole extant will of a burgess of the Frankish Kingdom, and we learn from it that Saliba had a male slave and a female slave who had already been baptized, and another male slave and female slave whom Saliba was now *ordering* to be baptized. We have, then, four Christian converts in a single Acre household![18] One can only wonder how many converted slaves were mentioned in the acts of Acre's notaries—acts that unfortunately have not survived.[19] We do however possess several documents of a different kind: accords drawn up between the Mamluks and various Frankish rulers in the years 1267–83. These accords refer repeatedly to Muslims fleeing from Mamluk to Frankish territory and converting there, and vice versa.[20] And the Muslim chroniclers Ibn al-Furat and al-Maqrizi tell about Mamluks of the Sultan Baybars who fled to Acre and Tyre and converted there. They also tell of a Muslim girl who was ransomed from the Franks and then seized by them and forced to convert. Al-Maqrizi adds that such forced conversions were frequent, but his assertion is not corroborated by other sources.[21]

Details on Muslim conversion in the Frankish Kingdom of Jerusalem can be gleaned also from two papal bulls preserved solely in canon law collections. In the first, dating from 1193, Pope Celestine III replies to que-ries by Theobald, bishop of Acre, regarding cases of Saracen conversion; some of these sound rather hypothetical. The second, which Pope Innocent III sent in 1201 to a bishop of Tiberias, proclaims the validity of consan-guineous marriage between converts, the inadmissibility of polygamy among them, and the ineffectiveness of a non-Christian divorce that precedes one's conversion.[22] Such problems appear to have recurred time and again. In 1274, when a papal legate set out for the Frankish Levant, he was autho-rized to permit converts to retain the wives they had married before their conversion, although the parties were related in a degree of consanguinity that was forbidden to Christians.[23]

Thus, the evidence of various sources—Frankish law, canon law, west-ern and oriental chronicles, treaties, a will, etc.—points to a significant number of conversions among local Muslims, mostly from the lower strata of their community. Was this conversion encouraged by the Franks? We have seen that lords opposed the conversion of their slaves. Yet the very law that promised manumission to a baptized slave indicates that some Franks did wish to further Muslim conversion; indeed, the first manifesta-tion of such a wish precedes the crusader conquest of Jerusalem. More-over, in the early 1120s the hermit Bernard of Blois left the Frankish realm to preach Christianity to a Muslim ruler, probably Nur al-Dawla Balak of Aleppo. This feat, anticipating by about a century the famous preaching of Francis of Assisi before al-Malik al-Kamil of Egypt, became known only recently.[24] In the thirteenth century, Franciscans and Dominicans endeav-ored to bring about Muslim conversion in the Holy Land, and Pope Gre-gory IX proclaimed these missionary efforts to be as commendable as cru-sading.[25]

Besides the numerous reports of the conversion of Muslims, there are three pieces of evidence on Jewish conversion to Christianity. The leaders of the Karaite community in Ascalon tell in their above-mentioned letter that upon the conquest of Jerusalem in 1099, several Jewish prisoners con-verted after they despaired of being ransomed.[26] Pope Innocent III wrote in 1198 to the archbishop of Tyre regarding a legal difficulty resulting from the conversion of Jews.[27] In Urban IV's letter of 1264 he mentions, in addi-tion to Muslims, impoverished Jews arriving in Acre for the purpose of converting.[28]

We also hear of Christians converting to Judaism in the Frankish King-dom. A law of King Baldwin II deals, inter alia, with Franks who go to a Muslim country to denounce Christianity and become Jews or Saracens. It would appear that the law deals with two cases: renunciation of Christian-ity while escaping to a Muslim-ruled territory, and conversion to Judaism or Islam while remaining in the Frankish Kingdom.[29] Conversion to Judaism within the kingdom is also suggested by a responsum Maimonides sent to the sages of Tyre, affirming that a Jew may instruct a Christian in the commandments of Judaism and may perform circumcision on Christians and Muslims. Maimonides also wrote a responsum to a proselyte by the name of 'Obadyah, a former Christian living in the Holy Land.[30] However, one may assume that only a few Franks converted to Judaism.

But there are many instances of Franks converting to Islam. Latin and Arabic chronicles tell of repeated instances in which Christian warriors could not withstand the hardships of battle, crossed the enemy lines, and converted to Islam. Such cases occurred during the Second Crusade as well as in Saladin's time and during the Fifth Crusade.[31] Crossing the lines for the purpose of converting to Islam was so frequent that when Francis of Assisi came to the Muslim camp to preach Christianity to the Egyptian sultan, the Muslims asked whether he had crossed the lines to be converted to Islam![32] Also, many Frankish prisoners converted to Islam.[33]

However, not all cases of conversion to Islam were carried out in the thick of battle or in its aftermath. The crusader law deals with Franks—including Frankish knights—who have decided to accept the law of Mahomet.[34] Parallel testimonies are found in canon law. In the above-mentioned letter of Pope Celestine III, we read about a Frank who moved to a Muslim country, converted to Islam, and then returned to Frankish lands along with his wife and Muslim children.[35] From another papal bull we learn that an archbishop of Tyre—perhaps the chronicler William of Tyre—wrote to Pope Alexander III that in the ecclesiastical province of Tyre, it frequently happened that a husband or wife went over to Muslim territory, whether of their own free will or by force, converted to Islam, and raised a new family. The pope is requested to decide whether the spouse who remains a Christian is permitted to remarry.[36]

Conversion of the Muslim enemy was an important component of the fantasy world of the western knight, and contemporary literature tells time and again of the yearning to convert a Muslim rival to Christianity or of the desire to lead a beautiful Muslim maiden to the baptismal font.[37] Yet there is reason to believe that the Muslims harbored the parallel fantasy of converting a beautiful Frankish woman to their faith. Evidence for this appears in a source hitherto ignored by scholars of the period: *A Thousand and One Nights*. On night number 894, Shahrazad begins spinning the following tale, which needs no commentary.[38] A Muslim merchant comes to Frankish Acre three years before the Battle of Hattin, to sell linen from Upper Egypt. One of his customers is a Frankish woman, who goes about the market streets with her face unveiled according to Frankish custom, and whose beauty dazes the merchant's wits. He sells her his wares at ever lower prices, hoping to entice her to return to his store. Finally, he speaks with the old woman who accompanies her, and agrees to pay fifty dinars if the beautiful girl would come to him. At nightfall she arrives at his house overlooking the sea, and the merchant ascends with her to the roof, as it is summer. They eat and drink and lie down in the moonlight, and gaze at the stars reflected in the sea. Suddenly the merchant is beset with shame for disobeying Allah with a Christian woman and vows to abstain from her. The Frankish woman rises at dawn and returns angrily to her abode. The merchant sits in his shop and suddenly catches sight of her passing, "as she were the moon," together with the old woman. Her beauty confounds him again, and he cajoles the old woman to bring her to him a second time in return for one hundred gold pieces. But when she comes, the merchant again feels remorse and abstains from her. The third time the old woman demands five hundred dinars, and the distraught merchant is about to put all his earnings in her hand—but just then a crier passes and proclaims that the truce has ended and all Muslim traders must conclude their business within one week and depart. The merchant winds up his affairs, moves to Damascus, and starts trading in slave girls, hoping thus to occupy his mind and allay his yearning for the Frankish woman of Acre.

Three years pass. Saladin defeats the Franks at Hattin, and Damascus is filled with prisoners. Our merchant sells a beautiful girl to Saladin for one hundred dinars, and since at the time there are only ninety dinars in the treasury, "because he had expended all his moneys in waging war with the Franks," the merchant is told to pick a Frankish girl-prisoner in lieu of the remaining ten dinars. He looks over the prisoners and finds among them the Frankish woman of Acre—it transpires now that she is the wife of a Frankish knight—and carries her to his tent. When the woman learns that the merchant, whom she had agreed to see in exchange for five hundred dinars, has now bought her for only ten, she is immediately convinced of the truth of Islam and is converted there and then. The merchant for his part vows not to approach her until she has been set free and takes her to the qadi of Saladin's army, who marries them.

A short while later Saladin promises the king of the Franks that he will release all Frankish prisoners. These set out on their way, all except for our Frankish woman, who is now carrying the child of her merchant husband and refuses to be separated from him. Thereupon the envoy of the Frankish king gives him a chest sent by her mother. In it are her clothes and two purses of money, one of fifty and the other of one hundred dinars, untouched since he had tied them up in Acre. Thus he obtains the woman he desires and his money as well.

To sum up, our sources indicate that in the Frankish Levant, passages from Islam to Christianity and vice versa were not rare at all. Muslims, especially of low social standing, opted for the religion of their conquerors; Christians converted to Islam, whether of their own free will or by force. A few Jews converted to Christianity; a few Christians converted to Judaism. Thus, on the fringes of Frankish society there was some interfaith mobility, which we cannot measure accurately by the sources at our disposal, but the existence of which cannot be questioned.[39]

NOTES

1. Albertus Aquensis, *Liber christianae expeditionis pro ereptione, emundatione et restitutione sanctae Hierosolymitanae ecclesiae*, bk. VI, chap. 5, in *Recueil des Historiens des Croisades* (hereafter *RHC*): *Historiens Occidentaux* (hereafter *Occ.*) (Paris: Imprimerie Nationale, 1879), 4:469.

2. For an English translation of the Ascalonites' letter see S. D. Goitein, "Contemporary Letters on the Capture of Jerusalem by the Crusaders," *Journal of Jewish Studies* 3 (1952): 172; see also Goitein, "Geniza Sources for the Crusader Period: A Survey," in *Outremer: Studies in the History of the Crusading Kingdom of Jerusalem Presented to Joshua Prawer*, ed. B. Z. Kedar, H. E. Mayer, and R. C. Smail (Jerusalem: Yad Izhak Ben-Zvi Institute, 1982), 313. According to Moshe Gil's reading of the text, the Jewish captive tells the crusaders "that it is unheard of for a priest to become a Christian" (Gil, *A History of Palestine, 634–1099*, trans. E. Broido [Cambridge: Cambridge University Press, 1992], 833).

3. For details, see B. Z. Kedar, *Crusade and Mission: European Approaches toward the Muslims* (Princeton: Princeton University Press, 1984), 42–52, 93–94.

4. Albertus Aquensis, *Liber*, VI, 42–44, in *RHC: Occ.* 4:491–93.

5. Fulcher of Chartres, *Historia Hierosolymitana*, bk. II, chap. 4, par. 4, ed. H. Hagenmeyer (Heidelberg: C. Winter Universitätsbuchhandlung, 1913), 374–75.

6. William of Tyre, *Chronique*, 11, 14, ed. R. B. C. Huygens, Corpus Christianorum. Continuatio Mediaevalis 63 (Turnhout: Brepols, 1986), 518.

7. Guibert of Nogent, *Historia quae dicitur Gesta Dei per Francos*, in *RHC: Occ.* 4:262.

8. J. Richard, "Les Turcoples au service des royaumes de Jérusalem et de Chypre: musulmans convertis ou chrétiens orientaux?" *Revue des études islamiques* 54 (1986): 259–70.

9. Abu Shama, *Kitab al-rawdatayn*, extracts ed. and trans. A. C. Barbier de Meynard, in *RHC: Historiens Orientaux* (Paris: Imprimerie Nationale, 1898), 4:205.

10. A part of the treatise, preserved in a Damascene manuscript, has recently been transcribed and translated into Hebrew by Daniella Talmon-Heller in her master's thesis, Hebrew University of Jerusalem, 1990 (the conversion story ap-

pears on p. 39). And see Talmon-Heller, "The Shaykh and the Community: Popular Hanbalite Islam in 12th–13th Century Jabal Nablus and Jabal Qasyun," *Studia Islamica* 79 (1994): 103–20.

11. For details on the legal situation in Frankish Jerusalem and in Catalonia see Kedar, *Crusade and Mission,* 76–77.

12. *Assises de la Cour des Bourgeois,* c. 255, ed. A. A. Beugnot in *RHC: Lois* (Paris: Imprimerie Royale, 1843), 2:191; cf. J. Prawer, *Crusader Institutions* (Oxford; Clarendon Press, 1980), 209.

13. *Lettres de Jacques de Vitry, évêque de Saint-Jean d'Acre,* ed. R. B. C. Huygens (Leiden: E. J. Brill, 1960), 87–88.

14. The letters are printed in Kedar, *Crusade and Mission,* 212–13, and discussed on 147–49.

15. Mansi, *Concilia,* vol. 26, cols. 317–18. Cf. B. Z. Kedar, "Ecclesiastical Legislation in the Kingdom of Jerusalem: The Statutes of Jaffa (1253) and Acre (1254)," in *Crusade and Settlement: Papers Read at the First Conference of the Society for the Study of the Crusades and the Latin East and Presented to R. C. Smail,* ed. P. W. Edbury (Cardiff: University College Cardiff Press, 1985), 226, reprinted in B. Z. Kedar, *The Franks in the Levant, 11th to 14th Centuries* (Aldershot: Variorum, 1993), Article XVII, 226.

16. Mansi, *Concilia,* vol. 26, col. 350A.

17. The letter is printed in Kedar, *Crusade and Mission,* 215; for a discussion see 151.

18. J. Delaville Le Roulx, ed., *Cartulaire général de l'Ordre des Hospitaliers de Saint-Jean de Jérusalem, 1100–1310,* 4 vols. (Paris: E. Leroux, 1894–1906), Doc. 3105, 3:191–92. Cf. H. E. Mayer, "Latins, Muslims and Greeks in the Latin Kingdom of Jerusalem," *History* 63 (1978): 187, reprinted in his *Probleme des lateinischen Königreichs Jerusalem* (London: Variorum, 1983), Article VI, p. 187.

19. The extant acts of contemporary Genoese notaries refer to numerous Muslim slaves who converted to Christianity: see for instance A. Haverkamp, "Zur Sklaverei in Genua während des 12. Jahrhunderts," in *Geschichte in der Gesellschaft. Festschrift für Karl Bosl,* ed. F. Prinz et al. (Stuttgart: A. Hiersemann, 1974), 209; M. Balard, "Remarques sur les esclaves à Gênes dans la seconde moitié du XIIIe siècle," *Mélanges d'archéologie et d'histoire publiés par l'Ecole française de Rome* 80 (1968): 645, 648; Charles Verlinden, *L'esclavage dans l'Europe médiévale* (Gent: Rijksuniversiteit, 1977), 2:437, 445; S. Epstein, *Wills and Wealth in Medieval Genoa, 1150–1250* (Cambridge: Harvard University Press, 1984), 191.

20. P. M. Holt, "Qalawun's Treaty with Acre in 1283," *English Historical Review* 91 (1976): 810–11; Prawer, *Crusader Institutions,* 206.

21. U. Lyons and M. C. Lyons, *Ayyubids, Mamlukes, and Crusaders: Selections from the Tarikh al-duwal wa'l-muluk of Ibn al-Furat,* 2 vols. (Cambridge: Heffer, 1971), 1:168–69 (text), 2:132–33 (translation); E. Quatremère, *Histoire des sultans mamlouks par Makrizi* (Paris: Firmin Didot Frères, 1837–42), 2 vols. in 4,

vol. 1, pt. 2, 68–69; M. H. Chéhab, *Tyr à l'époque des croisades*, 2 vols. (Paris: A. Maisonneuve, 1975), 1:536.

22. For a detailed discussion see B. Z. Kedar, "Muslim Conversion in Canon Law," *Proceedings of the Sixth International Congress of Medieval Canon Law*, ed. S. Kuttner and K. Pennington, Monumenta Iuris Canonici, Series C, Subsidia (Città del Vaticano: Biblioteca Apostolica Vaticana, 1985), 7:322–26, reprinted in Kedar, *The Franks in the Levant*, Article XIV: 322–26. See also Kedar, *Crusade and Mission*, 80–82.

23. *Reg. Grégoire IX*, no. 565.

24. See B. Z. Kedar, "Gerard of Nazareth, a Neglected Twelfth-Century Writer in the Latin East: A Contribution to the Intellectual and Monastic History of the Crusader States," *Dumbarton Oaks Papers* 37 (1983): 67, 73, reprinted in Kedar, *The Franks in the Levant*, Article IV: 67, 73; A. Jotischky, *The Perfection of Solitude: Hermits and Monks in the Crusader States* (University Park: Pennsylvania State University Press, 1995), 29, with note 28.

25. To the data assembled in Kedar, *Crusade and Mission*, 136–58, 213, one should add the account according to which a qadi at Safed tells two Franciscans that they brought back to Christianity erstwhile converts to Islam: Fidenzio of Padua, *Liber Recuperationis Terre Sancte*, in G. Golubovich, *Biblioteca bio-bibliografica della Terra Santa e dell'Oriente francescano*, 1st ser., 4 vols. (Quaracchi: Collegio di S. Bonaventura, 1906–23), 2:25.

26. Goitein, "Contemporary Letters," 166, 172.

27. For the letter see *Decretales Gregorii IX*, 4.14.4, in *Corpus Iuris Canonici*, ed. E. Friedberg, 2 vols. (Leipzig: B. Tauchnitz, 1879–81), 2:702. For discussion, see B. Z. Kedar, "Jews and Samaritans in the Latin Kingdom of Jerusalem," *Tarbiz* 53 (1984): 400–401 (Hebrew); J. Prawer, *The History of the Jews in the Latin Kingdom of Jerusalem* (Oxford: Clarendon Press, 1988), 254–55.

28. See note 17. For discussion see B. Z. Kedar, "Notes on the History of the Jews of Palestine in the Middle Ages," *Tarbiz* 42 (1973): 411–12 (Hebrew); Prawer, *History of the Jews*, 276.

29. *Livre des Assises des Bourgeois*, chap. 235, in *Les livres des assises et des usages dou reaume de Jérusalem*, ed. E. H. Kausler (Stuttgart: A. Krabbe, 1839), 270. For discussion see Kedar, "Jews and Samaritans," 402–3.

30. R. Moses ben Maimon, *Responsa*, ed. J. Blau, 2d ed., 4 vols. (Jerusalem, 1986), 1:282–85, nos. 148–49, 2:584, note 1 to no. 293. This Obadyah should not be identified with the far more famous Obadyah the Norman, who appears to have converted in 1102 to Judaism in Muslim territory: cf. J. Prawer, "The Autobiography of Obadyah the Norman, a Convert to Judaism at the Time of the First Crusade," in *Studies in Medieval Jewish History and Literature*, ed. I. Twersky (Cambridge: Harvard University Press, 1979), 110–34.

31. The evidence is surveyed in T. W. Arnold, *The Preaching of Islam: A History of the Propagation of the Muslim Faith*, 2d ed. (London: Constable, 1913), 88–95.

32. *Chronique d'Ernoul et de Bernard le Trésorier,* ed. L. de Mas Latrie (Paris: J. Renouard, 1871), 432.

33. For a detailed discussion see G. Cipollone, *Cristianità—Islam: Cattività e liberazione in nome di Dio, il tempo di Innocenzo III dopo il 1187* (Rome: Editrice Pontificia Università Gregoriana, 1992).

34. *Livre au Roi,* c. 23, ed. A. A. Beugnot, in *RHC: Lois,* (Paris: Imprimerie Royale, 1841), 1:622.

35. See note 22.

36. *Decretales ineditae saeculi XII,* ed. S. Chodorow and C. Duggan, Monumenta Iuris Canonici, ser. B, vol. 4 (Città del Vaticano: Biblioteca Apostolica Vaticana, 1982), Doc. 94, pp. 166–67.

37. For studies of this motif see, for example, F. M. Warren, "The Enamoured Moslem Princess in Oderic Vital and the French Epic," *Publications of the Modern Language Association of America* 29 (1914): 341–58; C. Meredith-Jones, "The Conventional Saracen of the Songs of Geste," *Speculum* 17 (1942): 221; A. R. Harden, "The Element of Love in the *Chansons de Geste,*" *Duquesne Studies: Annuale medievale* 5 (1964): 73–74; D. Metlitzki, *The Matter of Araby in Medieval England* (New Haven and London: Yale University Press, 1977), 136–77.

38. *The Book of the Thousand Nights and a Night,* trans. R. F. Burton, 12 vols. (London: H. S. Nichols, 1897), 7:99–104. A different version of the story, without the Thousand-and-One-Nights frame, was published by Varsi, "Anecdote des croisades," *Journal Asiatique* 4, 16 (1850): 75–92.

39. An earlier version of this article appeared, in Hebrew, in B. Z. Kedar, ed., *The Crusaders in Their Kingdom, 1099–1291* (Jerusalem: Yad Izhak Ben-Zvi Institute, 1987), 93–100.

CONTRIBUTORS

LAWRENCE G. DUGGAN received his Ph.D. from Harvard University. He is a professor of history at the University of Delaware.

JONATHAN M. ELUKIN received his Ph.D. from Princeton University. At present he is an independent scholar working in Washington, D.C.

LEONARD P. HINDSLEY O. P. received his Ph.D. from Rutgers University. He is an associate professor of German at Providence College.

JENNIFER R. GOODMAN received her Ph.D. from Harvard University. She is an associate professor of English at Texas A&M University.

JOHN M. HOWE received his Ph.D. from the University of California at Los Angeles. He is an associate professor of history at Texas Tech University.

RUTH MAZO KARRAS received her Ph.D. from Yale University. She is an associate professor of history at Temple University.

BENJAMIN Z. KEDAR received his Ph.D. from Yale University. He is a professor of history at the Hebrew University of Jerusalem.

RASA MAZEIKA received her Ph.D. from Fordham University. She is an archivist and curator at a museum in Toronto, Canada. She has also taught at the University of Klaipeda in Lithuania.

JAMES MULDOON received his Ph.D. from Cornell University. He is a professor of history at the Camden College of Arts and Sciences of Rutgers University.

CORDULA NOLTE received her Ph.D. from the University of Berlin. She is a research assistant in the Historical Institute of Ernst-Moritz-Arndt University, Greifswald, Germany.

FREDERICK H. RUSSELL received his Ph.D. from Johns Hopkins University. He is an associate professor of history at the Newark College of Arts and Sciences of Rutgers University.

JAMES D. RYAN received his Ph.D. from New York University. He is a professor of history at the Bronx Community College of the City University of New York.

INDEX